21世纪经济与管理精编教材

金融学系列

# 国际金融函电

（第二版）

## International Banking Communication

肖曼君 ◎ 编著

图书在版编目（CIP）数据

国际金融函电 / 肖曼君编著. —2版 —北京：北京大学出版社，2019.5
21世纪经济与管理精编教材·金融学系列
ISBN 978-7-301-30449-5

Ⅰ. ①国… Ⅱ. ①肖… Ⅲ. ①国际金融—英语—电报信函—写作—高等学校—教材 Ⅳ. ①F831

中国版本图书馆CIP数据核字(2019)第073626号

| | |
|---|---|
| 书　　　名 | 国际金融函电（第二版） |
| | GUOJI JINRONG HANDIAN（DI-ER BAN） |
| 著作责任者 | 肖曼君 编著 |
| 责任编辑 | 付海霞　兰　慧 |
| 策划编辑 | 张　燕 |
| 标准书号 | ISBN 978-7-301-30449-5 |
| 出版发行 | 北京大学出版社 |
| 地　　　址 | 北京市海淀区成府路205号　100871 |
| 网　　　址 | http://www.pup.cn |
| 微信公众号 | 北京大学经管书苑（pupembook） |
| 电子信箱 | em@pup.cn　QQ：552063295 |
| 新浪微博 | @北京大学出版社　@北京大学出版社经管图书 |
| 电　　　话 | 邮购部010-62752015　发行部010-62750672　编辑部010-62752926 |
| 印　刷　者 | 北京富生印刷厂 |
| 经　销　者 | 新华书店 |
| | 730毫米×1020毫米　16开本　22.75印张　454千字 |
| | 2009年10月第1版 |
| | 2019年5月第2版　2019年5月第1次印刷 |
| 定　　　价 | 49.00元 |

未经许可，不得以任何方式复制或抄袭本书之部分或全部内容。
**版权所有，侵权必究**
举报电话：010-62752024　电子信箱：fd@pup.pku.edu.cn
图书如有印装质量问题，请与出版部联系，电话：010-62756370

# 第二版前言

随着金融、经济全球化和人民币国际化进程的加速，国际银行业务模式日益创新，尤其是 CIPS（China International Payment System）的推出，使国际银行间的人民币跨境结算业务更趋于方便、简单、快捷。为了适应国际银行业务模式日新月异的发展，培养适合新时代的高素质国际化金融人才，我们有必要根据国际银行业务的最新发展，对《国际金融函电》的内容进行更新和改编。

## 新版说明

本教材在讲授传统的国际银行业务模式及应用文特征的基础上，更新了国际银行业务及其多元化案例的 SWIFT 报文，注重专业基础与英语语言运用相结合，融国际银行业务知识、最新业务模式、复杂的业务环节与英语电文的语言特征和表达技巧等为一体。

在第二版中，我们延续了第一版教材的编写风格，删除了过时的或者不常用的国际银行业务的书信和电文；拆分、合并和新增了部分章节，新增了大量的 SWIFT 报文和往来电文的实际案例等内容。

首先，我们将教材内容分为四个部分：第一部分为银行书信写作的基础知识；第二部分为国际银行业务的书信样例；第三部分为电报、电传和 SWIFT 业务；第四部分为其他业务函件样例。

其次，我们删除了第一版教材中第 6 单元的部分银行查询业务和第 8 单元的非国际贸易结算业务，并将部分内容整合或并入第 5 单元的会计业务和第 6 单元的国际贸易结算业务。

最后，我们新增了 SWIFT 业务（第 8 单元），其中包括 MT799 信用证业务、MT4xx 托收业务和 MT760 担保函业务等，它们基于进口方银行和出口方银行，按照每个业务不同环节必经的业务内容或可能出现的问题编排SWIFT报文和案例等，并对每份报文进行注解说明。

## 组织结构

第一部分包括两个单元，详细介绍了国际金融函电中书信写作的基本知识、写作技巧、语言特征、写作风格和写作原则（第1单元），以及书写格式、结构和信封特征等（第2单元）。第二部分包括四个单元（第3、4、5、6单元），详细阐述了国际银行业务中的代理行业务书信写作及样例分析（第3单元）、银行资信业务的书信写作及样例分析（第4单元）、银行会计业务的书信写作及样例分析（第5单元）和国际贸易结算业务的书信写作，包括信用证、托收和汇款业务的样例分析（第6单元），等等。

接着我们进入第三部分，这是本教材第二版中新增内容最多的部分，也是本教材的重点部分。首先，我们介绍了传统电文形式Telegram（电报）和Telex（电传）的语言特征、写作风格和写作技巧，然后呈现了大量的电文样例来诠释传统电文的特色（第7单元）；其次，我们重点介绍了SWIFT业务的报文，详细阐述、分析和注释了不同国际结算业务中各环节的SWIFT报文的语言特色、组织结构和篇章内容等（第8单元）。

第四部分介绍了其他业务函件的写作特色和语言特征（第9单元）。结尾部分以附录的形式，分别对国际金融函电常用开头语和结束语、国际金融函电常用缩略词进行归纳和诠释，最后附上各章练习的参考答案。

## 教学指导

本教材每章以学习目标开始，引导学生学习该章的主要内容；以每种国际业务样例书信和SWIFT报文样例为范本，附上详细注解，帮助学生学习和了解本章的要点与主要内容；以总结和归纳常用业务句型与习题结尾，帮助学生温习本章的关键知识和句型要点，也供学生检验对本章书信和报文写作的掌握程度。

本教材的各章节大部分自成一体，因此为教学内容的安排提供了很大的灵活性。本教材第1、2单元的写作基础知识和第3单元的代理关系较为重要，需要首先让学生掌握，其他章节可以依据教师的教学目标合理选取。授课教师可以优先和重点讲授第6单元的国际贸易结算业务，并选取第三部分第8单元中相同业务的SWIFT报文样例配合讲授。当然，如果学期课时允许，教师也可以按照本书的章节顺序授课，从而不省略任何章节，完成整本教材的教学。

# 致 谢

本教材的再版工作得到我的家人以及中国农业银行总行国际结算单证中心（合肥）进口部高级专员张煜同志、中国农业银行深圳分行国际结算部谢靖同志、中国农业银行广西壮族自治区分行国际结算部田艳丽同志等的大力支持和帮助，我在此对他们表示衷心的感谢。本教材的出版得益于湖南大学金融与统计学院吴志明副院长的鼎力支持和帮助，得益于湖南大学2018年度教研教改与教材建设项目的资助，得益于北京大学出版社张燕编辑和付海霞编辑的大力支持和辛勤工作，我在此向他们表示深深的谢意！

肖曼君

2019年5月

# 第一版前言

随着经济、金融全球化和一体化的趋势不断深化，以及我国改革开放的不断深入，我国各行各业与国际接轨的步伐逐步加快，因而迫切需要既精通专业知识又精通外语的高素质人才。为了适应这种需要，教育部从2001年起大力推动国内双语教学。金融专业便是教育部要求率先实行双语教学的六大专业之一，这是由金融学科本身的国际化特点决定的。而国际金融函电则是金融专业中一个重要的工具性课程。本课程的教学理念是：突破专业学习的英语语言瓶颈，培养学生的金融全球化视野，跟踪全球金融业务的发展，弥补单纯专业外语教育的低效与不足，提高国际竞争力，培养新世纪高素质的金融实践人才。

但从国内经济、金融专业双语教材的建设来看，传统的教材由于采用中文编写，内容和体例也具有较大的局限性，已经不能适应当前高校教育教学国际化实践的需要，因此目前国内双语教学大多选用引进版英文教材。但由于"国际金融函电"课程是一门操作性较强的实务课程，国际市场上没有合适的英文原版教材。为了满足国内的双语教学需要，我们编写了《国际金融函电》这本双语教材。

作为教育部首批100门双语教学示范课程建设项目"国际金融"方向的系列教材之一，以及湖南大学金融学专业国家级教学团队课程建设的成果之一，本教材在内容与形式上均有创新之处。在内容上：（1）本教材既秉承了传统的银行应用文的特质，又与时俱进地增加了现代银行业务模式特色的内容；（2）注重专业基础和语言运用相结合，融英语知识和国际金融业务知识为一体。在编写形式上：（1）每章都编有学习导航和本章的学习目的，在保持全书统一编写体例的基础上，各章又根据不同的业务内容自成体系；（2）全教材采用英文编写，同时辅以关键的中文注释，因此具有很强的专业性、可操作性和实用性。

本教材的目的是帮助学生了解国际金融业务的英语信函、电报电传和SWIFT等的语言特征和文体风格,掌握国际银行业务的各类书信写作知识和写作技巧,通过案例函电的学习,培养和提高他们的金融英语应用文写作能力,为他们毕业后走向工作岗位能迅速进行业务操作打下坚实的理论和业务知识基础。此外,本教材对国际金融业务人员、参加全国金融英语证书考试的考生也有很高的实用价值。

本教材的编写得到我的家人以及湖南大学金融学院研究生夏荣尧、周平、田艳丽、张煜和贺文宏等同学的大力支持和帮助,我在此对他们表示衷心的感谢。本教材的出版得益于湖南大学金融学院张强教授、杨胜刚教授的鼎力支持和帮助,得益于北京大学出版社张燕编辑和谢超编辑的辛勤工作,我此向他们表示深深的谢意!

肖曼君

2009 年 10 月

# CONTENTS 目录

## Part I  THE BASICS RELATED TO BANKING LETTERS
### 第一部分  银行书信写作的基础知识

**Unit One   Language Features and Writing Skills**
第1单元   语言特征和写作技巧 ………………………………………………… 3

**Unit Two   Layout and Structures of a Banking Letter**
第2单元   银行书信的格式和结构 ……………………………………………… 13

## PART II  LETTERS RELATED TO INTERNATIONAL BANKING BUSINESS
### 第二部分  国际银行业务的书信样例

**Unit Three   Agency Relationship**
第3单元   代理关系 …………………………………………………………… 33

**Unit Four   Credit Inquiry**
第4单元   资信调查 …………………………………………………………… 52

**Unit Five   Accounting Business**
第5单元   会计业务 …………………………………………………………… 69

**Unit Six　　Settlement Related to International Trade**
第6单元　　国际贸易结算业务 ·················································· 88

## PART III　TELEGRAM, TELEX AND SWIFT BUSINESS
## 第三部分　电报、电传和 SWIFT 业务

**Unit Seven　　Telegram & Telex Business**
第7单元　　电报和电传业务 ···················································· 123

**Unit Eight　　SWIFT Business**
第8单元　　SWIFT业务 ························································· 146

## PART IV　LETTERS ON OTHER ITEMS
## 第四部分　其他业务函件样例

**Unit Nine　　Other Items**
第9单元　　其他业务函件 ······················································· 291

**Appendix I　　Opening Sentences and Closing Sentences Commonly Used in Banking Communication**
附录 I　　国际金融函电常用开头语和结束语 ································· 314

**Appendix II　　Commonly Used Abbreviations in Banking Communication**
附录 II　　国际金融函电常用缩略词 ··········································· 320

**Appendix III　　Keys to Exercises**
附录III　　练习参考答案 ························································ 340

# Part I

## THE BASICS RELATED TO BANKING LETTERS
## 第一部分　银行书信写作的基础知识

Unit One　Language Features and Writing Skills
第1单元　语言特征和写作技巧
Unit Two　Layout and Structures of a Banking Letter
第2单元　银行书信的格式和结构

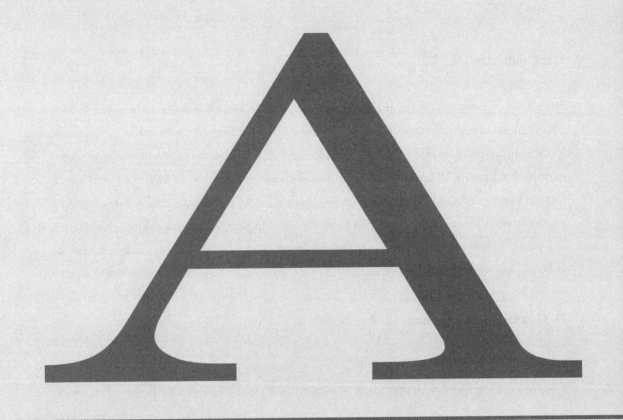

## Unit One  Language Features and Writing Skills

## 第1单元  语言特征和写作技巧

**After studying this unit, you will be able to:**
- Learn how to prepare yourself before writing a banking letter
- Recognize the features of practical writing, esp. international banking letters
- Identify some skills you will need in your writing banking letters
- Master the seven Cs writing principles of banking letters writing
- Identify the language barriers to a good banking letter
- Evaluate your banking letters writing skills by completing the self-test checklists in the unit

## I. Introduction（概述）

Since China's entry into WTO, the world economy has developed globally in fast speed. With RMB's internationalization and The Belt and Road（B & R）Initiative announced by Chairman Xi Jinping in 2013, we have made great development in large scale in international trade, multinational business and international finance business such as international settlement, international credit, foreign exchange dealings etc. As a communication tool, banking communication plays an important role in all these business. Generally speaking, the function of a banking letter is to get or convey banking information, to deal with varieties of international banking transactions and business.

## II. Quality to The Writer（作者应具备的素质）

Practical English writing does not call for flowery language because it isn't literary words, but it is required to express your own views accurately in a plain language that is very clear and is readily understood, and catch the readers' attention and persuade the readers into believing what you said. To achieve its purpose, before learning how to write, the writer should have:
1. a good command of standard modern English;
2. all kinds of social knowledge;
3. knowledge of technical terms;
4. knowledge of social psychology;
5. knowledge of various profession, such as secretary, management, banking theory and practice, etc.

## III. Preparation Before Writing（写作前的准备工作）

As a writer, you should make preparations for your creative works before taking up the pen. Generally speaking, the following should be drawn attention to:
1. Studying your reader's interest, that is, thinking of what your reader thinks.

    To achieve this, you should "put yourself in your reader's place" and try to imagine how he will feel about what you write. Ask yourself constantly, "what are his needs, his wishes, his interests, his problems to be solved, and how can I meet his requirements".
2. Planning what you will write and writing effectively.

In order to plan what you write and to write effectively, you should draft an outline before writing.

Every language has its own features. For Chinese students, English is not a native but foreign language. It is not easy for them to effectively and accurately use proper words and sentence structures in writing. Some of them tend to write in Chinese first, then translate it into English. But in this way the expression will appear to be stiff and awkward. So you'd better learn to think and write in English and draft an outline before writing. For example, if you are to write a letter of credit inquiring, firstly you should draft an outline like this:

1）states your intention of writing this letter;

2）states in detail the information about the inquired party you need to know, i.e. its financial standing, credit status and business modes etc.;

3）your commitment;

4）close.

3. Deciding to adopt the proper layout, tone and style.

As stated before, there are many kinds of practical English writing in different international banking business, which has different layout, tone and style, and will be discussed in relevant units. If you are a writer, it is very important for you to well know and properly adopt the relevant layout, tone and style in your writing that you can express yourself appropriately.

4. Writing naturally and sincerely.

Writing naturally and sincerely is to reveal your true feelings between lines, make sure what you write sound sincere and natural and try to avoid the affected words and florid style with little content. Besides, as a writer, you should also learn to use polite language and be considerate to your readers.

## IV. Writing Principles and Language Features（应用文写作的原则和语言特点）

Banking communication writing is a kind of practical English writing with its main function to inform or remind the counterpart or the public of a certain thing or the reader to act based on the rules stipulated in relative practices. Such a practical writing has its specific language style, i.e. the essential language features which are called the "7Cs": completeness, courtesy, consideration, clarity, concreteness, conciseness and correctness.

### 1. Completeness（完整）

An English banking letter is very successful and highly effectively written only when it contains all the necessary information to the readers（the counterpart or the public）and answers all the questions and requirements put forward by the readers. See to it that all the matters should be stated and discussed, and all the questions should be answered or explained. Incompleteness of the practical writing, such as banking communication, will lead to the unfavorable result, thus causing unnecessary disputes and lawsuit. In order to verify the completeness of what you write, five "Ws" ( who, what, where, when and why ) and one "H" ( how ) should be used. For example, if you write a letter of claim for reimbursement, you should make it clear that who will reimburse you, what ( the amount ) you need, when and where he will reimburse you. If some special requirements should be put forward, you would explain why you would do so.

## 2. Courtesy（礼貌）

Courtesy is an important language feature of practical English writing for international business, particularly for international banking letters. It is a favorable introduction card, helping to give the reader a good impression, thus strengthening your present business relations between you and them. Beautiful and courteous words do not necessarily mean having courteous attitude. It comes from your genuine sincerity and respect for others. To show courtesy, one should follow closely the suggestions given:

1) Be sincerely tactful, thoughtful and appreciative;

2) Take a personal, friendly and modest tone;

3) Omit expressions that irritate, hurt or belittle;

4) Be prompt in reply.

To express courtesy, you can express in such language styles or ways as follows:

(1) Change the commanding tone into requesting tone, i.e. change the imperative sentence into general question with the word "will" or "would" at the beginning. e.g.

    A: Return to us the documents previously sent to you at your earliest convenience.

    B: Will you/Would you/Will you please return to us the documents previously sent to you at your earliest convenience?

(2) Use the past subjective form. e.g.

    A: We would…

    B: We wish you would…

    C: We should be grateful if you…

(3) Use mitigation tone and avoid overemphasizing your own opinion or irritating your reader. e.g.

    In order to avoid overemphasizing your own opinion or irritating your reader, you should use mitigation tone, such as: we are afraid that…, we would say…, we may ( might ) say…, we (would) think…, it seems (would seem) to us that…, we would suggest that…, as you are aware…, it appears that…, etc.

(4) Use passive voice instead of active voice.

Sometimes passive voice appears more courteous than active voice because it can avoid blaming the doer of the act.

(5) Try to avoid using the words with forcing tone or arousing unpleasantness.

Some words or expressions such as demand, which has the forcing tone, should not be used, and should be changed into request; the word refuse which has minatory tone, should be expressed in other ways such as regret to be unable to accept or decline etc.

(6) Use the words or expressions with the meaning of joy, thanks and regret etc.

Expressions on joy and willingness are: it's my pleasure that…; we are pleased (glad, delighted, happy) to…; it's a pleasure for us to…; we are gratified to….

Expressions on thanks are: thank you for…; we are appreciative of sth.; it will be appreciated if…; we shall appreciate it very much if…; we shall be grateful (thankful, obliged) if…

Expressions on regret are: be sorry to…; regret one's inability to do…; regret being unable to…; regret to do…; wish to express one's regret…; much to one's regret, be regretful that…; it's regrettable that…

Finally, in our writing, when we express politeness, we must differentiate humbleness from the courtesy. Such words as beg, or allow etc. usually express one's humbleness to others.

## 3. Consideration (体谅)

A letter functions well if it can influence its recipient by impressing proper tone for words and sentences. To gain such a favorable impression and influence, you should put yourself in the position of the recipient, taking into consideration his demand, hope, interests, etc. Every body may have his own inconvenience. Thoughtful consideration enables you to better understand your recipient, thus your letter will be expressed in a more practical and understandable tone. When writing, you should pay attention to the following:

1) Taking the recipient's attitude, i.e. "You" attitude, and avoid taking the writer's attitude, i.e. "We" attitude. Some scholars say, as a writer you should always remember that the word "BUSINESS" contains both "U" (you) and "I", but the letter "U" comes before the letter "I", which is for you to remember. e.g.

   A: We are pleased to announce you that…

   B: You will be pleased to know that…

2）But "YOU" attitude is not always suitable to every occasion to express consideration. For instance, when the recipient has made a mistake, "YOU" attitude is not proper.

## 4. Clarity（清楚）

To make sure that your letter is so clear that it cannot be misunderstood. You should first have a concrete idea in your mind of what you are going to achieve. You can express clearly only with a clean mind. What is more important is to get yourself understood, so it is advisable to write in a certain language that makes the reader understand the main points. To do these, as a writer, you should:

1）Choose plain, simple words, and words that are short, familiar, conversational, straightforward.

2）Pay attention to the position of the modifier. The same modifier will function and imply differently when it is put in different position of the sentence.

3）Pay attention to the object of the pronoun and then the relations between the relative pronoun and the antecedent.

4）Pay attention to the rationality in logic, the variety in sentence structures, the compactness in plot and the coherence in meaning.

5）Build effective sentences and paragraphs. Generally, the average length for sentences should be about 17 to 20 words. Short paragraphs encourage one to finish reading a letter quickly and to the point. Usually a paragraph in a letter consists of less than 10 lines.

6）Aim at unity, coherence and emphasis in your expression.

7）Pay attention to the logicality of full text. Before writing, you should consider the order of expressions, and the proper arrangement and paragraphing. Usually one paragraph only contains one topic idea and/or one problem to be dealt with.

## 5. Concreteness（具体）

Any kind of practical English writing should be specific, definite and persuasive instead of being general, vague and abstract. In a general and vague message, everything seems to be mentioned but actually few are fully expounded. The readers only have a vague impression of what you try to achieve, so he or she is at a loss how to react upon reading your message. Especially for arrangements, agreements, announcements, notices, posters, advertisements and banking letters calling for specific reply, concreteness must be always stressed. Using specific facts, figures and time can help to write concretely and vividly. As a writer, you should keep in mind the following guidelines:

1）Use specific facts and figures.

2）Put action in your verbs. Prefer active verbs to passive verbs or words in which action is hidden.

3) Choose vivid, image-building words.

4) Pay close attention to word orders, put modifiers in the right place.

In a word, if you want your letter to be concretely expressed, you have to use specific expressions rather than general language, more active voices rather than passive ones.

## 6. Conciseness（简洁）

Conciseness is often considered to be the most important writing principle and language feature. To carry out this principle, when writing you have to use the fewest possible words by avoiding wordiness and very long sentences, thus enabling to save both the writer's and recipient's time. In addition, conciseness means that you should express clearly what you want to say in a short and pithy style as possible as you can without sacrificing completeness, concreteness and courtesy. To do so, the following guidelines must be observed:

1) Make a long story short and try to avoid wordiness. Try to use a word or phrase to express your idea as much as possible instead of using a long sentence or cause. e.g.

| You shouldn't use: | You'd better use: |
| --- | --- |
| at this time | now |
| come to a decision | decide |
| during the time | while |
| express a preference for | prefer |
| due to the fact that | because |
| enclosed herewith | here |
| in case | if |
| in due course | soon/in time |
| in accordance with your request | as requested |
| in compliance with your request | at your request |
| in spite of the fact that | although |
| in the event that | if |
| in view of the fact that | because |
| under separate cover | separately |
| with the result that | so that |
| … | … |

2) Avoid using the general and out-of-date commercial jargons and try to express your idea in modern English.

(1) Avoid the unusual words and try to use everyday expressions. e.g.

| You shouldn't use: | You'd better use: |
| --- | --- |
| concur | agree |
| initiate | begin |
| consummate | complete |
| interrogate | ask |
| terminate | end |
| deem | think |
| remuneration | payment |
| utilize | use |
| ult. | last month |
| prox. | next month |
| inst. | this month |

（2）Avoid the out-of-date commercial jargons and try to use modern English. e.g.

| Out-of-date commercial jargons: | Modern English: |
| --- | --- |
| acknowledge receipt of | have received… |
| be in receipt of | have received… |
| as per | as, according to… |
| at an early date | soon |
| at this time, at present | now |
| attached hereto | enclosed |
| beg | ask, request, hope |
| enclosed please find | enclosed, here |
| awaiting the favor of your early reply | we look forward to your early reply |
| at your earliest convenience | as soon as you can |
| take into consideration | consider |
| this is to inform you of | we are pleased to tell you |
| your goodselves | you |
| your esteemed bank | your bank |
| your esteemed favor | your letter |

3) Control the number of the words and build effective sentences and paragraphs. Generally speaking, the average length for sentences should be 10 to 20 words, not over 30 ones. Usually a paragraph consists of no more than 10 lines because short paragraphs encourage the readers to finish reading over the passage.

## 7. Correctness（正确）

Banking letters must be correctly written, otherwise they may be misunderstood and run the risk of going astray. Usually we can by banking letters handle various financial documents such as drafts, checks, letters of credit etc. which are concerned with the rights, title or obligations, etc. of parties involved, thus calling the writer's special attention.

By correctness, we mean your grammar, punctuation, spelling, sentence structure, phrases etc. must be correct. The figures and information stated in your letter must be correct and accurate. In order to guarantee the correctness of banking writing, you should keep in mind the following:

1）Choose the only accurate facts, words and figures. Pay attention to the correct understanding and all the banking terms and jargons you use.

2）Take a matter of fact attitude to state what you will say. Don't overstate or understate the fact.

3）Use the correct level of language, including the structure of the sentences, the spelling of the words, the use of the punctuations and capitalized letters, etc.

## V. Notes（注解）

1. **WTO**　世界贸易组织，World Trade Organization 的缩写
2. **The Belt and Road**　一带一路
3. **flowery language**　华丽的辞藻
4. **commitment** *n.*　承诺
5. **tactful** *adj.*　得体的
6. **thoughtful** *adj.*　周到的，体贴的
7. **appreciative** *adj.*　感谢的
8. **irritate** *adj.*　使人不舒服的
9. **mitigation** *n.*　缓和词语
10. **recipient** *n.*　收信人
11. **rationality** *n.*　合理性
12. **unity** *n.*　统一性
13. **coherence** *n.*　连贯性
14. **logicality** *n.*　逻辑性
15. **expound** *v.*　解释、说明
16. **jargon** *n.*　难懂的行话，术语

## VI. Exercises（练习）

1. What does the "7Cs" refer to?

2. In order to express courtesy in your writing, what kind of suggestions you should follow?

## Unit Two  Layout and Structures of a Banking Letter

## 第2单元  银行书信的格式和结构

**After studying this unit, you will be able to:**
- Distinguish many types of formats of a banking letter
- Identify each part of a banking letter and its functions
- Understand the most important parts in a banking letter
- Learn some special attentions and notes in writing
- Learn how to draft an envelope

# I. The Structure of A Banking Letter（银行书信的结构）

A complete banking letter usually consists of 14 parts: Letterhead, date, reference, inside address, attention note, salutation, subject line, body of letter, complimentary close, signature, enclosure, reference initials, carbon copy and postscript.

## 1. Letterhead（信头）

Letterhead, as the first and most obvious part of a banking letter, has two functions: ① to identify where the letter comes from, and ② to form one's impression of the writer's bank, or company. A printed letterhead in a banking letter includes the name and address of the sender's bank, telephone number, telex number, cable address and/or fax number, post office box number or post code, etc. They are normally printed at the top margin of the writing paper with the following order:

- name of the sender's bank
- detailed address
- house no.
- name of street
- name of city and country, postcode
- then followed by phone no., telex no.
- cable address SWIFT no.

The printed letterhead is usually artistically designed in four forms as follows:

1）Letterhead in the middle of the top margin of the writing paper:

**Specimen A**

- name: BANK OF CHINA, HUNAN BRANCH
- address: 71 Wuyi East Road Dong District
  Changsha 410000
  P. R. China
- cable: CHUNG CHANGS
- telex: 98107 HNBOC CN
- SWIFT: BKCHCNBJ × × ×
- fax : 0086 731 82299514

2）Letterhead is typed or printed from the left margin to the right hand in the top margin of the writing paper:

**Specimen B**

- name: BANK OF CHINA, HUNAN BRANCH
- address: 71 Wuyi East Road Dong District, Changsha (410000), P. R. China
- telex: 98107 HNBOC CN  fax: 0086 731 82299514  cable address: CHUNG CHANGS
- SWIFT: BKCHCNBJ×××

3) Letterhead in the right or left margin of the top of the writing paper:

**Specimen C**

- BANK OF CHINA, HUNAN BRANCH
- 71 Wuyi East Road Dong District
- Changsha (410000)
- P. R. China
- phone: (0731) 82244514
- fax: 0086 731 82299514
- cable add.: CHUNG CHANGS
- SWIFT: BKCHCNBJ×××

4) Letterhead with the name and rank of the person who is in charge of the institution before the name of the institution:

**Specimen D**

- directors: Richard Thomas, John Smith, Sarah David, M.W. Beevers
- BARCLAYS BANK PLC, International Services Branch
- P.O. Box No. 34 Barclays House Wimborne Road
- Poole Dorset BH15 2BB, Scotland
- tel: (0203) 678345

## 2. Date（日期）

Every letter should be dated. We never send out a letter without a date. It is usually typed 2 to 4 lines below the letterhead either in right or left margin of the writing paper based on the style or format used. There are several ways of writing the date:

A. 4th May, 2018——British style

B. May 4th, 2018——American style

C. May 4, 2018——American style

When writing the date, please pay more attentions to the followings:

Attentions:

1) The year is to be written in complete form with 2018 instead of 18.

2) The date is to be written not in this way e.g. 4/5/18, but in 4th May, 2018.

3) The month can be in such socially accepted written forms as: Jan., Feb., Mar., Apr., May., Jun., Jul., Aug., Sep., Oct., Nov., and Dec.

4) The specific date can be written either in cardinal number (1,2,3,4,5,…) or in ordinal number ( 1st, 2nd, 3rd, 4th, 5th,…).

5) A comma must not be used between the month and date, but before the year.

6) Date can be written in British style or American style. The former is DATE-MONTH-YEAR; the latter is MONTH-DATE-YEAR.

## 3. Reference（发文编号）

The reference number, which is not indispensable, is generally used as an useful indication for bank's file as well as convenience for the institution or individual to keep correspondence. It is often placed 2 to 4 lines below the date line.

It may include a file number, department code or the initials of the signer of the letter, followed by the typist's initials in the following fashion:

A. Our ref.: GW/345            B. Our ref.: JS/gp
   Your ref.: PB/789              Your ref.: PC/jc

## 4. Inside address（封内地址）

In a modern banking letter, the Inside Address, which includes the name and address of the addressee (receiver), is usually typed at the left margin of the writing paper 2 to 4 lines below the Date line or Reference line if any, no matter what style the letter is. It appears exactly the same way as on the envelope.

When the addressee is an institution, the inside address should be typed as follows:

**Specimen A:**

- The Chase Manhattan Bank N.A.
- 1 Chase Manhattan Plaza
- New York, N.Y. 10005
- U.S.A.

**Specimen B:**

- Citibank New York N.A.
- 339 Park Ave.
- New York, N.Y. 10021
- U.S.A.

**Specimen C:**

- BARCLAYS BANK PLC, International Services Branch
- P.O. Box No. 34 Barclays House Wimborne Road

- Poole Dorset BH15 2BB, Scotland

When the addressee is an individual, the person's name should be preceded by the courtesy title-Mr., Mrs., Miss, or Ms, then followed by his/her title or rank-Director, Manager, General Manager, etc. e.g.

- Mr. Zhou Haitao
- General Manager
- International Business Section
- Bank of China
- 410 Fuchengmen Nei Dajie
- Beijing 100818
- P. R. China

When writing the inside address, more attention should be paid as follows:

1) Inside address should be written in the following order:
   - The name of the bank
   - House number; name of street
   - name of city; postcode
   - name of country

2) There is no comma between the house number and name of street, but one between the city and country to separate them.

3) In the British style, the inside address should be written with a comma in the end of each line (PLS see Specimen C).

4) If the receiver is not a specific person, but a person in charge of the department, put a "the" before his rank instead of his name. e.g.

The General Manager
BANK OF CHINA, HUNAN BRANCH
71 Wuyi East Road Dong District
Changsha, 410000
P. R. China

## 5. Attention note（经办人代号）

When the letter addressed to a bank is intended to be directed to the attention of a specific person or section, the Attention Note line is necessary to be typed either flush with the left margin or in the center, 2 to 4 lines below the Inside Address, then followed by the name of the specific person or the section. e.g.

**Specimen A:**
- Citibank N. A.
- 339 Park Ave.
- New York N. Y. 10021
- ATTN: Ms. Sarah David, Int'l Dept.

**Specimen B:**
- Citibank N. A.
- 339 Park Ave.
- New York N. Y. 10021
- Attention of Mr. J. White

**Specimen C:**
- Citibank N. A.
- 339 Park Ave.
- New York N. Y. 10021
- Attention: Mr. J. White
- General Manager

## 6. Salutation（称呼）

The salutation is merely a polite way of beginning a letter. It is normally typed 2 to 4 lines below the Attention Note line in the following forms:

- Dear sirs, (letters to groups, commonly used in UK)
- Gentlemen: (letters to groups, commonly used in USA and Canada)
- Dear Mr. Harrison, /Mr. Harrison, (letters to individuals, for male)
- Dear Mr. President, /Mr. President; Dear Mr. Chairman, /Mr. Chairman, (letters to individuals with some ranks or title)
- Dear Madam…, /Dear Madame…, (letters to individuals, for female)
- Dear Madams, (letters to two or more females)
- Dear Miss Smith, /Miss Smith, (letters to unmarried females)
- Dear Mrs. Smith, (Letters to married females)
- Dear Ms. Smith, (letters to married or unmarried females)

## 7. Subject line（标题）

The subject line is a brief introduction of the content of the letter with a few key words, it is used in a banking letter just for the convenience of the addressees to obtain quickly the main idea of the letter. It can begin with or without "Re:" or "Subject:", but should always denote what the letter is about. The subject line is usually typed 2 to 4 lines below the salutation, flush with the left margin, in the center, or in the following forms:

1) Your Amendment to Your L/C No. 123

2) Re: OUR NEW TEST KEY

3) Your Montreal Office L/C No. …

4) Our BP No. … For…

## 8. Body of letter（正文）

The body of letter is the main part of a banking letter, beginning 2 to 4 lines below the subject line. It usually consists of three main parts:

1) the opening paragraph or sentence

2) the purpose paragraph or the actual message of the letter

3) the closing paragraph or sentence

The body should be carefully planned and paragraphed with only one topic in each paragraph.

The opening paragraph or sentence can begin with the following fashion:

- Expressing your thanks for…
- Acknowledging receipt of a letter (or cable, telex, fax) from the addressee.
- Referring to a certain matter shown in the subject.
- Referring to the matter expressed in the previous letters.

The actual message, which is the most important part of a banking letter, usually states something specific or some problems; or asks the recipient to do something or solve the relative problems, etc.

The closing paragraph or sentence generally states the writer's wish, request, expectation or future action, etc. e.g.

- We are looking forward to your early reply.
- We are awaiting your favorable reply.
- We wish you greater business volume.

Sometimes it is impossible to write the entire banking letter on one sheet of paper, the continued sheet must be used with the second-page heading (name of the addressee, number of the page and the date) typed down from the top margin of the writing paper.

There are two forms of second-page heading:

1) Block form (used when the letter is in block style)

    CITIBANK N. A.

    Nov. 28, 2018

    Page 2

    Mr. John Smith

Dec. 2, 2018

Page 2

2）Horizontal form (used for semi-block or modified block style)

CITIBANK N. A.　　–2–　　　　Nov. 28, 2018

Mr. John Smith　　–2–　　　　Dec. 2, 2018

## 9. Complimentary close（结束礼词）

The complimentary close is a polite way of ending a letter. It is typed 2 to 4 lines below the last line of the body of the letter, flush with left margin in full block letter, or in the right margin of the paper in semi-block letter. It should match the Salutation in the style. e.g.

| **Salutation** | **Complimentary Close** |
|---|---|
| • Dear sirs, | Yours faithfully, |
| | (commonly used in Britain) |
| • Gentlemen: | Truly yours, |
| | (commonly used in USA and Canada) |
| • Dear Mr. … | Yours sincerely, |
| | (commonly used between persons known to each other) |

## 10. Signature（落款）

All letters must be signed. Unsigned letters have no authority. The signature is typed 2 to 4 lines below the Complimentary Close line, and also flush with the latter one. A banking letter should be signed by hand and in ink, then followed by typed name, then followed by his job title or position, otherwise with no authority. It includes the names of the authorities and their ranks or titles. The following are examples of different ways of signing a banking letter:

**Specimen A:**

- Truly yours,
- Citibank N. A.
- (signature)
- Jackson Brown
- General Manager

**Specimen B:**

- Yours sincerely,
- (signature)
- John Smith
- General Manager
- China Department

- International Banking Group

**Specimen C:**

- Yours faithfully,
- (signature)
- Tom Harrison
- Assistant to Mr. Jackson Brown
- Vice President

**Specimen D:**

- Yours faithfully,
- Per Pro/P. P William & Co.
- (signature)
- Jackson Brown

**Specimen E:**

- Yours sincerely,
- For General Manager
- (signature)
- Zhou Tao

**Specimen F:**

- Faithfully yours,
- (signature)
- Yang Ming
- Deputy Manager
- Bank of China, Int'l Clearing Center

## 11. Enclosures（附件）

This part is not indispensable to all banking letters either. It is used when there is something to be enclosed in the letter. The enclosure(s) is (are) typed 2 or 4 lines below the signature flush with the left margin in the following forms:

1）"Enc." or "Encl." for single enclosure;

   "Encs." or "Encls." for two or more enclosures.

2）"Encls.(2)" or "Encls. (4)" for actual number of enclosures.

3）"Encls.: 2 invoices

   1 B/Lading

   1 Product Certificate" for enclosure with the name of the enclosures

4）"Encls. : as stated." for the name and the number of enclosures which have been stated in the body of the letter.

## 12. Reference Initials（经办人首写）

Reference initials is also termed as "Identification Marks". When the letter asks for it, it is typed flush with the left margin 2 to 4 lines below the Signature line. Generally, it includes the initials of the writer and the typist of the letter. Both initials can be typed in capitals or non-capitals with a colon(:) or a slant(/) between them. However, this line is not used in a letter written by a Chinese bank. e.g.

- JS/sr  (John Smith/ Sheely Reese)
- GW: GP (George William: Grace Parson)

## 13. Carbon copy（抄送件）

The carbon copy is used only when the copies of the letter are needed to be sent to others. It is typed flush with the left margin, 2 to 4 lines below the enclosure notation. e.g.

- C.C.: George William
- cc:  Bank of China, Chengdu
- c/c:  Bank of China, Beijing

(George William or Bank of China, Beijing, etc. is the person or institution that will receive the copies of the letter)

## 14. Postscript（附言）

A postscript is rarely used in a banking letter unless there is something new to add or something to emphasize. It is typed 2 to 4 lines below the last line of the part preceding it, flush with the left margin. It is normally in the abbreviation form "P.S." or "p.s." and then followed by what the writer wishes to add.

## II. The Format of A Banking Letter（银行书信的格式）

There are several acceptable formats for a modern banking letter. The three commonly used forms are: the block style, the indented style and the semi-block style, but now the most adopted one is the block style.

### 1. Full block style（完全平头式）

All parts contained in a banking letter should be typed from the left margin to the right without any blanks left. e.g.

（1）BANK OF CHINA, HUNAN BRANCH
　　　71 Wuyi East Road Dong District

Changsha 410000

P. R. China

Phone: (0731)84422312

Telex: 98107 HNBOC CN

Cable Add.: CHUNGKUO CHANGS

Fax: 0086 731 82299846

SWIFT: BKCHCNBJ×××

(2) March 5th, 2018

(3) Our Ref.: L/C1234

(4) CITIBANK, N. A.

339 Park Ave.

New York, N. Y. 10021

U. S. A.

(5) ATTN: Mr. Johnson Smith, Int'l Dept.

(6) Gentlemen:

(7) Re: Your Reference Number:

Our letter of credit number: 25910

Draft Amount: USD 61812.50

(8) We have accepted the above-mentioned draft maturing on 06/01/18:

——The draft is held in our portfolio.

——The draft is attached kindly acknowledge receipt by signing and returning the copy of this advice.

——We shall effect payment at maturity per your instructions.

(9) Very truly yours,

(10) (Signature)

International Department

Bank of China, Hunan Branch

(11) GW/dp

(12) Enc. …

(13) C.C. …

(14) P.S.

## 2. Indented style（缩行式）

The main feature in indented style is that each line of the letterhead and the inside address should be indented 2 to 3 spaces, and the first line of each paragraph should be indented 3 to 5 spaces. e.g.

---

（1）　　　Chase Lincoln First Bank, N. A.
　　　　　　International Trade Banking Department
　　　　　　　One Lincoln First Square
　　　　　　　　Rochester, New York 14643
　　　　　　　　　Cable Address: Chase Lincoln First RCA 235921 LINF UF
（2）　　　　　　　　　　　　　　　　　　　　　　　Date: Nov. 3rd, 2018
（3）Our Ref.:
（4）Bank of China
　　　　Bank of China Bldg.
　　　　　410 Fuchengmen Nei Dajie
　　　　　　Beijing, China
（5）Attention: …
（6）Gentlemen:
（7）　　　Re: …
（8）　　……………………………………………………………………………
　　　……………………………………………………………… .
　　　　………………………………………………………………………..
　　　………………………………………………………………………………
　　　…………………………………………………………………………………
　　　　……………………………
　　　　…………………………………………………………………………
（9）　　　　　　　　　　　　　　　　　　　Sincerely　yours,
（10）　　　　　　　　　　　　　　　　　　　(Signature)
　　　　　　　　　　　　　　　　　　　　　　…
　　　　　　　　　　　　　　　　　　　　　　…

（11）GW/dp
（12）Enclosures:

## 3. Semi-block form:（半平头式或混合式）

The semi-block form is similar to the block form with the exception of the date, complimentary close and signature on the right margin of the writing paper and the first sentence of each paragraph indented 3 to 6 spaces. e.g.

---

（1）            Chase Lincoln First Bank, N. A.
                        International Trade Banking Department
                        One Lincoln First Square
                        Rochester, New York 14643
                        Cable Address: Chase Lincoln First RCA 235921 LINF UF

（2）                                         Date: Nov. 3rd, 2018

（3）Our Ref.:
（4）Bank of China
       Bank of China Bldg.
       410 Fuchengmen Nei Dajie
       Beijing, China
（5）Attention: …
（6）Gentlemen:
（7）       Re: …
（8）…………………………………………………………………………
………………………………………………………….
…………………………………………………………………………………
……………………………
………………………………………………………………………………

（9）                                          Sincerely yours,
（10）                                        (Signature)
                                              …
                                              …

（11）GW/dp
（12）Enclosures:

## III. Addressing Envelope（信封的书写）

The address on the envelope must be correct, legible and placed in the appropriate location.

1. The name and address of the sender's should be placed at the left corner in the top margin of the envelope.
2. The name and address of the receiver on the envelope should be begun one third of the way across the envelope from left to right and half way down from top to bottom.
3. The stamp should be placed at the right corner above the envelope.
4. The name and address on the envelope are usually typed in form of block style according to the following order:

   Name:

   Address: the house number

            the street name

            the name of the town or city

            or the name of the State or the Province

            the postcode

            the country's name

5. Some special post notations on the envelope should be remembered and placed in the bottom left-hand corner. e.g.
   - Via Airmail/PAR AVION
   - Registered Mail
   - By Airmail Registered
   - Top Urgent
   - Express
   - Hot Hasten
   - Confidential etc.
   - Secret
   - Top Secret
   - Printed Matter

6. Some envelope specimens are given below:

**Specimen A:**

| | |
|---|---|
| CITIBANK N. A.<br>339 Park Ave.<br>New York N. Y. 10021<br>U. S. A.<br><br>Air Mail Registered | Stamp<br><br>Bank of China, Hunan Branch<br>71 Wuyi East Road<br>Changsha 410000<br>Attn: Clearing Dept. |

**Specimen B:**

| | |
|---|---|
| CITIBANK N. A.<br>339 Park Ave.<br>New York N. Y. 10021<br>U. S. A.<br><br>Private | Stamp<br><br>Mr. Wang Hai Tao<br>Ex-Deputy President<br>c/o BANK OF CHINA, BEIJING<br>410 Fuchengmen Nei Dajie<br>Beijing 100818<br>P. R. China |

**Specimen C:**

| | |
|---|---|
| CITIBANK N. A.<br>339 Park Ave.<br>New York N. Y. 10021<br>U. S. A. | Stamp<br><br>Bank of China, Beijing<br>410 Fuchengmen Nei Dajie<br>Beijing 100818<br>P. R. China |

**Specimen D:**

```
CITIBANK N. A.                          Stamp
339 Park Ave.
New York N. Y. 10021
U. S. A.


                      Mr. John Smith
                      By kindness of Mr. Li Ming
Private
```

**Notes:**

1. c/o in Specimen B is the short form of "care of", which means that the letter will be passed on to the real reader by the one followed c/o, who receives the letter.

2. The envelope in Specimen C is a window envelope. The address is identical with the inside address. Window envelope is commonly used for the sake of saving time and convenience.

3. The envelope in Specimen D means that the letter is delivered by one person but not by mail. So it's not needed to write down the address of the receiver in the envelope but needed to add the name of the person who will send it, preceded by some expressions such as: By courtesy of, Kindness of, Through courtesy of, By favor of. etc.

# IV. Notes（注解）

1. **Barclays Bank PLC.**　英国巴克莱银行（PLC.是英国国有银行 public limited company 的缩写）
2. **cardinal number**　基数
3. **ordinal number**　序数
4. **The Chase Manhattan Bank N. A.**　美国大通曼哈顿银行（N. A.是美国国民银行 National Bank 的缩写）
5. **Citibank New York N. A.**　纽约花旗银行
6. **Ave.**　街道，avenue 的缩写，美式用法
7. **Amendment** *n.*　修改
8. **block form**　平头式
9. **horizontal form**　水平式

## V. Exercises(练习)

1. How many parts does a banking letter usually consist of? What are they?
2. Give an example to show the full block style of a banking letter.
3. Suppose you are asked to write a letter on behalf of your bank, Bank of China, Hunan Branch, located at 123 Furong Rd, Changsha(410021), P. R. China, to the Clearing Center of Citibank N. A. New York, located at 339 Park Ave. New York, 10021, USA. Please draft an envelop based on the situation above-given.

# PART II

## LETTERS RELATED TO INTERNATIONAL BANKING BUSINESS

## 第二部分 国际银行业务的书信样例

Unit Three　　Agency Relationship
第3单元　代理关系

Unit Four　　Credit Inquiry
第4单元　资信调查

Unit Five　　Accounting Business
第5单元　会计业务

Unit Six　　Settlement Related to International Trade
第6单元　国际贸易结算业务

## Unit Three　Agency Relationship

## 第3单元　代理关系

**After studying this unit, you will be able to:**
- Understand the importance of setting up an agency relationship between two banks in international banking business
- Learn how to set up an agency relationship between two international banks
- Recognize the features of writing banking letters on agency relationship after learning sample letters
- Learn how to write letters related to the agency relationship
- Master the language skills of this respect
- Evaluate your writing skills by completing the self-test checklists in the unit

# I. Introduction（概述）

International banking business can be conducted through the cooperation among the commercial banks all over the world. It is very important and necessary for international banking business to establish an agency relationship between commercial banks in international cooperation, which enables the business to be simplified in procedure, thus saving the business time and relative costs.

When setting up the agency relationship, the two banks involved should supply each other with their services information, such as payments, collections, letter of credit, foreign exchange business, international lending, trade finance etc. for their mutual reference in cooperation. In addition, after signing the agency agreement they should exchange the control documents inclusive of specimen signatures, telegraphic test keys and tariffs conditions. But before signing the formal agency agreement, both parties should take into consideration the followings: ① Is it necessary for both parties to set up the agency relationship? i.e. is the business volume large enough to set up the agency relationship between them? ② Is it possible to set up the agency relationship? i.e. is the counterparty friendly to us? Is their credit reliable? Do they have strong financial standing? etc. If proper credit inquiry finds the credit standing, capital structure and business scope of the counterparty in order, and your business volume needs such an arrangement, the agency relationship between you and them is necessary to be established.

Generally speaking, letters on request for setting up an agency relationship usually consists of:

(1) State the intention of writing this letter, i.e. setting up a direct agency relationship.
(2) State the necessity of setting up the agency relationship between both parties, and give some reasons. e.g. if there is no agency relationship between both parties, any documents related to letter of credit, collection and remittance business have to be authenticated by the third bank, thus both affecting the working efficiency of the banks and increasing the business cost of the customers.
(3) State the proposals and plans, i.e. the business scope involved under the agency agreement and how to use control documents etc.
(4) If acceptable or agreeable, express your wishes, and ask for some information such as annual reports.

On the other hand, reply to letters on request for setting up an agency relationship usually consists of:

(1) Referring to the received letter (indicating the date and reference number of the letter) and express your thanks.

（2）Express your idea, i.e. whether you accept their proposal? If agreeable, you may tell them your plan and confirm the control documents. If disagreeable, you may first appreciate their goodwill and express your thanks, then state your reasons and decline their suggestions, finally express your future wishes, or reverting to the good wishes.

（3）Complimentary close.

## II. Specimen Letters（样例信件）

### 1. Request for the establishment of an agency relationship（要求建立代理关系）

**Sample letter 1**

Dear Sirs,

Agency Relationship

We are very glad to learn from the letter of the Midland Bank of Ltd., London addressed to our Head Office that your bank has just been founded and we hereby extend our heartfelt congratulations to you.

In this connection, we would avail ourselves of this opportunity to state that as a designated bank dealing in foreign exchange transactions, we are always ready to offer you our best service. In view of the continuous development of trade between our two great countries, we believe that the establishment of a direct agency relationship will contribute much to the mutual benefit of our two banks, and we would therefore put forward this proposal for your favorable consideration. If agreeable, we shall be pleased to receive your control documents in due course.

We assure you of our sincere service and look forward to your favorable reply at an early date.

Yours faithfully,

(Signed)

**Notes:**

1. This is an established bank's request for setting up an agency relationship with a newly founded bank. Note all the phrases and sentences in the letter, which are suitably and courteously worded.

2. **address** *vt.* 致函（常用介词"to"引间接宾语）

   e.g. We address this letter to you in order to ascertain whether an agency relationship between us would be established.

   [同义词语] write, forward

3. **extend** *vt.* 给予

   extend sth. to sb, or extend sb. sth

   e.g. It is only in view of our long friendly relationship that we extend you this accommodation.

   If you require any further information, we shall be pleased to extend it to you on hearing from you.

   〔同义词语〕give, accord, afford

   extend, afford 和 accord 是书面用语，远不及 give 常用。

4. **in this connection**　在这种情况下，在这方面，在这一点上

   e.g. In this connection, we hope you send us your latest specimen signature.

   We wish you would give us understanding in this connection.

   〔同义词语〕in this respect

5. **avail oneself of**　利用

   e.g. We avail ourselves of this opportunity to express our thanks to you for your close cooperation.

   〔同义词语〕make use of, take advantage of

6. **designate** *vt.*　指定，委派，任命（过去式 designated 作形容词用）

   e.g. This bank is designated by Chinese government to specialize in foreign exchange dealings.

   〔同义词语〕appoint, name

7. **deal in**　从事……业务，经营

   e.g. This corporation deals in products imported.

   〔同义词语〕handle, trade in, in…line, specialize in

8. **offer** *vt.* 给予，提供

   常用结构为：offer sb. sth. 或 offer sth. to sb.

   e.g. We shall offer you this special accommodation.

   〔同义词语〕give, grant

   offer you our best service=place our sincere service at your disposal=our service will be entirely at your disposal.

9. **in view of**　鉴于

   e.g. In view of the increasing business volume between our two banks, we wish to propose the establishment of an agency arrangement.

   〔同义词语〕considering, in consideration of, bearing in mind

10. **contribute** *vi.*　有助于，促进

    常用结构为：contribute to sth. 或 contribute to doing sth.，很少接动词不定式。

e.g. These measures contributed greatly to improvement of the quality of our service in this respect.

11. **for one's consideration**　供某人参考

    [同义词语] for one's information, for one's reference, for one's study

12. **control documents**　控制文件

    It consists of specimen signatures（印鉴）, test keys（密押）and tariffs（费率）.

13. **in due course**　及时

    e.g. We have received the L/C No. 123 issued by Citibank N. A. in due course.

    [同义词语] in time, duly

14. **assure** *vt.*　向某人保证, 担保

    常用结构为：

    （1）assure sb. of sth

    　　e.g. We assure you of our close cooperation in this connection.

    （2）assure sb. that…

    　　e.g. We assure you that we are always ready to place our best service at your disposal.

    [同义词语] guarantee, ensure

    guarantee 是保证或担保比较正式而具体的事情, 其他担保则用 assure 与 ensure, 不过二者在结构上不同, ensure + n 或 ensure + v-ing /that, 而以物作为主语时, assure, ensure 可通用, 做一般的"保证"讲。

# Sample letter 2

Gentlemen:

Re: Agency Relationship

We are pleased to note that the volume of business between your Mexico Branch and our Hunan Branch has been increasing during recent years. But as there is no agency relationship between us, the credits received from you have to be authenticated through a third bank, and this always unavoidably results in delay in business.

In order to cope with the increasing business volume, we would like to propose the conclusion of an Agency Arrangement with your bank. Should the proposal meet with your approval, please send us your latest specimen signatures for our future use and take the establishment of cable/telex authentication arrangements into consideration.

We trust that our proposal will be found mutually beneficial.

Truly yours,

(Signed)

**Notes:**

1. This is also a letter on proposal for establishment of an agency relationship put forward by one established bank ( Hunan Branch) to another established bank ( Mexico Branch). It states the writer's intention, shows their reasons for this, and express their wishes and it's a forceful letter with plain and courteous languages.

2. **note** *vt.* 注意到，获悉（主语或逻辑主语为 you）

   e.g. We are somewhat surprised to note that you have now met with difficulty in opening the L/C in Renminbi.

   ［同义词语］learn, know

3. **volume of business** 业务量，营业额

4. **authenticate** *vt.* 确证……真实性，查证

   e.g. We would inform you that as we are not in possession of your Specimen Signatures, we are unable to authenticate the signatures appearing on your L/C No. 123.

   ［同义词语］identify, verify

5. **result in** 导致，引起

   e.g. We assure you that the establishment of an agency relationship between us will result in a consistent development of business between us.

   ［同义词语］lead to, cause

6. **cope with** 赶上

   e.g. In order to cope with the increasing business, we would offer this proposal for your consideration.

   ［同义词语］catch up with, keep up with

7. **propose** *vt.* 建议

   常用结构为：

   （1）propose to do sth.

   e.g. We propose to pay by Bill of Exchange at 30d/s(days), documents against acceptance. Please confirm if it is acceptable to you.

   （2）propose + doing sth.(较为普遍)

   e.g. We propose paying by T/T when the shipment is ready.

   （3）propose + that… ( 从句中用 should 或虚拟语气现在时 )

   e.g. We propose that the direct agency relations (should) be established between our two banks.

   ［同义词语］suggest, 但 suggest 不可接不定式。

8. **specimen signature** 印鉴，是象征有关业务权力的压印符号、图章或标志以及本

人的亲笔签名。印鉴一般是用在给银行的具体指示上，包括开立和修改信用证的信函、授权银行执行指令并进行支付的凭据（如支票、借据、信汇委托书等）。往来银行通常持有对方银行有关业务权威人士的印鉴样本，以便在执行具体业务指令时核对，以证实其真实性和可靠性。

9. **take…into consideration**　考虑到

   e.g. We may take the matter into consideration when we honor the documents.

10. **mutually beneficial**　互惠互利的

    e.g. We are always anxious to cooperate with you closely with a view to furthering a mutually beneficial trade.

## 2. Reply to the request for setting up an agency relationship（要求建立代理关系的回信）

### Sample letter 3

Dear Sirs,

Re: Agency Relationship

We thank you for your letter dated September 20th, 2018, from which we learn that you wish to establish an agency relationship with us, which coincides with our desire.

In order to keep us with the increasing trade development between the clients of our two countries, it is necessary for us to conclude such kind of arrangement with your bank.

Enclosed you will find our control documents including the specimen signatures, telegraphic test keys and tariffs and a draft agreement for your comments, please return the latter to us for our finalization.

We are confident the conclusion of the arrangement will lead to a consistent development of business between our two banks.

Yours sincerely,

(Signed)

**Notes:**

1. This is the Mexico Bank's acceptance of Hunan Branch's proposal. Note the first and last paragraphs, which are suitably worded to promote their future business between two banks.

2. **coincide with one's desire**（wishes, ideas, views, opinions）　同某人的愿望、主意、看法一致。

3. **enclose** *vt.*　把……附在信中，随函附寄

e.g. We are enclosing one copy of the relative L/C opened by our bank.

Enclose 在金融函电中的常用结构有：

e.g. Enclosed is a check.

Enclosed please find (Pleased find enclosed, Enclosed you will find) one duplicate of the Invoice No. 123.

4. **tariff** *n.(c)* 费率表

5. **draft agreement** 草拟协议

## Sample letter 4

Dear Sirs,

Agency relationship

We have received your letter of Sept. 12th, 2018 and quite understand your wish for setting up an agency relationship with us.

In reply, we would like to state that we fully understand your goodwill in this respect. However, after serious consideration, we do not think conditions are ripe to do this at the present stage as our bank has just been formed and business volume is too small. We shall revert to it when our bank is in better condition.

We hope you will appreciate our position and expect that there may be opportunity to cooperate with each other in the near future.

We wish you a greater business volume.

Yours faithfully,

(Signed)

**Notes:**

1. This letter is selected because it is not only a non-acceptance of the counterparty's good proposal but also demonstrates the new concept of a good bank letter, i.e. the use of formal language with its preciseness, plainness, courtesy and restraint so that it will not hurt the recipient's feeling.

2. **understand** *vt.* 理解

3. **state** *vt.* 表明，指出

4. **ripe** *adj.* 成熟

5. **revert to** 下次再谈，回复到，重议

6. **appreciate** *vt.* 理解，谅解

   常用结构为：appreciate + *n* 或 appreciate + that…

e.g. We hope you will appreciate our situation and cooperate with us.

We appreciate that you disagree to our proposal.

7. **expect** *vt.* 期待

   常用结构为：

   （1）expect + *n*

   e.g. We are expecting your early reply.

   （2）expect + that…

   e.g. We expect that you will open the relative letter of credit by the end of this month.

   （3）expect sb. to do sth.

   e.g. We expect you to amend the clause 1 on the letter of credit No. 123.

   [同义词语] look forward to, await, anticipate

## 3. Agency arrangement between Bank A and Bank B（A 行与 B 行间的代理协议）

### Sample 5

**Agency Arrangement**

**Between**

**Bank A and Bank B**

（1）Office Concerned

　　①Bank A Head Office and Shanghai Branch

　　②Bank B International Department, Osaka

（2）Control Documents

Bank A's office and Bank B's office mentioned above are supplied with general list of authorized signatures and schedule of terms and conditions of the other party.

Bank B's telegraphic test keys are supplied to Bank A's office for mutual use.

（3）Currency for transactions

　　U. S. Dollar, Japanese yen

（4）Credit facilities

Credit facilities of both banks shall be subject to separate arrangement.

（5）Transactions originated with Bank A

　　① Drawings

Bank A's office mentioned above may directly draw on Bank B's office mentioned above by drafts, mail transfer or telegraphic transfer.

At the time of drawing, cover is to be remitted as follows: for U.S. Dollar... The

Chase Manhattan Bank, New York A/C No. 910.

for Japanese yen… Bank of Tokyo, Tokyo A/C No. 010.

② Commercial Letter of Credit

Bank A's office mentioned above may issue by mail or cable irrevocable letter of credit directly through Bank B's office mentioned above. Appropriate instructions are to be embodied in each credit advice with regard to reimbursement.

③ Collections

Bank A's office mentioned above may send collections directly to Bank B's office above with specific instructions in each individual case regarding disposal of proceeds.

(6) Transactions originated with Bank B

① Drawings

Bank B's office mentioned above may directly draw on Bank A's office mentioned above by drafts, mail transfer or telegraphic transfer.

At the time of drawing, cover is to be remitted as follows: for U.S. Dollar… Bank of China, New York A/C No. 987.

for Japanese yen… Bank of Tokyo, Tokyo A/C No. 675.

② Commercial Letter of Credit

Bank B's office mentioned above may issue by mail or cable irrevocable letter of credit directly through Bank A's office mentioned above. Appropriate instructions are to be embodied in each credit advice with regard to reimbursement.

③ Collections

Bank B's office mentioned above may send collections directly to Bank A's office above with specific instructions in each individual case regarding disposal of proceeds.

Signed on Sept. 30, 2007

| Bank A | Bank B |
| --- | --- |
| Senior Managing Director | Senior Managing Director |

**Notes:**

1. This is an agency agreement signed by both banks (Bank A and Bank B), which contains all the clauses indicating the responsibilities held by both parties and relative terms and conditions.

2. **currency for transactions**  交易货币

3. **credit facilities**  信贷便利

4. **drawings** 出票

5. **draw** *vi.* 开具汇票 [= draw *(vt.)* a draft]

   常用结构为 : draw on sb. for a sum

   e.g. We have drawn on you for this amount at sight through Bank of China.

6. **demand draft, mail transfer, telegraphic transfer** 票汇，信汇，电汇

7. **cover** *n.* 头寸，清偿款

8. **appropriate instructions** 适当的须知

9. **credit advice** 贷记通知

10. **collection** *n.* 托收

11. **disposal of proceeds** 托收款的处理

12. **Senior Managing Director** 高级常务董事

## Sample letter 6

Dear Sirs,

Amendment to the Agreement Between… Bank and…

…Bank and…International Hong Kong have, through friendly consultation, made the following amendments to some of the agency agreement signed on March 27, 2018 between the…Bank and CITIBANK Hong Kong on commissioned sales of… Credit Card (hereinafter briefly referred to as the Agreement).

Under Article 4:

The percentage of the collected charges as the sales agency's income should be changed from 2% to 1.5%, whereas that for…income be changed from 2% to 2.5%.

Under Article 5：

The sales agency should, after encashment under… Credit Card, claim reimbursement for the paid amounts plus 1.5% instead of 2% service charges on the issuer.

The above amendments shall come into force on… 2018.

Signed on…                                                Signed on…

   …                                                              … Bank

**Notes:**

1. This is an amendment to the Agency Agreement of the Credit Card between the two banks on the adjustment of the relative service charges.

2. **consultation** *n.* 磋商，商议

e.g. We confirm that, as agreed upon through consultation, the validity of Agency Agreement has been extended for two years, from April 15, 2016 to April 15, 2018.

3. **through friendly consultation**   经过友好协商
4. **amendment**  n.(c, u)
   （1） n.(c) 修改（通知书），修改
   
   常用结构为：
   
   ① make amendments（常与动词 make 搭配使用）
   
   e.g. In case you like to make some amendments on the terms of the Agreement, please do not hesitate to communicate with us.
   
   ② …amendments to/of sth.
   
   e.g. Upon receipt of your amendments to L/C No. 123，we shall immediately make shipment of the goods.
   
   （2） n.(u) 修改（行为）
   
   ① 常与动词 make 搭配使用
   
   e.g. When you find anything to the contrary in the L/C, please cable us so that we can make amendment accordingly.
   
   ② 常接用介词 to
   
   e.g. We wish to inform you that the item was crossed off the delivery note but the corresponding amendment was not made to the invoice.
   
   [同义词语] alteration, modification, change  amendment 常意味着规章、单证等文字的改变；alteration 意味着部分、表面的改变；modification 常意味着轻微的改变；change 是一般用词，使用最广泛，常意味着全部、本质的改变。

5. **commissioned sale**   委托销售
6. **issuer**  n.   发行人
7. **service charges**   服务费


## 4. The usage of the control documents（控制文件的使用）

### Sample letter 7

Dear Sirs,

Unverifiable Signatures on Your L/C No. 8878 Dated…For…

With reference to the subject letter of credit, we wish to inform you that we are unable to verify the signature appearing thereon after comparing it with your list Authorized Signatures in our possession.

For good order's sake, please supply us with the specimen signature of the gentlemen who signs on your behalf on the captioned L/C, or else inform us of the page number on which his specimen signature appears.

Thanking you for treating this matter urgent, we remain.

Yours sincerely,

(Signed)

**Notes:**

1. This is a request for supplements to existing specimen signature. But it is an old-fashioned letter. The style is too old for today, particularly the last sentence, "Thanking you…, we remain" is so outdated that it is no longer much used now, which could be replaced by "Thank you for treating this matter urgent" or "Please treat this matter urgent". In addition, the first sentence "With Reference to…, we wish to inform you…" is a very formal beginning of a letter.

2. **unverifiable signatures**　签字走样

3. **with reference to**　关于

   常用于书信开头，但是有学者认为此用法过于正规，而且还较陈旧，不宜仿效。用 refer to 比较合适。

   ［同义词语］Referring to, with regard to

   e.g. Referring to your letter dated June 1, 2017, we regret that we are unable to accept your suggestion.

4. **subject** *adj.*　标题下的

   ［同义词语］captioned, above-mentioned

5. **inform** *vt.*　通知，告知

   常用结构：inform sb. of sth. or inform sb. that…

   e.g. We shall inform you of our decision.

   　　We regret to inform you that we are unable to accept your proposal.

   ［同义词语］advise, notify, instruct

   其中 instruct 的结构有所不同：instruct sb. to do sth.

   e.g. Please instruct Bank of China, Hunan Branch to issue the relative letter of credit as soon as possible.

6. **compare…with**　拿……比较

   e.g. Compared with the specimen signatures, we found the signature appearing on your L/C No.123 irregular.

7. **authorized signature**　印鉴

8. **in one's possession =in one's hand**　在……手中

e.g. Please destroy the relative documents in your possession.

9. **for good order's sake**   为了手续齐全，为了规范起见

10. **supply sb. with sth.**   给某人某物

   e.g. We shall supply you with our latest control documents.

   ［同义词语］provide sb. with sth., furnish sb. with sth.

11. **on one's behalf**   代表某人

   e.g. I, on our General Manger's behalf, hereby express our sincere thanks to you for your kind cooperation.

12. **treat** *vt.*   对待，处理

   常用结构：treat sth. as +*n/adj/v*-ed

   e.g. We shall treat all this information as confidential.

   A portion of each installment can be treated as payment of interest.


## Sample letter 8

Dear Sirs,

Re: Fixed, Serial and Rotation Numbers

In reply to your letter of November 5, 2018, ref. SZH/GP, we send you herewith, under sealed cover, a new set of Serial and Rotation Numbers together with the relative Fixed Number to be used in conjunction with Test Key forwarded to you by our Head Office for authentication of cables dispatched by our bank.

Please acknowledge receipt to us.

The said control documents will be effective from December 5, 2018. Please cancel and destroy the old ones now in your possession.

Yours sincerely,

(Signed)

**Notes:**

1. This is a letter on sending telegraphic Test Key, instructing the corresponding bank how to use the relative test key numbers.

2. **Test Key**   密押：供开各类电报电传或SWIFT单据时使用，只有密押数相符的电文，银行才予认可。密押有两种：一种是双方银行共用一方银行所提供的密押表，即该表由一方制定后寄给各分行和代理行；另一种是各银行分别用各自制定的密押表，双方互寄，互相确认，并凭此核对密押数。密押表包括定数（fixed number）、次数（serial number）和转数（rotation number）。以这三个数字为基础，加上该票据的日期、金额等代号数字，即为某电报的密押数。密押表属银行机密文件，非有关人员不得使用。

3. **under sealed cover**  密封件

   e.g. We shall send you under sealed cover the documents upon receipt of your letter of consent.

4. **in conjunction with**  与……配合，与……合作

   e.g. The new test key can be used in conjunction with the old ones.

5. **dispatch** *vt.*  发送

   e.g. If you fail to dispatch the statement of account in time, we shall hold you responsible for any dispute occurred in future.

   ［同义词语］send, forward

6. **effective** *adj.*  生效的, 能实行的

   e.g. The agreement shall become effective as soon as it is signed by both parties.

   ［同义词语］in effect, operative

   be effective=go into effect=come into effect =come/enter into force=be brought into effect= be put into effect

   e.g. The agreement shall be effective/go (come, enter, be put, be brought) into effect from October 11, 2007.

## Sample letter 9

Dear Sirs,

Telex Not Tested

We have received your telex dated September 27, 2018 notifying us of your payment of our banking charges USD 1,895.00 by debiting your account with us. However, we would like to point out that the telex is not authenticated by a test key. And it is not the first time that your telex or cable have been sent without tested authentication.

We would think that for cables, telexes or SWIFT involving your authorization or commitments, such as advice of money transfer, amendments to letter of credit, etc., it would be best to have them tested as a means to safeguard your interest and enable us to avoid unnecessary troubles in carrying out your instructions.

We anticipate your urgent attention to this matter.

Yours sincerely,

(Signed)

**Notes:**

1. This is a plain and forceful letter. It is forceful as it puts down in plain and courteous language all facts that would prove the recipient's carelessness in handling business and

the possible troubles incurred if he should fail to use test key to authenticate the relative authorization.

2. **banking charges** 银行业务费

3. **debit** *vt.* 借记

常用结构为：debit one's a/c with…

e.g. We wish to inform you that we have debited your account with Citibank N. A., Ningbo Branch with a sum of USD 2,102.00 for settlement of the above-mentioned charges.

4. **point out** 指出，指明

e.g. Please point out the discrepancies after checking the statement of account for May 2018.

5. **SWIFT.** 全球同业银行间金融电讯协会（Society for Worldwide Inter-bank Financial Telecommunication）

6. **advice of money transfer** 资金转账通知

7. **amendments to letter of credit** 信用证修改通知书

8. **test** *vt.* 加密

e.g. We wish to inform you that all these messages must be tested, otherwise void.

9. **carry out** 执行

10. **attention to...** 处理某事

## Sample letter 10

Gentlemen:

Re: Telegraphic Test Key

Having examined our test key arrangements, we find that the testing facilities between our two banks have not been used for a long time. As you are well aware, keeping and administering these documents would entail superfluous costs which could otherwise be avoided.

For this reason, we would propose a cancellation of the existing test key arrangements. If there is a need in future, however, such arrangements can be easily resumed.

Accordingly, please destroy the testing documents as soon as you receive this letter and confirm that fact by returning the enclosed copy of this letter duly signed.

We expect your cooperation in this respect and thank you in advance for your kind assistance.

Sincerely yours,

(Signed)

**Notes:**

1. This letter express a request for a cancellation of testing arrangements owing to extra administering cost of some not commonly used test keys. The tone of this letter is rather formal, perhaps for emphasizing the reasons and the consequent extra cost occurred.

2. **keeping and administering**　管理

3. **entail** *vt.*　招致，使需要

    e.g. Authenticating these credits through a third bank would entail additional expenses.

4. **superfluous cost**　多余费用，额外成本

5. **resume** *vt.*　恢复

    e.g. We are pleased to inform you that we have arrived home safe and sound and resumed our work.

6. **expect** *vt.*　期待

    常用结构：

    （1）expect + *n.*

    e.g. We are expecting your early reply.

    （2）expect + that…

    e.g. We expect that you will open the relative letter of credit by the end of this month.

    （3）expect sb. to do sth

    e.g. We expect you to amend the clause 1 on the letter of credit No. 123.

    ［同义词语］look forward to , await, anticipate

## III. Sentences Commonly Used on Agency Relationship（关于代理协议的常用句型）

1. In order to ensure the speedy handling of the relevant banking transactions along with the increasing trade volume, we would like to propose the establishment of a direct correspondent banking relationship with your bank.
2. As there is no agency relationship between us, the relative credits directed to us have to be authenticated through a third bank.
3. We believe that this step would enable us to avoid any possible delay that may occur in handling business to the benefit of clients on both sides.
4. We are sending you herewith a copy of our control documents together with our annual report for the fiscal year 2018 for your reference.
5. You are requested to send us your latest specimen signatures and terms and conditions for our

future use.

6. We should appreciate it very much if you would send us your control documents in return.

7. As soon as the exchange of control documents is completed, both parties may start direct business with each other.

8. We fully understand your desire to set up an agency relationship with us.

9. As you well understand, the trade exchange between our two banks is limited with a small volume at present.

10. We therefore do not intend to expand our agency network in the near future.

11. We hope you will give us understanding in this respect.

12. We are forwarding to you, under separate cover, one set of our control documents consisting of our Authorized Signature, Terms and Conditions and Telegraphic Test Key for your future use.

13. To facilitate business exchange between us, we would propose…

14. We look forward to a consistent business growth between us.

15. Thank you in advance for your kind cooperation in this matter.

16. We have ventured to draft a schedule of Agency Agreement which is enclosed for your study.

17. We wish to assure you that our services will be entirely at your disposal.

18. We are unable to identify the signatures on your L/C No. 123 of Nov. 12 according to the numbers given.

19. We shall be obliged if you send us a complete set of your up-to-date Authorized Signatures at an early date.

20. Please note that the fixed number remains the same as that we sent you on October 5th, 2018 which is on your hand.

21. We take pleasure in sending you our test key for the authentication of cables dispatched/exchanged between our two banks.

22. We wish to inform you that up-to-this-date we do not appear to have received any acknowledgement from you.

23. To complete our files, we would request you to send us your latest supplements, if any, to your specimen signature book.

24. Please look into the matter and let us know whether you have sent the above two specimen signatures, together with others to update the Booklet in our possession.

25. We hope everything in regard to your Test Key is now in order.

26. We hope you will do likewise in future before the establishment of an agency relationship between our two banks.

## IV. Exercises（练习）

1. Suppose you are asked to write a reply with 120 to 150 words to letter of Apr. 12, 2018 from the ABC Bank (located in 34 Main Ave. New York N.Y. 10021, U.S.A.) and agree to accept their proposal of setting up an agency relationship between them and your bank (Bank of China, Hunan Branch, 168 Furong Road Changsha 410000, P. R. China) with the following particulars:

   （1）他们的建议正合你意。
   （2）由于双方的业务量日渐增长，为了便利双方之间的业务处理，很有必要建立这种关系。
   （3）你行将随函附寄有关控制文件以及草拟协议以供他们参考。
   （4）客套结尾。

2. Imagine you work in Bank of China, Beijing (located in Fuchengmen Neidajie Beijing 100818), a direct correspondent relationship was set up in 2018 between your bank and Barclays Bank PLC (12 Barclays House, Wimborne Road Poole Dorset BH152BB, England). Now you are asked by your Deputy General Manager to write a letter to them asking for Amendment of Agency Arrangement with the following points:

   （1）自从建立直接的代理关系以来，你行和我行之间的业务量日渐增长，这令人高兴。
   （2）鉴于我们两国之间的贸易量在稳步增长，我行认为此时提出修改我们之间的代理安排最合适不过了，即让我行与你行的如下分行进行直接的业务往来：…Branch, …Branch。
   （3）我们相信你方上述分行的加入将进一步促进我们之间已有的互惠互利的业务关系的发展。
   （4）一收到你方同意函，我行就将有关控制文件包括定数、次数表寄送你方分行。
   （5）对对方的友好合作表示谢意并盼复。

3. Translate the following letters：

   （1）收到我北京总行通知，他们同意贵行 2018 年 6 月 2 日函中的建议，即他们双方互发电文时使用我行密押核对，现寄上次数和转数表供贵行发电使用，请注意，定数与我行 2017 年 5 月 5 日向贵行提供的相同。收件后请发送回执。
   （2）我行客户要求我们证实你行直接寄去的你行米兰分行号码为 XXX、金额为 XXX 的信用证。因为我行没有贵行的印鉴本，特要求将以上签字交由我行伦敦分行核对。因此，他们特转达我行受益人的意见，即如果贵行今后的信用证通过该行核对，对他们将非常方便。

## Unit Four  Credit Inquiry

## 第4单元  资信调查

**After studying this unit, you will be able to:**
- Understand the necessity of credit inquiry business in international banking business
- Recognize the features of credit inquiry after learning sample letters
- Learn how to write letters related to credit inquiry and credit report
- Master the language skills of this respect
- Evaluate your writing skills by completing the self-test checklists in the unit

## I. Introduction（概述）

Credit inquiring is one of indispensable business in international banking business. Generally before the agency relationship between two banks is to be set up, one party should take the credit standing of the other party into their consideration to see whether their counterparty is reliable and trustworthy. In addition, sometimes a bank is entitled by one of her clients to supply some credit information on another client, which enables them to judge whether these clients are capable and reliable in doing business. Any credit information on the financial standing, credit status, capital composition, balance sheet, income statement, business scope and business mode etc. can be obtained through the established corresponding banks and other channels. When such information is to be provided, the recipient is asked to take it in confidence.

Usually letters on credit inquiry consists of the followings:

Ongoing letter:

1. Stating the intention of this letter.
2. Specifying what you are going to know about the investigated bank or company.
3. Making relative promise to the information supplier that you treat these as confidential, and not hold them responsible for these.
4. Close.

Reply to the investigating letter:

1. Referring to the received letter ( date, reference number).
2. As requested, furnishing relative credit information or credit report.
3. Indicating wishes or requirement: asking the recipient to treat any information in private etc.

## II. Specimen Letters（样例信件）

### 1. Request for information on credit status（要求获取资信信息）

**Sample letter 1**

Dear Sirs,

Request for a Report on the Credit Standing of … Bank

As we are going to conclude an Agency Arrangement with the captioned bank, at 223 Park Ave. New York 10022, U.S.A., we should be grateful if you would furnish us with detailed information regarding the means, credit standing, and trustworthiness etc.

Please be assured that any information you may give will be treated as private and confidential and without any responsibility on your part.

We thank you very much for your kind assistance in this respect and would be pleased to reciprocate your service any time in the future.

Sincerely yours,

(Signed)

**Notes:**

1. This is a letter written by an established bank which wants to know credit information on another bank through a third bank before they setting up an agency relationship. Note all the phrases and sentences in the letter, which are suitably and courteously worded.

2. **conclude** *vt.* 达成，议定

    e.g. We are pleased to have concluded business with you in the captioned goods.

    Our bank could not conclude an agency arrangement with that financial institution.

3. **grateful** *adj.* 感激的，感谢的

    常用结构为：

    （1）be grateful + if. …

    e.g. We should be grateful if you would let us know whether you consider this firm creditworthy.

    （2）be grateful to sb. (for sth.)

    e.g. We shall be grateful to you, if you will furnish us with detailed information on the above-mentioned bank.

    We should be grateful for any further information you may give us about our counterpart.

    （3）be grateful to do sth.

    e.g. We shall be grateful to receive your remittance.

    ［同义词语］obliged, indebted, thankful

4. **regarding** *prep.* 关于

    e.g. We would like to go into detail regarding agency arrangement.

    ［同义词语］as regards, in regard to, with regard to（regarding 较为通俗些）

5. **means** *n.* 财力，收入

    e.g. Messrs John Smith & Co. possesses ample means and is trustworthy.

6. **standing** *n.* 地位，情况

    e.g. As to our financial (credit) standing, we wish to refer you to our bank.

    ［注意］financial/credit standing 有时简化为 standing（财务状况，资信情况）。

    e.g. We shall appreciate your giving us particulars as to their standing and reliability for our reference.

7. **trustworthiness** *n.* 信誉可靠

8. **assured** *adj.* 感到放心的，感到有把握的

   常用结构为：

   （1）Please be/rest assured of…

   　　You may be/rest assured of…

   　　e.g. If we can be of service in any way, you may rest assured of our interest and help.

   　　Please be assured of the prompt attention which you have had in the past.

   （2）Please rest/be assured + that…

   　　You may be/rest assured + that…

   　　e.g. Please rest/be assured that we will do everything necessary to cooperate with you.

   　　You may be/rest assured that everything will be in order.

9. **treat** *vt.* 处理，对待

   常用结构为：be treated in + *n.*/be treated as…

   e.g. Any information you supply will be treated in strict confidence.

   The above information you give us will be treated as strictly private and confidential.

10. **without any responsibility on one's part** 不让某方承担任何责任

11. **thank** *vt.* 感谢

    常用结构为：

    （1）thank sb. for sth. (sth. 前可用物主代词)

    　　e.g. Thank you for your letter dated May 4 requesting for the establishment of an agency relationship between us.

    （2）thank sb. for doing sth. (doing 前不可用物主代词)

    　　e.g. Thank you (Many thanks) for calling our attention to the fact.

    　　［同义词语］appreciate, be grateful

    　　［注意］thank 用在函电中一般表示收到东西、得到帮助等时候的感谢，而其他情况多用 appreciate。另外，thank 指语言、文字上的"感谢"，是一种动作，不是感谢的心理状况——"感激"。

    　　如不可以说：

    　　［误］We thank them.

    　　［正］We are grateful to them.

12. **reciprocate** *vt.* 报答，答谢，酬谢

    e.g. We trust that we may have the opportunity to reciprocate your courtesy.

    We shall, on a similar occasion, be pleased to reciprocate.

## Sample letter 2

Dear Sirs,

Private and Confidence

As we are on the point of executing a considerable order from Messrs John Smith & Anderson Pierce Inc. at 286 Lincoln Str. Washington, we should be much obliged if you would inform us, in confidence, of their financial standing and modes of business.

The reference they have given us is the Standard Chartered Bank, Washington Branch. Will you please be good enough to approach the said bank for all possible information we require?

It goes without saying that any information you obtain for us will be treated as strictly confidential and without any responsibility on your part.

We thank you in advance.

Yours faithfully,

China National Imp. & Exp. Corp

**Notes:**

1. This is a letter inquiring for credit information of an unknown customer in USA sent to a bank by its business client, who is going to do business with the unknown customer. They wish to obtain credit information through their domestic bank approaching the reference, Standard Chartered Bank, Washington Branch for these information. Note the first sentence in the first paragraph, and the closing sentence in the last paragraph, which are courteously worded but with the second sentence in the second paragraph over-courteous.

2. **on the point of** 正要……的时候，正准备

3. **execute** *vt.* 执行

   e.g. We always do our best to execute our contracts to the full.

   ［同义词语］carry out, fulfill, fill, perform

   ［注意］在表示"执行订单"时，execute, fulfill, fill 可替换使用。

4. **Str.** 街道，street 的缩写

5. **oblige** *vt.* 使感激

   常用结构为：

   （1）be obliged by…

   　　e.g. We should be obliged by your early reply.

   （2）be obliged to sb. for sth.

   　　e.g. We shall be obliged to you for a prompt reply.

   （3）be obliged to sb. for doing sth.（doing 前不能接用物主代词）

e.g. We are much obliged to you for giving us such an accommodation in this respect.

（4）be obliged + if…

e.g. We should be greatly obliged if you would give us more detailed information on the said bank.

［同义词语］indebted, grateful

6. **in confidence**　秘密地

e.g. We should be very grateful to know in confidence if you have found this firm reliable and prompt in settling their account.

7. **Inc.**（有限责任的）公司代号，Incorporated 的缩写形式。Inc.=incorporated with limited liability（有限责任的），美国常将其置于公司名称后，相当于英国的 Ltd。

8. **modes of business**　经营方式

9. **reference** *n.*　资信证明人

e.g. The buyers ask for credit and have given the CITIBANK N. A., New York as a reference.

10. **Standard Chartered Bank**　渣打银行

11. **approach** *vt.*　接洽，联系

e.g. Please approach your bank for amendment of the L/C without delay.

［同义词语］contact, get in touch with, get in contact with

12. **require** *vt.*　需要

e.g. Please send us as soon as possible the control documents we require.

［同义词语］need, want

13. **be good enough**　善意，惠予

14. **goes without saying**　不用说，不言而喻

e.g. It goes without saying that as soon as we receive your confirmation, a letter of credit will be opened through the Bank of China, Shanghai Branch.

［同义词语］needless to say

15. **obtain** *vt.*　获得，得到

e.g. We regret that we are unable to obtain the information you required.

［同义词语］get, secure, procure

［注意］get 是通俗用语，使用广泛；obtain 是一般用语；secure 含有"难得获得"的意思；procure 含有"经过努力而获得"的意思。

16. **in advance**　预先

［同义词语］beforehand

### Sample letter 3

Dear Sirs,

Request for Information on Messrs John Smith & His Son Inc.

The captioned company wishes to obtain a large amount of loan from us. You are cited as a reference. We would be grateful if you would provide us with some information with respect to the financial standing, credit standing and business modes of this company, located at 21 Park Ave. New York.

We assure you that any information you kindly give us will be treated in strict confidence, and without any responsibility on your part.

We thank you very much for your assistance.

Sincerely yours,

(Signed)

**Notes:**

1. This letter is a request sent by one bank to another bank for some credit information of a foreign company which applied for a credit line from the writer's bank. To eliminate the risk of this loan business, it's necessary for the bank to know the credit information concerning the applicant before signing the loan agreement.

2. **Messrs.** 法语词,是先生的复数形式,一般用于以人名命名的公司名称前,表示尊敬。

3. **captioned** *adj.* 标题下的

   [同义词语] subject, above-mentioned

4. **cite** *vt.* 列举,引证

5. **with respect to** 关于

   [同义词语] with regard to, as to, on, concerning etc.

6. **financial standing** 财务状况

7. **located at** 位于

8. **Ave.** 街道,avenue 的缩写,美式用法。


## 2. Replies to request for information on credit status(要求获取资信信息的回信)

### Sample letter 4

Dear Sirs,

Private and Confidential

This is in reply to your letter dated… concerning the credit status on…Bank at 223 Park Ave. New York 10022, USA.

> The bank, founded in 1964, is one of the leading international banks in this city and has… branches at home and abroad with its head office in New York. Since 1970, this bank has been a fully paid-up member of the Local Bankers' Association.
>
> The bank has enjoyed fine reputation for its abundant resources with registered capitals US$… and wide business scope all over the world.
>
> The president of this bank is Mr.… We regard Mr. … and his management as reliable and capable.
>
> Any above information must be treated as strictly private and confidential. We shall have no responsibility for any irregularity therein.
>
> Yours sincerely,
>
> (Signed)

**Notes:**

1. This letter is a reply to sample letter 1, which provides detailed credit information on a would-be corresponding bank of the recipient, an international bank in New York. Usually this kind of letter firstly should contain what the reader needs, secondly should contain specific and concrete information based on the facts, avoiding vague and general messages.

2. **in reply (to)** 答复

    e.g. We regret to say that we have not heard from you in reply to our two letters of May 6 and 21.

    In reply to your letter dated…, we are pleased to inform you that we have accepted your proposal.

    ［同义词语］in answer to, in response to

3. **credit status** 信用状况

4. **Ave.** 街道，avenue 的缩写，美式用法

    ［同义词语］street, road

5. **found** v. 建立，创立，缔造

    e.g. This business company was founded in 1927.

    ［同义词语］establish, form

6. **at home and abroad** 国内外

7. **head office** 总部

8. **paid-up** 已缴的，已交款的

9. **Local Bankers' Association** 当地银行协会

10. **enjoy fine reputation** 享有良好声誉

11. **abundant resources** 资金雄厚

12. **registered capital** 注册资本

13. **business scope**　业务范围

14. **president**　总经理，董事长，行长

15. **regard** *vt.*　考虑

    常用结构为：regard…as…

    e.g. We regard the above-mentioned bank as trustworthy.

    [同义词语] consider, reckon

16. **private and confidential**　机密

17. **irregularity** *n.*　异常情况，不合规定，走样

## Sample letter 5

BANK OF CHINA

Shanghai Branch

Shanghai 220000

P. R. China

TEL:　　Telex:　　Fax:　　SWIFT:

April 12, 2018

China National Imp. & Exp. Corp.

Shanghai Branch

Shanghai 220002

China

Dear Sirs,

Private & Confidential

　　In response to your letter of April 1st, 2018, we wish to inform you that we have now received from the Standard Chartered Bank, Washington Branch the information you require.

　　Messrs John Smith & Anderson Pierce Inc. at 286 Lincoln Str. Washington, was established in 1970 with a capital of US $30,000. Their chief line is in the import and export of machine tools and electric goods. Their suppliers' business with them is reported to have been satisfactory. We consider them good for small business engagement up to an amount of US $3000. For large transactions we suggest payment by sight L/C.

　　The above information we offer is strictly confidential and is not given any responsibility on this bank and our bank.

Yours faithfully,

Bank of China

Shanghai Branch

**Notes:**

1. This is a reply to sample letter 2 supplying detailed credit information on Messrs John Smith & Anderson Pierce Inc. through the Standard Chartered Bank, Washington Branch. This letter is properly worded with specific and concrete information that the reader needs.

2. **Standard Chartered Bank** 渣打银行

3. **with a capital of**… 拥有资本……

4. **chief line** 主要业务（范围）

5. **machine tools** 机床

6. **electric goods** 电器商品

7. **supplier** *n.* 供应商

8. **consider sb. good for sth.** 认为某人适合某事

9. **engagement** *n.* 约定，经营

10. **up to** 达到，等于（某数量，金额，规格等）

    e.g. We can supply up to 10,000 Forever Brand bicycles from stock.

11. **Suggest** *vt.* 建议

    常用结构为：

    （1）suggest + *n.*

    e.g. We suggest payment by irrevocable letter of credit at sight.

    （2）suggest + *v*-ing

    e.g. They suggested substituting payment by D/P for payment by D/A.

    （3）suggest + that… （从句中要用 should 或虚拟语气现在时）

    e.g. We suggest that you should instruct your bank to issue the relative L/C without delay.

    ［注意］suggest 后不可接用不定式或宾语 + 不定式

    ［误］We suggest you to accept our opinions.

    ［正］We suggest that you should accept our opinions.

    ［同义词语］propose

12. **sight L/C** 即期信用证

13. **payment** *n.*(*u*) 支付，付款条件

    e.g. Payment will be made by Letter of Credit in London against shipping documents.

    Could you agree to payment by D/P?

## Sample letter 6

CITIBANK N. A.
339 Park Ave.
New York N. Y. 10023
U. S. A.
TEL:    Telex:    Fax:    SWIFT:

May 24th, 2018
Gentlemen:
Re: Credit Report on Messrs John Smith & His Son Inc.
This is to certify that Messrs John Smith & His Son Inc. is one of the companies specialized in import and export of mechanical, electric, instrumental products and complete machinery equipments in the United States.
The corporation has been our client since the year of 1981, it maintains an active current account with us. We have granted them banking facilities on the base of partial security, and handle their documentary L/Cs with satisfactory result. For the time being, the corporation always keeps good financial standing and is considered as trustworthy counterpart.
The above information is given for reference only, without any responsibility on our bank or any of its staff.
Faithfully yours,
For and on behalf of
Citibank N. A., New York
(Authorized Signature)

**Notes:**

1. This letter is a reply to Sample letter 3, providing some credit information on business scope, financial standing and credit standing of Messrs John Smith & His Son Inc. All these information is only for the reader's reference owing to lack of specific figures. It's better to do further investigation to ensure the least risk before signing a loan agreement.

2. **certify** *vt.*  证明

    e.g. This is to certify that the abovementioned bank is one of our correspondent banks.
    ［同义词语］evidence, prove, verify
    ［注意］prove 为普通用语，含义广泛，可指各种"证明"。evidence 是指某事物的表面现象就可"表明"或"证明"另一事物如何。certify 指"用文字宣称而证明"。verify 指"证明"某事是"正确的、真实的"。

3. **specialize** *vi.* 专门从事

   常用结构为：specialize in…

   e.g. We specialize in a variety of silk piece goods.

4. **instrumental products** 仪器产品

5. **complete machinery equipment** 全套机械设备

6. **current account** 往来账，活期存款

7. **banking facilities** 银行便利

8. **on the base of**… 以……为基础

9. **security** *n.* 抵押品，证券，担保

10. **handle** *vt.* 处理

    e.g. We hope you will handle the matter with utmost care.

11. **trustworthy counterpart** 可靠的合作伙伴

## 3. Request for recommending counterpart（要求推荐商业伙伴）

### Sample letter 7

Dear Sirs,

Re: Asking For Recommendation

Our valued clients, China National Textiles Import & Export Corporation, Hunan Branch, handling the export of Chinese traditional silk goods and enjoying very good reputation all over the world, approach us with the request that they be introduced to importers at your end who are interested in the import of:

White Steam Filature, Silk Piece Goods, Silk Embroideries, Silk-Wear and other Silk Ready Made products.

In view of the very pleasant relations between our two institutions, we would request you to kindly introduce some big firms at your end, who may show interest in the import of the above goods. We send you here with some samples, which please distribute to the relative firms.

We trust that your endeavor, for which we thank you beforehand, will be successful, and we hope that this will lead to the further increase of business between our two banks.

In the meantime we shall be obliged if you will furnish us with a credit report on them and we thank you once again for your kind cooperation.

Yours sincerely,

(Signed)

**Notes:**

1. Letter of recommendation is one of the supporting business of a bank. In recommending and introducing a client to a foreign client, this kind of letter should be worded with facts simply, properly and courteously but not over-exaggeratedly. This letter recommends one of bank's clients who needs to expand its business to foreign markets.

2. **enjoy very good reputation** 享有极好的声誉

3. **approach** *vt.* 接洽，联系

   常用结构为：

   （1）approach + *n*

     e.g. Please approach your bank for the amendment of the L/C without delay.

   （2）approach + 宾语 + 动词不定式

     e.g. You are requested to approach them to clarify this matter immediately.

   ［同义词语］contact, get in touch with, get in contact with

4. **request** *n.* 要求，请求

    e.g. We are in a difficult position to meet your request.

    Your request for the establishment of an agency relationship with us is being considered by our bank.

    We note your request that an agency relationship (should) be set up between our two banks.

5. **at your end** 在你处

6. **White Steam Filature** 白色蒸汽缫丝机

7. **Silk Embroideries** 丝绸绣制品

8. **Silk-Wear** 丝绸服装

9. **Silk Ready Made Products** 丝绸制成品

10. **request** *vt.* 要求，请求

    常用结构为：

    （1）request + *n.*（表动作的名词）

      e.g. We request the extension of the L/C validity for 30 days.

    （2）request sb. to do sth.

      e.g. We request you to advise it to the beneficiary without delay.

    （3）request + that 从句

      e.g. We have cabled you requesting that the stipulations in the L/C (should) be in conformity with the terms and conditions in the Contract No. 123.

    ［注意］request 后不可同时接用 sb.（宾语）和从句。如：

［误］We requested them that they immediately look into the matter.

应改为：

We requested that they immediately look into the matter.

We requested of them that they…

We requested them immediately to…

［同义词语］ask, demand

ask 为日常用语，使用广泛。request 较正式而客气，函电中常用。demand 表示理直气壮地提出要求，语气强硬。

11. **trust** *vt.* 相信，热切希望

e.g. ABC Company would like to know if you could appoint them (to be) your sole agent in their country.

## Sample letter 8

Dear Sirs,

Re: Recommendation for Counterpart

We have received your letter dated…asking us to introduce to you some of clients in our country who are in the market for the Silk goods.

In compliance with your request we take pleasure to recommend our clients Messrs Anderson & Peter Co. at 123 Park Street, Manchester, who are interested in such commodities as mentioned in your letter. Kindly advise your clients to communicate with them direct stating our recommendation.

In order to help your clients have more information, we enclose without responsibility on our part a report on the above-mentioned company for your reference. Please treat it as private and confidential.

Yours sincerely,

(Signed)

Enc. …

**Notes:**

1. This letter is an answer to Sample letter 7, introducing to the Chinese bank a client which intends to import the silk goods made in Hunan. The letter is properly and courteously worded except a wordy phrase in the first sentence of the second paragraph.

2. **be in the market for**　想买

　　［同义词语］be interested in

3. **in compliance with**　按照

［同义词语］at one's request, as requested, as per, according to

4. **communicate with**　与……联系

5. **state** *vt.*　注明, 说明

## III. Sentences commonly used on credit business（资信业务的常用句型）

1. We shall be obliged if you will kindly furnish us with detailed information regarding the capital composition, credit standing and business operations of…Bank.

2. The information attached hereto is strictly private and confidential and is provided at your request without any responsibility what so ever on the part of our bank or on any of our branches.

3. Please be assured that any information you may give us will be treated in strict confidence.

4. Principal shareholder and managing director is Mr. …aged about…, who is reported to be a capable and energetic banker.

5. The bank has a staff of…and can meet its commitments and obligations duly and is generally considered as financially strong and reliable and trustworthy in cooperation and with its counterpart.

6. The said bank is one of the leading banks in Canada. With its turnover in 2018 for US$… and last year's profit of US$ …and paid up capital of US$…

7. Any information sent to us will be held in strict confidence by this company and its officers and entail no obligation on your part.

8. We thank you very much for your assistance and would be pleased to reciprocate your service any time in the future.

9. We have asked them to contact you direct, or you may approach them, if that suits you better.

10. The corporation maintains an account with…Bank and is generally regarded strong in financial position and reliable in business operation.

11. We should appreciate it very much if you would furnish us with the credit standing, financial condition, business status and general reputation of the following firms.

12. We thank you in advance for your kind cooperation and shall be happy to reciprocate your assistance at any time.

13. We take pleasure in introducing to you China National Metals and Minerals Import & Export Corporation. …Branch, who are interested in the commodities mentioned in your letter dated…

14. For your reference we enclose a report on the corporation for your private use only.

15. We thank you for your letter of 4th May ref. …enclosing a list of some valued firms who wish to be brought into contact with our clients.

16. We have passed on the information to our clients, and upon your recommendation, they are now communicating with the relative firms direct.

17. We reiterate our thanks for your cooperation.

18. We should be very much pleased if you would be able to furnish us with information as to the annual demand for the said commodity in your market, the import exchange control, customs regulations, and the necessary formalities in connection with the importation into your place of woolen textiles.

19. We would take this opportunity to express our cordial desire to reciprocate your kindness in this respect.

20. We shall therefore be much grateful if you would kindly recommend to them through us, some reliable importers who are interested and well experienced in the marketing of the above-mentioned commodities.

21. This company is likely to be reliable for a credit line up to USD150,000.00.

22. They are reported by their counterpart that they can settle their accounts promptly.

## IV. Exercises（练习）

1. You are asked to write, on your bank's behalf, a reply to a letter of May 4th, 2018, written by Midland Bank, London inquiring for one of your clients (China National Animals By-Products Import & Export Corporation, …Branch) on credit status and financial standing etc. with the following particulars：

   （1）该公司经营各类皮革进出口业务，信誉可靠，实力雄厚，注册资本达××元人民币。该公司系我行推荐客户。

   （2）为了便于你行了解情况，我们随函附寄一份有关该公司的资信报告，仅供你行内部参考。

2. Suppose you work in Bank of China, Beijing. Now you are entrusted by one of your clients to write a letter to Eastern Bank, London, asking them to recommend one of their clients to your client, who wishes to establish business relations with it according to the followings：

   （1）我行客户中国纺织品进出口公司××分公司，专营各类纺织品，现想与你方有兴趣进口纺织品特别是毛织品的客户建立直接的商业关系。

   （2）希望你行提供有关上述商品在你地市场的年需求量、进口外汇管理、海关规章以及毛织品进入你地市场的必要手续等信息。
（3）你行如能提供对此感兴趣的你方客户的名称、地址及上述各项信息，我行将不胜感激。
（4）随函寄去有关上述公司情况的报告一份，供参阅。

## Unit Five  Accounting Business

## 第5单元  会计业务

**After studying this unit, you will be able to:**
- Understand the importance of accounting business in international banking business
- Learn how to write letters related to bank account and bank accounting
- Grasp the language skills and features of this respect
- Evaluate your writing skills by completing the self-test checklists in the unit

# I. Introduction（概述）

International payment in international trade is generally to be made by corresponding banks of both parties. In order to deal with accounting business in international settlement, the agency agreement between both corresponding banks is to be entered into. The accounting relationship is established after the signing of the accounting arrangement.

As to the clearing or settlement business in bilateral trade, based on the trade agreement, both parties are to lay down relative regulations and rules of handling bank accounting business on clearing house, opening account, clearing currency, payment methods, credit line, reverse entry, statement of account and closing account etc.

In international settlement business, there are two kinds of accounts, one is bilateral clearing account opened by corresponding banks of both countries to serve the relative debts free of charge and interest. The other is bilateral exchange account opened based on such conditions confirmed by accounting banks as initial deposit, overdraft, interest rate, value rule, time of sending statement of account etc.

In the process of dealing with accounting business, esp. when checking the statement of account, one may find some errors accrued, e.g. omission, overcharged item, less balance, omitted interest, error of interest, error of value date, error of credit and debit, etc.

All the above-mentioned business are to be handled by accounting departments of the corresponding banks through banking letters, which are mostly in standardized format and formal style.

# II. Specimen Letters（样例信件）

## 1. Terms and conditions of opening bank accounts（开立银行账户的条款和条件）

### Sample letter 1

Gentlemen:

<u>Our U.S. Dollar Account</u>

We are very pleased to refer to your letter dated… 2018 with regard to the transfer of our US dollar account from your New York Branch to your Head Office in Montreal. We have carefully studied your proposed conditions therein and discussed the matter with Mr. John Smith, your Group Head, and Mr. Huston, your resident representative in a cordial way. We agree to wind up our US dollar account with your New York Branch and reopen a new one with your Head Office in Montreal under the following conditions:

1. Interest shall be computed on all credit balances on our US dollar account.

2. The credit interest is to be computed at the US prime interest rate minus 1%. In case of temporary overdraft, interest shall be charged at the US prime rate plus 1%.

3. Interest shall be computed on a monthly basis, with the first date of the next interest period as the value date. Your statement of interest should indicate all credit and debit balance in order of their value date and shall be sent to this Head Office along with your relative advices.

4. The supply of advices and bank statement :

   A credit/debit advice shall be made out in duplicate for each item passing through our account with original (including cables/telexes , SWIFT message ) to be sent to our branch concerned and a copy attached to your daily statement of account to this Head Office. Within 20 days after receipt of your last statement of account for each month, we shall confirm the account balance to you and point out discrepancies, if any.

5. Both banks shall collect charges on each other according to their respective tariff and shall waive those in connection with the operation of the account, including inquiries and replies.

6. An inquiry shall be answered within 3 to 7 days. As for important or urgent matters, cable/telex should be applied in replying to the inquirer. Should the inquired side fail to do so, it shall bear the economic loss incurred on the other side because of the delay.

7. If you agree to the above, credit balance on our US dollar account with your New York Branch shall be transferred to the new US dollar account with your Head Office in Montreal on…, 2018. Outstanding items, if any, under the former account with your New York Branch shall be settled through our US dollar account with your Head Office in Montreal.

Sincerely yours,<br>（Signed）

C.C. Your Rep. Office, Beijing

**Notes:**

1. This letter refers to the terms and conditions in opening an U.S. dollar account, which is a very standardized letter with proper language and formal style.

2. **open** *vt.* 开立（账户，信用证等）

   e.g. We are desirous of opening an account with you.

3. **refer** *vi.* （后常接用 to）谈到，涉及

   e.g. We refer to your letter dated June 24, 2018 concerning the above collection for US$12,000.00.

Referring to your request in your letter dated May 4th, we enclose a copy of our latest specimen signatures.

［注意］referring to 一般常用于书信的开头，表示"涉及"相关的文件、电报等，有的人认为不宜仿效。

4. **transfer** *n. vt.* 转账，过户

5. **Montreal** *n.* 蒙特利尔（加拿大的一个城市）

6. **resident representative** 常驻代表

7. **cordial** *adj.* 友好的，亲切的

8. **wind up** 结束，终止

   e.g. Please wind up this Special Account after the termination of the operation of the Contract No. 1.

   ［同义词语］close, terminate

9. **compute** *vt.* 计算，估计

   e.g. The losses are computed at US$ 340.

10. **Prime Interest Rate** 美国最优惠贷款利率，基础利率

11. **in case of** 假使，如果

    e.g. In case of business, please see to it that the L/C be opened telegraphically without delay.

    ［同义词语］in the event of

12. **overdraft** *n.* 透支

13. **value date** 起息日

14. **statement** 报单

15. **credit and debit balances** 贷方和借方余额

16. **credit advice** 贷记报单，贷记通知书

17. **make out** 开列，缮制

    e.g. We wish to inform you that the relative documents should be made out in English and in triplicate.

18. **SWIFT** 全球银行间金融电信协会（Society for Worldwide Interbank Financial Telecommunication）

19. **collect** *vt.* 收取（款项），托收

    e.g. The bank will collect charges when they open the relative L/C for you.

    We have drawn on you at sight a draft for the invoice value to be collected through the Bank of China.

20. **waive** *vt.* 放弃（要求，权利等）

e.g. The buyer waived his right to lodge a claim on the defective goods.

[同义词语] give up, relinquish, 其中 waive 和 relinquish 是正式用语，而 give up 为日常用语。

21. **C.C.** 抄送件，carbon copy 的缩写
22. **Rep. Office** 常驻办事处，Representative Office 的缩写

**Sample letter 2**

Dear Sirs,

Barter Contract No. 123
Our Ref. No. …

At the request of our client, China National Import & Export Corporation, Hunan Branch at No. 36 Bayi East Road Changsha Hunan, and in accordance with the terms of the barter contract No. 123 signed between your and our clients on June 1, 2018, a special barter account should be established between our two banks to record and offset their transactions. Please note the followings:

1. We agree to establish the required barter account and suggest its name be called…

2. All documents presented to be settled through this barter account shall be handled in conformity with…

3. This account will bear no interest and charges and will work on a sequence year basis.

4. Statements shall be sent monthly by our two banks and within 15 days after receipt of the statements, the receiving bank shall verify the balance of the account and indicate discrepancies, if any.

5. All correspondence should be made in English and documents presented under this barter contract shall be expressed in clearing currency and marked "proceeds to be settle through the special barter account No. …"

6. After the termination of the contract concerned, the account shall be closed on mutual consent.

7. The balance of the account, if any, will be settled by both trade partners.

Please contact your client and if no objection, confirm your agreement to us by returning tested telex quoting our Ref. Number.

Yours truly,
(Signed )

**Notes:**

1. This letter refers to the terms and conditions in opening a special account under a barter

contract. As contract under barter trade needs no payment for goods but goods for goods, a special barter account needs to be opened between two banks of each client to record and offset their transactions, thus the terms and conditions under this kind of account are to be in more detail, thus avoiding subsequent trouble.

2. **at the request of …at one's request**　应……请求

　　e.g. We are sending you herewith our control documents at the request of your bank.

　　At your request, we reopen a new account with your Head Office in New York.

3. **in accordance with**　根据，按照；与……一致

　　e.g. The L/C should be opened in accordance with the terms and conditions of the contract.

　　The stipulations in the L/C must be in accordance with the terms and conditions in the contract.

　（1）［同义词语］according to, in conformity with, in compliance with, as per, 其中 according to, in accordance with 使用较普遍；in conformity with, in compliance with 较正式；as per 较陈旧，后者使用较少。

　（2）［同义词语］in agreement with, in conformity with, in accord with, in line with

　　［注意］第（1）组短语多用以引起副词性的短语，用作句中的状语；而第（2）组短语只用以引起形容词性的短语，用作句中的表语，不能用以引起副词性的短语。

4. **offset** *vt.*　抵消，冲销

　　e.g. We are supposed to be making economies to offset the increase in material cost.

5. **on a sequence year basis**　以一个连续年为基础

6. **verify** *vt.*　核查，证实

　　e.g. We would like to ask you to verify the matter with your banker.

　　［同义词语］certify, evidence, prove

7. **present** *vt.*　提交，呈递

　　e.g. We regret to inform you that the documents presented by you are not in conformity with the terms and conditions.

8. **clearing currency**　清算货币

9. **close** *vt.*　结束

　　e.g. Will you please send us a bank draft for the amount so as to enable us to close our books?

　　We are pleased to inform you that we have closed the account at the request of your bank.

10. **quote** *vt.*　引用，注明

　　e.g. The Buyer is requested to always quote the number of this Sales Confirmation in the L/C to be opened in favor of the seller.

## 2. Letters on opening and closing an account（关于开立账户和注销账户的书信）

### Sample letter 3

Dear Sirs,

Opening A Renminbi Account

During the past months, we have been asked to establish an increasing number of documentary credit denominated in renminbi by our clients.

In this connection, we feel that rather than asking you to draw in USD on our New York correspondent in reimbursement of each negotiation, it may be simple for us to open a renminbi account with your bank and to give you the authority to fund the account by drawing on CITIBANK, N.A. New York in certain amount of U.S. currency when funds are needed. Negotiations under our renminbi letters of credit can then be debited to the account in your books.

If you deem this arrangement agreeable to you, we will give you the necessary authority to draw on the said bank, whom we shall authorize to honor your drawings.

We are looking forward to your early reply.

Sincerely yours,

(Signed)

**Notes:**

1. This letter is a request for opening a renminbi account for the simplicity of work procedures, which are firstly to the point: stating the reasons and then describing how to process it in detail. It is sincere and reasonable. No matter whether the request is acceptable or not, the letter will leave a good impression which will help promote future business.

2. **establish** *vt.* 开立，建立

    e.g. Please establish the relative Letter of Credit as soon as possible.

    ［同义词语］open, write

3. **documentary credit** 跟单信用证

4. **denominated in** … 用……标价

5. **in this connection** 鉴于这种情况

    ［同义词语］in this respect

6. **draw on** … 向……开立汇票

7. **correspondent** *n.*   代理行
8. **in reimbursement of**   偿付
9. **negotiation** *n.*   议付款
10. **be debited to** …   借记……账户
11. **honor your drawings**   承付你方票据

**Sample letter 4**

Dear Sirs,

Winding up the Special Barter Account

Our Ref. … Your A/C No. …

With reference to the Special Barter Account captioned, we are informed by our client, (name and address), that both contractual parties have reached an agreement to terminate the operation of the contract No. … on which the said account was opened.

Therefore, at the request of our client, kindly convey our intention of winding up the barter account to your client, (name and address), and get consent from them under advice to us quoting our ref. number. Remaining balance of (amount), ending on (date), in favor of … will be adjusted and settled by trade partners themselves without engagement.

Yours sincerely,

(Signed)

**Notes:**

1. This letter is a request for closing a barter trade account owing to the ending up of the operation of the barter trade contract on which the said account was opened. Note all the words and sentences in the letter, they are all worded properly and reasonably with sincerity, but with some words and phrases too formal and outdated in the opening sentence "with reference to…".

2. **wind up**   终止,停止

   ［同义词语］terminate, end up

3. **with reference to**   关于

   常用于书信开头,但是有学者认为此用法过于正规,而且还较陈旧,不宜仿效。用 refer to 更为合适。

   ［同义词语］referring to, with regard to, we refer to…

4. **captioned** *adj.*   标题下的

   ［同义词语］subject, above-mentioned

5. **reach an agreement**   达成协议

6. **terminate** *vt.*  终止，停止

   ［同义词语］end up, wind up

7. **operation** *n.*  执行，运行，运作

8. **at the request of**   应……的要求

9. **kindly**   相当于"请……"的意思

10. **convey** *vt.*  传达，表达

11. **quote** *vt. vi.*  引用

12. **in favor of**   以……为抬头人或受益人

13. **engagement** *n.*  责任，约束

## 3. Letters concerning bank accounting business（关于银行会计业务的书信）

### Sample letter 5

From: ... Bank, Hong Kong

To: Bank of China, Hong Kong

Date: May 4, 2018

Dear Sirs,

Your Ningbo BP... for HK$...

Drawn by...

On...

Under Our L/C No. ...

We are pleased to advise having credited your current account in the books of our Hong Kong Office with the sum of HK$...being the captioned bill plus your commission HK$... Please credit the amount of ... to the account of your Ningbo Office under cable /airmail advice quoting the captioned reference. This amount is made up as follows:

| | |
|---|---|
| BP... | HK$12,407.00 |
| Charges | 138.00 |
| Your Commission | 20.00 |
| | HK$ 12,565.00 |

Yours faithfully,

(Signed)

C. C: Bank of China, Ningbo

**Notes:**

1. This letter is a credit note advising the recipient that the relative account has been credited with a certain amount of money. It is a good sample letter with facts.

2. **BP** 出口押汇，是 bill purchased 的缩写，指出口商将货物装运出后，即以货物单据（shipping documents）附在向进口商收取货款的汇票上，称"跟单汇票（documentary bill）"，转让给（议付）银行，收回现金，即称出口押汇。

3. **drawn by**... 由……出票

4. **credit** vt. 贷记，记入贷方

   常用结构为：

   （1）credit an amount to sb.

   e.g. We have credited US$5,000.00 to the ABC Textile Company.

   （2）credit one's account with an amount

   e.g. We advise that their account has been credited with a sum of US$4,500.00 through Bank of China, New York.

5. **under advice to sb.** 并同时通知某人

   e.g. Please instruct your bank to amend the relative L/C to allow partial shipment, under advice to us.

## Sample letter 6

From: CITIBANK N.A., New York

To: Bank of China, Ningbo Branch

Date: April 24th, 2018

Gentlemen:

Your Ref. BP No. ... for US$...

Our L/C No ....

Further to our telex dated April 18th, 2018, we wish to inform you that the drawees have paid the above bill and the matter is now in order. We are awaiting receipt of your confirmation that in settlement of the cost of our above telex you have remitted us ￥30.00 for the credit of our account with your Head Office, Beijing.

Yours faithfully,

(Signed)

**Notes:**

1. This is a follow-up letter advising that the payment has been effected and asking for confirmation. Note the language used in this letter, it is worded concisely and clearly to the point.

2. **further to** 继……之后

e.g. Further to our previous letter dated May 24th, 2018, we would have to inform you that up to date we have not yet received our reimbursement.

［注意］在函电中，further to 常用在书信的开头，表示多次去函电谈同一件事，再次去函电谈及此事。

3. **drawee** *n.* 受票人，付款人，支付人

4. **in order** （单据、手续等）齐全无误，符合要求，妥当；状况良好（多用作表语和补语）

e.g. We are pleased to inform you that we have found the documents in order.

Please confirm by return if everything is in order.

5. **settlement** *n.* （账款）偿付，（账目）结算

e. g. For a settlement of our account of US$1,800.00，please let us have your check.

We can promise you to make a remittance within 10 days in full settlement of this outstanding item.

6. **credit** *n.* 贷方

## Sample letter 7

Dear Sirs,

Statement of Our External Account

Upon checking your statement of our account ending August 31, 2018, we find that the amount of… dated August 15, 2018, appears on the debit side without particulars, which we are unable to trace in our records.

We shall be much obliged if you will inform us of the nature of the transaction and our reference so as to enable us to pass a corresponding entry on your part.

Yours faithfully,

(Signed)

**Notes:**

1. This is a letter advising the recipient of something on an outstanding item. Note the language used in this letter, it is worded concisely to the point in the first paragraph and courteously with the request in the last paragraph.

2. **trace** *vt.* 查找，追查

e.g. We are regretful that we are unable to trace this item.

3. **nature of the transaction** 这笔交易的原委

4. **pass a corresponding entry** 作相应的入账

## Sample letter 8

Dear Sirs,

<u>Omitted Interest on Our A/C No. ...</u>

In checking your statement of our US Dollar A/C No. ... for October, 2018, we found that on October 12th, 2018, you adjusted the value date of your credit of August 20th, 2018 for US$... back to August 13th, 2018. However, your statement of interest indicates that the above item was only back valued but interest was not calculated and credited to our account for the 7 days from August 13th to August 19th.

According to the Accounting Arrangements between our two banks, interest should be calculated on the adjusted item separately when adjustment is made for a credit or debit entry for a large amount.

You are therefore requested to credit our account with an amount of US$... as interest for the 7 days calculated at rate of 2.75% p.a.

Please look into the matter and advise the outcome as soon as possible to us for the attention of Mr. Wang qiang of International Clearing Dept.

We are expecting your early reply.

Sincerely yours,

(Signed)

**Notes:**

1. This letter is to advise the adjusted interest omitted. Note all the phrases and sentences in the letter, which are worded plainly, forcefully and reasonably. It is forceful by putting down in plain and courteous language all facts that would prove the recipient's carelessness in handling business and the troubles incurred, and finally by expressing the writer's requests and wishes reasonably.

2. **check** *vt.* 查对，核对

3. **adjust** *vt.* 调整

    e.g. As requested, we have adjusted the relative clauses in L/C No. 123.

4. **back value** 倒期计息

5. **calculate** *vt.* 计算

    e.g. You are requested to calculate the interest at US prime rate.

6. **Accounting Arrangements** 财务协定

7. **look into** 调查，查证

8. **for the attention of ...** 由……经办

**Sample letter 9**

Dear Sirs:

Our B/P No. … of …

For S.F… Under Your L/C No. 123

Referring to your letter dated 12th Jan., 2018, concerning the above item, we wish to advise that we have received the proceeds of S.F… and the interest of S.F… from our London Office as per their credit advice dated 20th Jan., 2018.

However, we have to point out that the interest originally claimed should be S.F…, for which you may refer to our letter of 4th Jan. and yours of 12th Jan. Besides, our charges, which amount to S.F… and are claimed under above schedule, are not paid yet. Therefore, we would request you to pay the difference of S.F… and our charges of S.F… to our London Office for the account of our Head Office, Beijing under advice to us.

Sincerely yours,

(Signed)

**Notes:**

1. This letter is to ask for the underpaid interest. All the phrases and sentences in the letter are worded plainly with the fact that the relative interest was underpaid, and with the request for claiming the less paid interest reasonably.

2. **S.F** 瑞士法郎，Swiss Franc 的缩写

3. **point out** 指出，指明

    e.g. We wish to point out that the relative stipulations in the L/C are not in accordance with the terms and conditions in the contract.

    Please point out the discrepancies after checking the statement of account for May 2018.

4. **claim** vt. 索偿，索取，要求

    e.g. To facilitate the settlement, we would ask you to reappoint your London agency as the reimbursing bank, from whom we can claim our reimbursement directly.

    We should like to claim the trade discount and intend to pay within 30 days.

    ［同义词语］ask，request，require，claim，demand 这些词都可译成"要求"。ask 为日常用语，使用广泛。request 较正式而客气，为"请求""恳求"，在函电中使用广泛。require 和 claim 有根据权利等而"要求"的意思。demand 表示理直气壮地、不断地"提出要求"，语气强硬。

5. **refer to** 查询

6. **amount to** 总额达……

7. **for the account of…**   收入……的账户

**Sample letter 10**

Dear Sirs:

<u>Your Debit Dated …, 2018 for US$…</u>

The subject debit represents the interest for… days from… to…, 2018 under the item of US$… upon inquiry of our… Dept., we understand that they requested your bank to debit our account with US$… on…, 2018. But the said debit was wrongly value dated… instead of…. As a remedy, we further authorized you on… via SWIFT… to correct it.

Accordingly, you should refund an interest amount of US$… by crediting our account. On the contrary, however, you wrongly passed the said amount to the debit of our account. Enclosed is the related booking information for your reference.

If our calculation is found in order, please refund US$… under advice to us.

Yours faithfully,

(Signed)

**Notes:**

1. This letter is to advise the items wrongly value dated and interest wrongly entered. All the phrases and sentences in the letter are also worded plainly and forcefully with the facts that the debit of account was wrongly value dated and relative interest was wrongly calculated and entered, and with the request for relative collection and refunding.

2. **subject** *adj.*   标题的

   e.g. We are enclosing a check of US$1,250.00 for settlement of the subject item.

   [同义词语] captioned

3. **inquiry** *n.*   询问，调查

4. **remedy** *n.*   补偿，赔偿

5. **accordingly** *adv.*

   该词在函电中有两种用法：

   （1）相应地，按照(要求，合约等)办事。多用于句尾。

   e.g. As soon as we receive the relative letter of credit from you, we will arrange shipment accordingly.

   （2）因此，所以。多用于句子的开头或中间。

   Accordingly, we have to ask you to extend the validity of the L/C.

   [同义词语] therefore

   accordingly 较 therefore 正式，但语意较轻。

6. **refund** *vt.* 归还，退还，偿还（款项）

   常用结构为：

   （1）refund + *n.*

   e.g. As you calculated the interest for January at the wrong interest rate, please refund the part overcharged.

   （2）refund+ 双宾语 /+ 直宾 to 间宾

   e.g. We shall refund you the premium upon receipt of your debit note.

   ［同义词语］repay, reimburse

   repay 和 refund，reimburse 的意义和用法相同，但是 repay 还可用于比喻方面，例如：

   e.g. We are sure that they will repay your kindness.

7. **on the contrary** 相反，反之

   e.g. As regards this proceeds, you should credit the amount to our account, on the contrary, you debit our account.

   ［同义词语］on the other hand, in contrast

   on the contrary 用于否定前面叙说的真实性。

   e.g. You said the amount due you paid was correct. On the contrary, we found the amount you credited our account underpaid.

   on the other hand 用于补充说明另一新的不同的事实。

   e.g. The quantity of the shipment is correct. On the other hand, the quality is not up to the usual standard.

   in contrast 用于说明两件不同而真实的事物，指两者惊人的不同。

   e.g. The contracted amount is US$1,200.00. In contrast, the paid amount is US$1,180.00.

## Sample letter 11

Dear Sirs,

Subject: Our D/N... for cable charge of...

We wish to advise that in answer to our inquiry about the above debit note, Eastern Bank Ltd., London informed us that the sum was already paid to us on June 2, through Midland Bank Ltd., London. However, up to date we do not seem to have received the relative credit advice from you. We would therefore, ask you to kindly look into the matter, and if necessary, approach Midland Bank Ltd., London for clarification, in order that the necessary entries might be passed.

For your information we enclosed the reproduced copies of the letter sent to us by Eastern

Bank Ltd., London which are self-explanatory.

Yours truly,

(Signature)

Enc. as stated

**Notes:**

1. This is an inquiry for cable charge of…, which is formal in language and style but not standardized in format.

2. **D/N**　借记报单，欠款账单，欠货单。Debit Note 的缩写形式。

3. **credit advice(C. A.)**　贷记通知书，收款报单

4. **entries might be passed**　转账

5. **For your information**　供你方参考

6. **Enc. as stated**　附件如文

## Sample letter 12

From: The… Bank, Ltd., London

Our Ref. …　　　　　Date: …

Your Ref. BP…

To: …

Dear Sirs,

Re: Letter of Credit…

Advice of Payment Account…

We acknowledge receipt of your letter dated May 14, 2018, forwarding to us documents drawn under the above credit valued at… charges…

This item has been duly paid/accepted and has been disposed of as indicated in "2" below.

1. Your account on our books has been credited with…

2. US$…has been paid to your London Office for the credit of your account.

3. We have responded to the debit in our account on your books of…

4. You may release/not release guarantee or reserve under which you negotiated or made payment.

Yours sincerely,

(Signed)

**Notes:**

1. This is a reply (to the inquiry) from…Bank, Ltd., London, which is simple and not as standardized as inquiry in format and style.

2. **forward** *vt.* 寄送，发送

   ［同义词语］send, dispatch

3. **for the credit of your account**　记入你的账户

4. **release guarantee / reserve**　撤保

5. **negotiate** *vt.*　议付

   e.g. The exporters must present shipping documents when they negotiate payments with the bank.

## III. Sentences Commonly Used on Accounting Business（会计业务的常用句型）

1. Our… Branch would like to open with you in the name of Forex dept. a RMB Dealing Special Account.
2. Outlined hereunder for your study are our proposed arrangements for operating the account.
3. Forex Dept. shall be responsible for the management of the account balance and the replenishment of funds to the Special Account.
4. Whenever the Special Account was overdrawn, replenishment is to be made by Forex Dept.
5. After receipt of your statements of account, our… Branch shall at any time inquire by telex of you about erroneous, omitted or duplicated items, if any.
6. They will confirm the correctness of your last statement of each month within 20 days after its receipt.
7. When an item was found cross-entered, the said Dept. shall be responsible for advising you to make necessary adjustment.
8. Please study the foregoing and confirm in writing, informing us of the account number so that an initial deposit can be remitted to you and our… Branch be notified to operate their Special Account.
9. Our account was credited /debited on… and again on… under the same reference number, please reverse the latter entry under advice to us.
10. As your statement of account ending… does not indicate particulars for the following amounts on the debit side, we are not able to trace them in our records.
11. There is a discrepancy between your advice and your entry on statement.
12. We have not received your statement of account from… to…
13. The two amounts were booked into A/C… through oversight but both have been transferred into A/C…
14. Please do likewise in your books and accept our apology for inconvenience caused to you.

15. Kindly do the needful in your books.

16. After checking your statement of account for Jan., 2018, we wish to confirm that the balance of US$… is correct except for the following items.

17. We deducted US$… being 3% commission from the invoice value as per letter of credit terms.

18. We have instructed your H.O Beijing by cable /mail to credit the following amount to your account with them.

19. We are informed by… Branch that your statement of account appears the following debit entry, which is not shown in our books.

20. We wish to bring your attention to the fact that till now your statement of account has not yet been received by us.

21. At the request of the above bank, we enclose our cashier Order /Demand Draft No. … for HK$… in settlement of captioned bill.

22. We refer your telex dated… and wish to inform you of opening on our books a special barter account for settlement under the above contract.

23. We are informed that both parties have fulfilled their contractual obligations under the above barter contract and that the account shows a balance of zero.

24. Please contact your client for their consent to close the account under advice to us.

## IV. Exercises（练习）

1. Write an English letter according to the followings:

    发　文：梅恩银行，香港

    主　送：中国银行，香港

    事　由：宁波中国银行汇票号 BP12345

    支付行：东亚银行，香港

    　　　　我行信用证号：5678，金额 125,600 港元（包括费用 280 港元）（我行汇票号 6789）

    　　　　应以上银行的要求，现寄上我行即期汇票 No. 6789，金额 125,600 港元，以结清以上款项。

    　　　　请将此金额贷记以上银行并引用它们的案号，用电报／航空通知它们。

    附　件：1 份

    抄　送：中国银行，宁波

2. Translate the following letter.

接我北京总行通知，在你方报单中有下述借记，但在我行账上却未见。

"2月6日……系有关货物退回上海的费用和我方有关费用，2,400.25美元"

因我行好像未收到你行的有关通知书，另外，你行报单上亦无引用我行案号，故我行无法核销此笔账。希望你行提供有关此事的详细资料，或对此作进一步说明，以供我行考虑。

3. Write an English letter according to the following particulars:

发文：美国银行，旧金山

主送：中国银行，成都

日期：2018年2月23日

事由：我行信用证号：

你行案号：

受益人：

账目：

金额：

称呼：

现将贵行2018年2月12日寄来的本金为……的提示单证退还贵行。

我行客户拒绝为这些单据付款，原因如下：

（1）货运起点不是成都而是上海。

（2）发票商品名称与信用证要求不符。

（3）空运提单没有签字。

（4）给买方的电文副本没有案号。

我们建议买卖双方直接联系。现我行即将勾销这笔业务。

附件如文。

## Unit Six  Settlement Related to International Trade

## 第6单元  国际贸易结算业务

**After studying this unit, you will be able to:**

- Understand international settlement as one of the most important business in international banking business
- Recognize the features of this kind of letters in the format and style after learning sample letters
- Learn how to write letters related to international payment methods inclusive of remittance, collection and letter of credits
- Master the language skills of this respect
- Evaluate your writing skills by completing the self-test checklists in the unit

## I. Introduction（概述）

With the increasing globalization of international trade, commercial bank as a financial intermediary of both buyers(importers) and sellers(exporters) has been important international clearing center, which provides special types of services directly to international payment and settlement, and not only makes fund transfer more speedy and convenient in international trade, but also supplies its clients with other useful services on economic information and credit inquiry needed.

Generally in international settlement there are three commonly used payment methods: Remittance, a commonly used one by payer making payment to payee through bank by means of Mail Transfer(M/T), Telegraphic Transfer (T/T), and Demand Draft (D/D); Collection, one consisting of clean bills and documentary bills, with the latter one classifying into time and sight Documents against Payment(D/P) and Documents against Acceptance( D/A); Letter of Credit, a main method in international payment, which is, a written undertaking by a banker in importer's country to the exporter or the beneficiary at importer's request, is available on condition of that a set of documents meet with the requirements, i.e. a complying presentation. The credit created for international settlement among banks not only provides a sense of security for traders involved, but also a reliable source of finance for foreign trade where required. There are several types of credits: documentary credit, clean credit, irrevocable letter of credit, confirmed and unconfirmed credit, transferable credit, among which, documentary credit is the most commonly used one.

What a bank usually does in international settlement related to international trade is to open credit, amend credit, examine credit and negotiate documents, claim for reimbursement and guarantee payment and deal with problems in processing of international settlement etc., all of which will be finished by means of letters, cables and SWIFT.

## II. Specimen Letters（样例信件）

### 1. Opening and advising relative letter of credit（信用证的开立和通知）

**Sample letter 1**

To:
From:
Date:
Dear Sirs,

Documentary Credit Application

We hereby request you to open for our account by airmail/SWIFT in full an irrevocable documentary letter of credit in favor of China National Chemicals, Imp & Exp. Corp. to the extent of US$56,700.00, say FIFTY SIX THOUSAND AND SEVEN HUNDRED ONLY. The contents of the credit are shown on the back page hereof.

 We hereby assure you of sufficient funds on our account with you on the date of payment to cover all payments, including expenses/charges incurred or interest occurred due to you or your agency banks.

 It is hereby stated that the shipping documents under the credit shall, after presentation to you but prior to your acceptance, be temporary lent to this corporation, whereas they are held in your name with the trust liability on us and consignments belonging to your bank, entirely free from any third party's interests.

 We guarantee that within three business days after we have received the above-mentioned documents as your trustee, notice shall be given to you in writing whereby you are authorized to act in the light of the following conditions:

（1）Provided that we inform you of our acceptance of the documents, you can make payment/accept bills of exchanges and/or confirm your liabilities for deferred payments.

（2）In case the documents are refused by us for any points which are not in conformity with the credit terms, you shall dispose of these documents thus returned to you with a statement of our refusal.

（3）If these points cannot be considered as discrepancies after a careful examination in the light of international practice, you have the right to effect payment/acceptance or confirm deferred payment, as the case may be, and return us the documents along with your advice of debit/acceptance/confirmation.

（4）Where no written notice is received from this company/corporation beyond three business days, you have the right to effect payment/acceptance/confirmation under the credit.

（5）You are authorized to debit our account with the invoice amount plus charges/interest, if any, at the time of your payment/acceptance/confirmation under advice to us.

（6）Your commitment for payment on maturity shall be established once you have made acceptance/confirmation under an usance/deferred payment credit and have so advised us. Then, we shall have no right to prevent you for whatever reasons from making payment when due.

 We are agreeable that all matters and procedures in respect of the establishment of a credit, amendments thereto, and examination of documents, payments or acceptance thereunder shall be subject to the Uniform Customs and Practice for Documentary Credits(2007 Revision), International Chamber of Commerce Publication No. 600.

> It is understood that you shall assure no liability or responsibility for the consequence arising out loss and/or delay in transit of any messages, letters or documents, or for delay, mutilation or other errors arising in the transmission of any telecommunication.
>
> The credit can be amended with our notice in writing and your consent.
>
> Applicant(Seal)<br>(Authorized Signature)

**Notes:**

1. This letter is an application for opening Documentary Letter of Credit by the importer to his bank. Note all the words and phrases in the letter and its writing style, which are worded formally, standardized and courteously.

2. **in full**  全部，详细（内容，数额等）

    e.g. They have established by airmail in full an irrevocable, confirmed Letter of Credit.

    The debt must be paid in full.

3. **Irrevocable Documentary L/C**  不可撤销的跟单信用证

4. **in favor of /in one's favor**  以……为受益人

    e.g. We inform you that we have opened an irrevocable letter of credit No. 123 in favor of ABC Trading Co. Ltd.

    We will instruct our banker to issue an L/C in your favor upon receipt of your confirmation of this order.

5. **thereof** *adv.*  它的

    书面用语，等于 of that, of it.

    e.g. You will find the instructions on the bank page thereof.

6. **sufficient fund**  足够的资金

7. **cover** *vt.*  偿付

    e.g. In order to cover our order, we have arranged with Bank of China, Hunan Branch, a credit for US$1,200.

8. **expense** *n.*  经费，费用

    用复数形式。

    e.g. The expenses in issuing an irrevocable, confirmed letter of credit would be a little bit heavier.

    [同义词语] charge, costs, fee

    expenses 多指劳务费用。costs 多指成本费用，如产品的原料、劳务等费用。fee 多指专业劳务费用，如支付医生、律师、学校等费用。charge 多指对某一项劳务、商品所索取的费用总和。

9. **due** *adj.* 应付的（款项），应到期的（票据）

常用结构为：

（1）置于名词后，引起定语

  e.g. We are sending you herewith a check for US$1,000 in settlement of our 5% commission due to you.

（2）用作句中的表语

  e.g. Your invoice No. 12 for US$5,500 worth of goods supplied on June 1st is due for payment at the end of this month.

（3）置于名词前作定语

  e.g. Due date of each payment is to be the 45th day, after the issue of Bill of Lading of the carrying vessel.

[同义词语] owing，但是 due 较 owing 正式。

10. **prior to** 在……之前

  e.g. It is hereby stated that the shipping documents under the credit shall, after presentation to but prior to your acceptance, be temporarily lent to this corporation.

11. **trust liability** 信托责任

12. **trustee** *n.* 受托人

13. **authorize** *vt.* 授权，批准

常用结构为：

（1）authorize sb. to do sth./be authorized to do sth.

  e.g. Mr. John Smith is authorized to sign the agreement with you.

（2）authorize + *n.*

  e.g. Our Head Office has authorized the agreement.

14. **in the light of** 根据，按照

  e.g. Both parties shall act in the light of terms and conditions in the contract.

15. **Bills of Exchange** 汇票

16. **deferred payment** 延期付款

17. **commitment for payment** 承担付款

18. **on maturity** 到期日

19. **usance payment** 远期支付

20. **prevent** *vt.* 阻止，妨碍

常用结构为：

（1）prevent + *n.*

  e.g. You'd better take all reasonable steps necessary to prevent economic loss.

（2）prevent sb. from doing sth.

    e.g. You have no right to prevent them from effecting payment when due.

（3）prevent sb. doing sth./prevent one's doing sth.（在非正式用语中）

    e.g. Circumstances prevent us effecting payment=Circumstances prevent our effecting payment.

21. **assume** *vt.* 承担（责任等）

    e.g. We wish to make it clear that we cannot assume any responsibility for the matter.

22. **in transit** 在运送中，在运输中

23. **mutilation** *n.* 残缺

## Sample letter 2

Date:

Dear Sirs,

We hereby establish our irrevocable commercial letter of credit No. H/IA021809/18.

Amount:US$56,700.00

Validity: 30 November, 2018 in P. R. China.

Applicants: Helm AG Hamburg, Germany

Beneficiaries: China National Chemicals, Imp. & Exp. Corp.

Available with us at sight in Hamburg against presentation of the following documents:

（1）Signed commercial invoice in 4 copies.

（2）Full set of 3/3 original plus 2n/n copies of clean on board ocean/marine bills of lading, original signed, issued to order and blank endorsed, notify: Helm AG, Hamburg marked "Freight Prepaid", evidencing shipment from P. R. China's main port to Rotterdam not later than 15 Nov., 2018 for MT=3FCL.

    – Transshipment not allowed; Container shipment: prescribed.

    – B/L to show container No. s. and to show always name, place, phone and telex-No. of the carrier.

（3）Certificate of Origin. Form 'A' showing P. R. China as origin, one original and one copy, legalized by a Commodity Inspection Bureau of the P. R. China and in accordance with rules agreed with EEC authorities.

（4）Packing/Weight-list 2 copies stating: kind, number, content, net weight, gross weight and measurements of each and total packages.

（5）Certified copy of SWIFT advice to applicants latest 2 days after shipment, showing quantity, product, total net and gross weight, date of B/L. vessel's name, B/L No., loading port, destination port, ETA, and No....

（6）Certificate of Analysis, 2 copies issued by the beneficiary:

Certifying: Citric Acid Anhydrous BP 80, giving full specifications description of goods: 60mt=3FCL of citric acid anhydrous BP 80.

China contract No.: 18CNC9-B00128

Unit price: US$995/mt net CFR Rotterdam, as per incoterms 2010 Packed: in 25 kg net multiply bags (export and seaworthy)

Marks: Citric Acid Anhydrous BP 80

   25kgs net

   Rotterdam 1.

Special conditions:

（a）Documents are to be presented within 15 days after bill of lading date

（b）This credit is subject to ICC publication No. 600

（c）All banking commissions and charges outside Germany are for account of beneficiary, also in case of non-utilization

（d）Any original documents, excl. Any kind of marine bills of lading, produced by automated or computerized systems or carbon copies, only acceptable if they are clearly marked as 'original' and signed by issuer in handwriting

（e）Documents including transport documents dated prior to the issuance of this credit are not acceptable

（f）Partial shipment not allowed

（g）Third party transport documents are not acceptable

（h）The amount of each drawing must be endorsed on the reverse side of the original instrument

（i）Payment will only be effected after receipt of first and second mail documents

（j）Please send the documents to the following address:

  Manufacturers Hanover Trust Company

  P.O. box 303630 Fehlandtstrasse 3

  2000 Hamburg 36, Germany

**Notes:**

1. This is an irrevocable documentary letter of credit at sight opened by importer's bank to the exporter, which is available with a complying presentation of all the documents listed in the D.C..

2. **n/n** 不可转让的（non-negotiable 的缩写形式）

3. **clean on Board Ocean/Marine Bill of Lading** 已装船的海洋清洁提单

4. **to order**　凭指定

5. **blank endorsed**　空白背书

6. **Freight Prepaid**　运费已付

7. **Rotterdam** *n.*　鹿特丹（荷兰一港口）

8. **FCL**　（集装箱）整箱装（Full Container Loaded 的缩写形式）

9. **prescribed** *adj.*　规定了的

   e.g. We feel it regrettable that you fail to establish your L/C within the time limit prescribed.

10. **carrier** *n.*　承运人

11. **Certificate of Origin**　原产地证明书

12. **P. R. China as Origin**　中国产

13. **origin/copy** *n.*　正本/副本

14. **legalize** *vt.*　使……合法化

15. **Commodity Inspection Bureau**　商检局

16. **EEC**　欧共体（European Economic Community 的缩写形式）

17. **packing list**　装箱单

18. **weight list**　重量单/磅码单

19. **Certificate of Analysis**　分析证明书，化验证明

20. **Citric Acid Anhydrous**　无水的柠檬酸

21. **mt**　公吨（metric ton 的缩写形式）

22. **incoterms** 2010　国际贸易术语解释通则2010版（incoterms 为 International Chamber of Commerce Terms 的缩写形式）

23. **multiply bags**　多层袋，夹层袋

24. **non-utilization**　没使用

25. **automated or computerized system**　自动化或计算机系统

26. **endorse** *vt.*　背书

27. **reverse side**　反面

## Sample letter 3

To:

From:

Date:

Dear Sirs:

We thank you for the letter of credit you have from time to time entrusted to us, to which our best attention has always been given, and we trust that they have been handled to your satisfaction.

However, we have observed that it is the practice of your good bank to mail only the original copy of credit. In this connection, we wish to suggest that, with the sole intent of rendering better service to you and safeguarding the interests of all parties concerned, we will also be provided with an extra copy of your letter of credit together with the original, and another copy to be sent by subsequent mail for our records. And this also applies to your cable confirmation and your amendment.

We trust that you will appreciate our position, and will therefore signify your agreement to our proposal, and we look forward to your favorable reply.

Yours faithfully,

(Signature)

**Notes:**

1. This is a request sent by advising bank for the dispatch of the original and copy of the L/C, which are worded reasonably, forcefully and courteously but with some words such as "your good bank" old-fashionable.

2. **practice** *n.* 惯例

3. **with the sole interest of** 本着唯一目的 / 意向

4. **safeguard** *vt.* 保护，维护

5. **by subsequent mails** 后寄

6. **signify** *vt.* （以行动）表示（尤指意见，建议等）

   常用结构为：signify one's agreement to sth.

   e.g. We trust that you will signify your agreement to our proposal.

## Sample letter 4

To:

From:

Date:

Dear Sirs:

Your L/C No. ... for... Dated...

We have received and advised your above credit to the beneficiary under reserve there is no correspondent relationship between us. For the sake of order, please invite another bank which is one of our correspondent banks to authenticate or confirm your credit.

Please give us your reply by telex.

Yours faithfully,

(Signature)

**Notes:**

1. This letter asks the issuing bank to authorize the third bank to verify the relative letter of credit, which has been advised to the beneficiary, as the advising bank is unable to authenticate it. As an usual practice, it cannot be dealt with like this.

2. **under reserve** 保留追索

3. **for the sake of order** 为了手续齐全

## 2. Amending relative credits（修改有关信用证）

**Sample letter 5**

To:
From:
Date:
Dear Sirs,
Your L/C No. … for… Dated…
Our Ref. …

It comes to our attention that the dates of shipment and expiration of your above credit are inversely given to be (date) and (date).

We presume it might be a clerical error and have reversed them for you before advising the credit to the beneficiary.

Please correct your records accordingly and confirm the rightness of our action by return.

Sincerely yours,
(Signature)

**Notes:**

1. This is a letter advising the issuing bank that the date of shipment and expiration of credit are wrongly given and then revised them on behalf of it.

2. **come to one's attention** 引起某人的注意

   ［同义词语］draw one's attention, attract one's attention, call one's attention

3. **date of shipment** 装船期

4. **date of expiration** 有效期

5. **presume** *vt.* 认为（依据客观事实进行的判断）

6. **clerical error** 笔误

## Sample letter 6

Your L/C No. ... for ... Dated ...

Our Ref. ...

We refer to your captioned L/C, we wish to inform you that we have found the amount of the said credit are different in figures and in words with (amount) and (amount) respectively. A check-up of the quantity and the unit price proves that the amount in figures is correct.

We have made the necessary correction for you before advising the credit to the beneficiary.

Please confirm our action in order by return and do like wise in your records.

Yours sincerely,

(Signed)

**Notes:**

1. This letter also informs the issuing bank of the amendments to the relative L/C concerning the amount in figures and in words.

2. **refer to**  提及，谈到某事（常用于开头）

   ［同义词语］with reference to，referring to（这几个短语显得过于正式，有点过时，尽量少用）

3. **amount in figures and in words**  小写和大写金额

4. **check-up**  检查

5. **unit price**  单价

6. **made the necessary correction**  做必要的更正

7. **do like wise**  做同样的事

## Sample letter 7

To:

From:

Date:

Dear Sirs,

Your L/C Nos. ... & ...

We are in receipt of your L/C Nos. ... and ... and find that both credits stipulate that the drafts are to be drawn on yourselves.

In this connection, we wish to advise that according to the usual practice, credit issued in terms of Pounds Sterling and credits of this kind are generally settled in London. And so far as our records show the drafts under quite a number of your previous sterling credits were drawn on your London Office. We shall therefore much appreciate it if you will agree to amend the relative clause to this effect in the present instance.

Thank you in advance for your kind cooperation.

Yours sincerely,

(Signature)

**Notes:**

1. This letter is a request for the Amendment to the relative Letter of Credit in which the negotiation places should be revised based on customary practice.

2. **stipulate** *vt.* 规定

3. **sterling credit** 英镑信用证

4. **settle** *vt.* 结算（账目等）

   e.g. We wish to advise that according to our usual practice, US Dollar credits are generally settled in New York.

   [同义词语] clear, clear up, 但注意 clear 与 clear up 虽有"清算"的含义，但不及 settle 通用。

5. **to this (that) effect** 大意是这（那）样

   e.g. We shall therefore much appreciate it if you will agree to amend the relative clause to this effect in the present instance.（如贵行能将有关条款作相应的修改，我行将不胜感激。）

## Sample letter 8

To:

From:

Date:

Dear Sirs,

Terms in SWIFT and L/C Not Identical

In checking the terms of your credits confirmation with that of your SWIFT opening them, we have found several cases where the credit terms do not conform to those contained in relative SWIFT. In this connection, we wish to revert to your letter dated…in respect of the code word "COMCREDIT" used for opening commercial credit telegraphically by your bank.

Furthermore, three stipulations in the confirmation are found at variance with those advised by SWIFT.

Firstly, your SWIFT states "transshipment not allowed", whereas the confirmation shows "transshipment allowed", we must be advised of the new steamer's name.

Secondly, as your cable/telex does not mention how many copies of the invoice are required under these credits, we have, in accordance with our arrangement, advised the beneficiaries that the invoice is made out in six copies, three of which are to be sent with the original set of documents. But your credit confirmation changed to call for seven copies, four copies to attached to the original documents.

Thirdly, the blacklist clause as shown in your confirmation is "documents showing any of the steamers…", which is also different from the original one as arranged between us.

We are much surprised to note the divergence of your confirmation with the relative SWIFT and your failure to adhere to the Arrangement as agreed between us. We wish to state that, should any question arise owing to your default, our bank shall assume no responsibility for it.

Your prompt attention to the matter will be highly appreciated.

Yours truly,

(Signed)

**Notes:**

1. This is a letter informing the issuing bank of Terms and Conditions in SWIFT L/C differing from that in written L/C. From the sentences and paragraphs, we note that they are worded reasonably and forcefully with the facts.

2. **conform** *vi.* 一致，符合

    常与介词 to 搭配，有时也接用 with

    e.g. The stipulations in the L/C must conform to/with the terms and conditions in the contract.

3. **code word** 电码

4. **at variance with** 不一致，不相符合

    e.g. The company's discriminatory business practices are at variance with the law of that country.

    ［同义词语］in contradiction with

    at variance with 不及 in contradiction with 语意强烈。

5. **call for** 要求，需要

6. **divergence** *n.* 差异

7. **adhere to** 坚持（原则，政策等）

    e.g. We wish to assure you that we adhere to the Agreement agreed upon.

    ［同义词语］insist on, persist in

8. **default** *n.* 违约，不履行债务

## Sample letter 9

Dear Sirs,

Your L/C No.…for…

With reference to the captioned Credit to which you ask us to add our confirmation, we wish to advise that in consideration of the pleasant relations between us and the fact that you are appointed bank authorized to handle letters of credit under China &…Trade and Payment Agreement, we have, at the time of our advising your credit to the beneficiaries, conveyed the above commendatory information to them for their consideration.

Now we are pleased to inform you that for the present Credit, the beneficiaries are agreeable to accept it without our confirmation.

We trust that the pleasant relations between our two banks will further develop, in view of the increase of business and trade between our two countries.

Yours sincerely,

(Signature)

**Notes:**

1. This is a letter advising the issuing bank that beneficiary agrees to accept the L/C without confirmation.

2. **add our confirmation** 加保（兑）

3. **in consideration of** 考虑到，由于，鉴于

   e.g. In consideration of the increasing business volume between our two banks, we agree to accept your proposal.

   ［同义词语］in view of, considering

4. **appointed bank** 指定银行

   ［同义词语］designated bank, authorized bank

5. **Trade and Payment Agreement** 贸易支付协定

6. **convey** *vt.* 转达

   e.g. Please convey my thanks to your president Mr. Li Ming.

7. **commendatory information** 赞意

## 3. Claiming for reimbursement（索偿）

### Sample letter 10

To:
From:
Date:
Dear Sirs,

Our BP No. 2345 for US$12,345.00

Under Your L/C No. 789

We have received your telex dated May 28, 2018, which informed us that you had already paid our captioned negotiation by crediting our account with our New York Branch.

We wish to state that according to the credit terms, payment of the above item should have been made right upon your receipt of the documents. But now, as it is, the payment was effected 22 days late, the time for normal postal voyage excluded. Our clients claim compensation for the loss of interest for the 22 days.

We wish to have your favorable reply.

Yours sincerely,

(Signed)

**Notes:**

1. This is a letter sent by the negotiating bank to the issuing bank informing them that the negotiation was delayed by the reimbursing bank, which states the seriousness of the delay in payment. Note the whole letter, it is worded with facts forcefully and reasonably and to the point.

2. **BP**　押汇，Bills Purchased 的缩写形式

3. **captioned negotiation**　标题下的议付款

4. **effect** *vt.*　进行，实施

   常用结构：effect + *n*; *n* + be effected

   e.g. effect payment（付款），effect shipment（装船），effect insurance（投保）

   ［同义词语］make

5. **the time for normal postal voyage excluded**　除去正常的邮递时间

6. **claim compensation for**　索赔

## Sample letter 11

Dear Sirs,

Your L/C No. …Our BP…Dated…

Upon claiming on Midland Bank Ltd., London, reimbursement of negotiation, we regret to understand that their authority to reimburse is limited to a total of US$1,800.00 only. Obviously payment was refused owing to their not having been informed of your amendment of 12th November, to increase the credit amount by US$500.00 to a total of US$2,300.00. Please look into the matter immediately and instruct them to effect payment under advice to us.

It is hoped that similar cases will not happen again in the future.

Yours faithfully,

(Signature)

**Notes:**

1. This letter states the problem of inadequate authority in the reimbursing process. In the letter the negotiating bank instructs the reimbursing bank to honor the claim. Note all the sentences in the letter, which are worded with facts properly and forcefully.
2. **claim on sb. reimbursement of** …  向……（谁）索偿……（金额）
3. **Their authority to reimburse is limited to**…  他们授权可偿付的金额仅限于……
4. **amendment**  修改通知书
5. **look into**  调查
6. **under advice to us**  同时通知我行

## Sample letter 12

Dear Sirs,

Your L/C No. … Our BP…

Upon claiming on Eastern Bank Ltd., London reimbursement of our negotiation under the above Credit, we are informed by our London Office that the payment was effected under reserve for the following reason:

"According to our records the letter of credit is overdrawn by…"

Having looked into our records, we find that the credit stipulates. "Difference of about 3% in quantity and amount is acceptable". In view of the fact that the amount we claimed falls within the said limit, we therefore request you to explain the matter to reimbursing bank and instruct them to lift the reserve under advice to us. In the meantime, we hope that

> similar cases will not occur in the future.
> Yours truly,
> (Signed)

**Notes:**

1. This is a letter sent by the negotiating bank to the issuing bank and asks it to instruct the reimbursing bank to release the reserve.

2. **under reserve** 保留追索权

3. **fall within** 属于

   e.g. Claims which fall within the responsibility of parties other than supplier will not be accepted by us.

4. **lift** *vt.* 解除，取消

   e.g. The unpopular tax has been lifted.

   to lift reserve 解除保留

5. **similar cases** 类似事件

6. **occur** *vi.* 发生

   e.g. The loss of message might occur en route.

## Sample letter 13

> Dear Sirs,
> Your Irrevocable Credit No. …
> Our BP No. 123…
> We refer to your letter of 11th May, 2018, wherein you inform us that your principals failed to pay the drafts under the above credit, and ask for our instructions as to the disposal of the same. In this connection, we wish to reiterate our views expressed in our letter of 8th February, 2018, that in respect to an Irrevocable Letter of Credit, the Issuing Bank is legally bound to fulfill the provisions for payment, acceptance and negotiation contained in the credit, provided the documents presented there complied with credit terms. In the present instance, therefore, we are fully justified, after taking up the documents prepared in full compliance with the terms of the credit, to debit the Irac Account for reimbursement of our negotiation, and we deem it unnecessary that we should be informed of your principals' failure to fulfill their obligations towards you, which is a matter we are in no way involved in.
> We regret, therefore, being unable to give you any instructions.
> Yours sincerely,
> (Signed)

**Notes:**

1. This letter is a reply to dealing with the matter concerning failure to pay the draft under the relative credit. Note all the sentences and phrases in the letter, which are worded forcefully and based on the rules and facts.
2. **refer to** 提及、谈到
3. **principals** *n.* 委托人
4. **in this connection** 鉴于此事
5. **reiterate** *vt.* 重申
6. **in respect to** 关于
7. **is legally bound to** 有法律义务地
8. **fulfill the provisions** 执行条款
9. **complied with** 与……一致
10. **are fully justified** 有充分理由地
11. **taking up the documents** 承兑单据
12. **fulfill their obligations** 履行责任
13. **a matter we are in no way involved in** 我行与此事无关

## Sample letter 14

Dear Sirs,

Our BP… Dated… Drawn at 90 Days Sight

under Your L/C No. … for US$…

We refer to the subject schedule which we sent you on April 30, 2018 by airmail together with the relative documents with the request that you pay the above amount at maturity to our London Office for the credit of our account.

Up till now, we do not appear to have received the remittance in respect of this item, although estimating the time, we think it must have already matured.

We should appreciate it very much if you would investigate the matter and inform us whether payment has been duly effected.

Faithfully yours,

(Signed)

**Notes:**

1. This is a letter asking for payment under L/C No.…, which is worded properly and courteously with a non-standardized format.
2. **at maturity** 到期日

3. **remittance** *n.* 汇款

4. **in respect of** 关于

**Sample letter 15**

Dear Sirs,

Your Documentary Remittance No. …

under Our L/C No. …

We have received the above documentary remittance, and regret to inform you that we are unable to effect payment on account of the following discrepancies:

Certificate of Quality and Quantity is issued by the beneficiaries, whereas the said credit calls for Manufacturers' or Public Recognized Surveyor's quality/weight certificate.

Payment, however, will be made after receipt of the quality/weight certificate issued by Manufacturer or Public Surveyor.

Kindly advice the beneficiaries.

Yours truly,

(Signature)

**Notes:**

1. This is a letter informing that payment is not to be made due to discrepancies in presented document and asking for the correct ones, which is worded with facts properly and reasonably.

2. **Documentary Remittance No.** 跟单汇兑号

3. **on account of** 原因是

   e.g. We have to lodge a claim on you on account of your failure to fulfill the contractual obligations.

   由于你方未履行合同的职责，我们不得不向你方提出索赔。

   ［同义词语］owing to, because of

4. **recognized surveyor** 公认的检验员

**Sample letter 16**

From: Main Bank, Hong Kong

Re: Your BP No. …, … Dated …

　　Our Ref. … under L/C No. …

　　Issued by Citibank N. A.

　　New York

Regarding your letter dated… concerning the delay in reimbursing payment for the captioned bills. We wish to inform you that the time lag between the receipt of documents and reimbursement was caused by the following reasons：

1. We received the documents on…and…, which were public holidays in Hong Kong.

2. Since ABC Company is not our client, it took more time for us to transfer the documents and message to them through their banker.

3. As the following discrepancies were found in the presented documents，they must be referred to applicant for their acceptance:

   （1）Invoice showing some alterations not authenticated and address of seller differs from that of shipping documents.

   （2）Custom Invoice showing a third party instead of L/C applicant as buyer.

   （3）Custom invoice not showing columns 2, 3, 8.

   （4）Invoice not bearing with specifications.

   （5）Inspection Certificate，Certificate of Quality instead of Inspection Certificate.

   （6）Bill of Lading mechanically signed.

4. Payment was received on…from the applicant's banker and we credited to your Beijing Head Office's USD account with us on the same day as per your instructions.

We hope that you will be satisfied with our above explanation.

Faithfully yours,

(Signed)

**Notes:**

1. This is a reply explaining the reasons for delayed payment, which is a standardized reply to inquiry.

2. **reimburse** *vt.* 偿付

   常用结构为：

   （1）reimburse sb. for sth. 表示偿还……费用

      e.g. We assure you that we shall reimburse you by remittance for the handling charges.

   （2）reimburse oneself（接用反身代词作宾语）

      e.g. Please reimburse yourselves through the Bank of China, Hunan Branch，to the debit of the government of Sri Lanka Account A for the year of 2018.

   ［同义词语］repay, refund

3. **time lag** 时间间隔，间隔期间

4. **transferor** *n.* 转让人

5. **transferee** *n.* 受让人

6. **substitution of document**　代用票据

7. **refer** *vi.*　提交……解决、处理等

   常用结构为：

   （1）refer sth. to sb.

   　　e.g. We shall refer the matter to the insurance company.

   （2）refer sth. to sb. for sth.

   　　e.g. Your inquiry for this item has been referred to us for attention.

8. **differ** *vi.*　不同，有差别

   常与 from 搭配

   　　e.g. As the figures in the captioned bill differed from that in the L/C, the bank dishonored the draft.

9. **applicant** *n.*　申请人

10. **Custom Invoice**　海关发票

11. **Inspection Certificate**　检验证书

12. **Certificate of Quality**　品质证书

13. **Bill of Lading**　提单

14. **make contact with**　与……联系

    　　e.g. Please make direct contact with them stating our recommendation.

15. **bear with**　注明

16. **ascertain** *vt.*　查实，确定

    常用结构为：

    （1）ascertain + *n*.

    　　Could you ascertain the possibility of setting up an agency relationship between us?
    　　你行能否确定我们之间有无建立代理关系的可能？

    （2）ascertain + 从句

    　　We have to ascertain whether the payment has been effected.
    　　我们仍需查核货款是否已支付。

## 4. Letters on collection and remittance business（关于托收和汇款业务的信件）

**Sample letter 17**

Dear Sirs,

Our Collection No. … Dated…for…

At the request of our clients, China National Tea & Native Produce Imp. & Exp.

Corporation….Branch, we wish to ask you to change the drawees of the captioned collection to ABC Trading Co. Manchester. We enclose herewith the new documents made out in the name of the new drawees.

Drafts –in duplicate

Invoice –in triplicate

Weight Lists–in triplicate

Inspection & Testing Certificates–in duplicate replacing the respective old ones which please return to us at your earliest convenience.

Furthermore, our clients state that they would have this item collected through your branch at…Manchester. Please follow this instruction and ask your said office to collect the proceeds from the new drawees.

Yours faithfully,

(Signature)

**Notes:**

1. This is a letter advising and asking the change of the name of drawee under Collection No.…

2. **native produce**　土特产

3. **drawee** *n.*　受票人

4. **made out**　填制

5. **in duplicate**　一式两份

6. **in triplicate**　一式三份

7. **weight lists**　重量单

8. **Inspection & Testing Certificates**　检验证书

### Sample letter 18

Dear Sirs,

Your T/T No.…Dated…for…

F/O… Our Ref. …

We refer to the above-mentioned item and regret to advise you that we have just received the cover of your captioned telegraphic transfer through…Bank.

In this connection, we have to point out that your reimbursement was delayed for days… and our usual practice is to overcharge overdue interest for such delay.

Considering the large amount and long time delay involved in this case, we would appreciate it if you could pay us…(amount) being our interest for…days calculated at rate of …% p.a. under advice to us. Otherwise, please let us have your reasons for it.

Yours faithfully,

(Signature)

**Notes:**

1. This letter is a request for the reason for delay in T/T reimbursement and claim for compensation of the interest.

2. **T/T**　电汇（Telegraphic Transfer 的缩写）

3. **F/O**　以……为受益人或抬头人（in favor of 的缩写）

4. **overcharge** *vt.*　加收，对（某人或某物）多收钱

   e.g. Our check for US$120 is enclosed for the amount that you were overcharged on our recent invoice.

## Sample letter 19

Dear Sirs,

Our Draft No. … of… for…

We refer you to the letter dated July 12th, ref.…, with regard to the subject item, and wish to advise that according to the remitter, China National Machinery & Equipment Imp. & Exp. Corp., Hunan Branch, the said draft was sent to the payee in payment of commission, and the correct name of the payee should be the Dean, Faculty of Engineering, Washington, and not Engineer Imp. & Exp. Inc.…The captioned draft is now returned to us for our cancellation.

You are now requested to cancel our Advice of Drawing of the above draft and in replacement, we hereby authorize you to pay the amount of…to the payee, the Dean, Faculty of Engineering, Washington University, Washington, Against payee's duly signed receipt.

After payment, please send to us the payee's receipt and the obsolete advice of drawing.

We thank you in advance for your kind cooperation.

Sincerely yours,

(Signature)

**Notes:**

1. This is a request for cancellation of Advice of Drawing of the Draft No.…

2. **refer sb. to sth.**　使（某人）参阅、询问、洽办等

   e.g. We refer you to our cable of March 24.

   　　We refer you to your insurance company for recovery of this fee.

3. **remitter** *n.*　汇款人

4. **in payment of**    偿付……（某费用、某单据等）款项

    e.g. This remittance is in payment of all commissions due to you up to date.

5. **the Dean, Faculty of Engineering**    工程学院系主任

6. **advice of drawing**    汇票通知书

### Sample letter 20

Dear Sirs,

Re: Your Ref. … dated… under Your Documentary Remittance

We refer to your documentary remittance dated…enclosing the above-mentioned documents, and as requested, return to you herewith the following drafts duly accepted by us:

Amount of Draft                 Date of Maturity

…                               …

If any one of these drafts is presented to you for payment at maturity, you may effect payment to the debit of our a/c with yourselves, and return the draft to us by airmail after payment.

Yours sincerely,

(Signed)

### Notes:

1. This is a letter returning the relative drafts accepted, which is worded simply, concisely and to the point.

2. **refer to**  谈及，关于

3. **accept** *vt.*  承兑

4. **Date of Maturity**  到期日

5. **present** *vt.*  提示

6. **effect payment**  付款

7. **debit** *n.*  借方

### Sample letter 21

March 18th, 2018

Dear Sirs,

State Commercial Bank, Rangoon D/D…

dd… Drawn on us for…

With reference to the captioned item, we are informed by the subject bank as per their advice dated 10th March, that in cover of our payment of the said draft, they have reimbursed us through your bank with the captioned amount.

As up to date we have not yet received any advice from you concerning this remittance, you are requested to kindly look into the matter and let us have an early reply.

We thank you for your anticipation in advance.

Yours sincerely,

(Signed)

**Notes:**

1. This is a letter inquiring whether the relative cover has been paid. Note all the words and sentences in the letter, which are suitably and courteously worded with facts and queries.

2. **State Commercial Bank, Rangoon**  仰光国家商业银行

3. **D/D=Demand Draft**  即期汇票

4. **dd=dated**  注明……日期的

5. **in cover of**  关于……的头寸

6. **up to date**  至今为止

　　e.g. We haven't yet received from you any advice regarding the cover up to date.

7. **kindly** *adv.*  请

函电中常见用 kindly 代替 please。

　　e.g. Kindly advise US when the payment will be effected.

　　　　You are kindly requested to effect immediate shipment upon receipt of our I/C.

8. **anticipation** *n.*  期望，预料

　　e.g. Please be assured that we shall treat your letter under anticipation strictly, confidential.

　　Thank you in anticipation = Thank you in advance. 〔注意〕这类句子已陈旧，不宜使用。

## Sample letter 22

Dear Sirs,

　　Your… Branch Draft  No….for US$…

From your letter dated 8th this month we note that the cover for the above draft was received by you on 1st October, 2018, but was not paid over to our London Office until your receipt of our claim for reimbursement.

We wish to mention that according to the standing agency arrangements between our two banks, you had to pay the said cover to our London Office for our credit immediately upon receipt of the relative advice of drawing from your…Branch, instead of holding it pending our claim for reimbursement. We are regretful that the above arrangements not being observed, payment was thus delayed.

For the sake of good order, we would call your attention to the matter in the hope that you will henceforth pay the relative cover immediately it is received in London in order to facilitate our mutual operations.

We are expecting your comments on this matter.

Yours sincerely,

(Signature)

**Notes:**

1. This letter is a request for immediate reimbursement based on the agency arrangements between two banks. Note all the phrases and sentences, which are worded properly and courteously but forcefully with facts.

2. **mention** *vt.* 说到，提及

    常用结构为：

    （1）mention + *n.*

    e.g. We regret that the invoice which you mentioned in your letter dated April 1st was not sent to us.

    （2）mention + that 从句

    e.g. We would like to mention that you have failed to fulfill the contractual obligations.

3. **the standing agency arrangements** 长期代理协定

4. **upon/on receipt (of)** 收到（……后）

    e.g. Upon receipt of the relative advice we shall pay the relative cover to you without delay.

    We will ship the goods to you with transshipment at Hong Kong right/immediately upon receipt of the L/C amendment.

    ［同义词语］after receipt of

    二者使用都很普遍。其使用上的区别是：after receipt of 句中可另加表示一段时间的状语如：within 15 days 等。upon/on receipt of 本身含有"收到后就立即"的意思，句中可另加表示"立即""迅速"等含义的时间状语,却不能另加表示一段时间的状语。

5. **for the sake of good order** 为了便于顺利工作；为了手续齐全

6. **call one's attention to…** 提请某人注意某事

    e.g. We wish to call your attention to the matter raised in our letter of April 25th.

    ［同义词语］bring/draw/invite/direct one's attention to

7. **in the hope** 怀着……的希望

    常用结构为：

    （1）in the hope of…

e.g. We contact you today in the hope of setting up an agency relationship between our two banks.

（2）in the hope that…

e.g. We are now writing to you in the hope that you will give this matter your further consideration.

8. **henceforth** *adv.* 从此以后

书面用语。

［同义词语］hereafter

9. **facilitate** *vt.* 促进，使……容易

常用结构为：facilitate + *n.*

e.g. In order to facilitate the economic exchange and trade between us, we agree to your proposal.

［注意］facilitate 不能接用不定式或在宾语后面加不定式。例如：

［误］This will facilitate us to settle the matter.

应改为：

This will facilitate our settlement of the matter.

10. **mutual operations**　双方良好的合作

11. **comment** *n. vt. & vi.* 评论，意见，解释

后面常接用介词 on/upon/about

e.g. We wish you would give your comments on this matter.


## Sample letter 23

Dear Sirs,

　　Re: Our Payment Order… Dated… for…

　　　　Your T/T No. …　　　　　

We have received your letter dated… informing us that on 23rd July a sum of US$15,858.00 was transferred to you by…(Bank), Stockholm in payment of the above item.

In this connection, we wish to confirm that the correct amount of payment should have been US$15,585.00 (instead of US$15,858.00 wrongly given in our original instructions to… bank), and we shall be pleased if you will refund to us the difference of US$273.00 quoting our above-mentioned reference.

Thank you for your cooperation.

Sincerely yours,

(Signed)

**Notes:**

1. This is a letter requesting for refunding the amount overpaid, which is worded suitably and courteously.
2. **Payment Order** 付款通知
3. **transfer** *vt.* 转账
4. **refund** *vt.* 退还
5. **difference** *n.* 差额
6. **quote** *n. vt. & vi.* 引用

## Sample letter 24

Dear Sirs,

Your M/T of… for Euro… f/o…

We have received your letter of 28 August, Ref.…In reply, we wish to inform you that payment of the above mail transfer was effected on 22 April, and on 1 May, we sent you the required receipt duly signed by the beneficiaries.

However, it is observed from your letter that the receipt might appear to have gone astray, and we have obtained from the beneficiaries a duplicate which we trust will meet your requirement.

Yours sincerely,

(Signature)

**Notes:**

1. This is a letter concerning sending the receipt duplicate as the original one seems to be lost in the mail transit.
2. **Euro** 欧元
3. **f/o** 以……为受益人（in favor of 的缩写形式）
4. **in reply (to)** 答复

　　（1）in reply 常用于书信一句话的开始（其实 in reply 可不用）

　　　　e.g. Thank you for your letter of April 2, 2016 requesting for the establishment of the agency relationship with us，In reply, we regret to say that we are unable to accept your proposal for the time being.

　　（2）in reply 有时也位于句中

　　　　e.g. With regard to the matter mentioned in your letter of April 5, 2018, we wish to give the following in reply:…

　　（3）in reply to 常用于书信的开头

e.g. In reply to your letter of 15th May, Ref...., we wish to inform you that payment of the above Telegraphic Transfer was effected on 24th Feb., 2018.

5. **go astray** （信件等）遗失；误投

e.g. We regret to say that the signed acknowledgement of receipt enclosed with previous letter of Jan. 6th, 2018 might have gone astray.

6. **meet** *vt.* 满足（需要等）

e.g. We hope that the information we provide you will meet your requirement.

［同义词语］meet one's need, meet one's demand

## III. Sentences Commonly Used on Settlement for International Trade（国际贸易结算业务的常用句型）

1. We have only received a confirmation of your telex/cable of…opening the captioned credit.
2. From the said copy of the credit we notice that it is addressed to us, but we cannot trace having received its original.
3. The original telex/cable does not appear to have reached us so far.
4. In order to save time, we have already notified the credit to the beneficiary against the cable confirmation.
5. For order's sake, please confirm by telex the opening of the above credit.
6. Please confirm by telex whether we can negotiate the relative transport documents against the duplicate, if the original should fail to come to our hand before the date of shipment.
7. It comes to our attention that the dates of shipment and expiration of your above credit are inversely given to be…and….
8. We presume it might be a clerical error and have reversed them for you before notifying the credit to the beneficiary.
9. Please make a corresponding correction in your records.
10. The above credit stipulated that the unit price is on FOB basis, whereas the Bills of Lading require the indication of "Freight Paid".
11. The two stipulations apparently do not tally with each other.
12. We have thereupon changed it for you to read "Freight Collected at Destination" before advising the credit to the beneficiary.
13. A check-up of the quantity of the goods and the unit price proves that the amount in figures is correct and whereas that in words is incorrect.

14. We have therefore made the necessary correction before advising it to the beneficiary.

15. Please confirm our action in order and do likewise in your records.

16. In view of the fact that the beneficiary is domiciled at…, China, and our Bank is authorized, in accordance with the credit terms, to claim reimbursement from…Bank, London, we should think that negotiation should be made in Mainland of China instead of "in Hong Kong SAR of China".

17. We wish to inform you that the said Credit is established in terms of Pounds Sterling and credits of this kind are generally settled in London.

18. With a view to facilitating settlement under your further credits, we should request you to appoint your London agency as the reimbursing bank from whom we can claim our reimbursement direct.

19. As we have no agency relationship with…Bank, we regret being unable to have any contact with you. Therefore, you are requested to designate another bank as your reimbursing bank.

20. We are in receipt of the captioned credit, which calls for the relative credit drafts to be drawn on your London Office.

21. It is however found that the covering letter of the said Credit says, "We will pay a depository bank of your choice through our New York agency".

22. Apparently this clause is inconsistent with the above stipulation and is therefore not acceptable to us.

23. Without further notice to the contrary, we shall, upon negotiation, claim reimbursement on your London office.

24. Referring to your telex dated…for stop-payment of the above item, we inform you that the true payee has today presented the original draft to us for payment.

25. To avoid any unfavorable effects, please reconsider the circumstances and authorize us to honor our draft by tested telex as soon as possible.

26. We paid the captioned M/T on…. As we do not seem to have received the relative cover from…Bank, please investigate the matter and give us an early reply.

27. We would also request you to take proper measures to ensure that in future you will transfer the cover to… Bank for our account at the time you send your mail transfer to us.

28. Enclosed please find the original remittance receipt duly signed by the payee for your reference.

## IV. Exercises（练习）

1. Write a letter on the following situation:

   Your bank, Bank of China, Hunan Branch (at No. 71 Wuyi East Road Dong District Changsha) has received a letter dated March 26 referring to the L/C Nos. 2314 and 2315 in favor of China National Tea & Native Produce Imp. & Exp. Corp. Hunan Branch issued by Commercial Bank, Chicago (located at 204 Haide Ave., Chicago). You are informed by the letter to transfer the balance of the L/C No. 2314 of US$…to L/C No. 2315. But now there is a difference between the transferred balance and the one mentioned in the incoming letter dated Mar. 26 according to the following particulars:

   （1）兹复你方3月26日函……告我行将你行2314号信用之余额361.19美元转入你行2315号信用证，我们已按来函作相应处理，特此奉告。

   （2）然而，受益人通知我行，他们虽同意你行将余额转让之要求，但同时指出截至2月28日2315号信用证之余额为8,387.15美元而不是来函所述7,732.00美元；并告我行其中相差655.15美元，系因未入11月19日和2月11日你方电告修正书之增加款额，该款额先后分别为300.05美元和355.10美元。

   （3）请尽快告我行截至2月28日上述信用证之准确余额。

2. Write two English letters according to the following situations:

   （1）你行，花旗银行中国香港分行（中国香港梅恩大街30号），收到伦敦米德兰银行（伦敦米德兰大街第4号）开来的第……号信用证。该证中包含有条款："本信用证有效期为5月15日，在中国香港议付。"由于该证的受益人居住在中国（内地）……城市，按信用证之规定，你行有权向……银行伦敦海外部索汇，所以你行认为议付地点应该在中国内地，而不是"在中国香港"。因此你行已冒昧代为更正，并同时将该证通知了受益人。现在你受你行国际结算部经理的委托，写一封信给开证行通知上述信用证修改一事并要求他们查证。

   （2）你行，中国银行上海分行（地址：上海市东区黄兴路第54号，邮编：220000），作为通知行于2018年10月18日收到位于纽约，罗彻斯特，林肯第一广场，邮编14643的蔡斯林肯第一银行（Chase Lincoln First Bank，N.A.）开来的日期为……金额为……的第3456号信用证。由于该信用证规定该货物的单价是按中国港离岸价计算，但却又要求提单需注明"运费付讫"。这两项规定显然互不相符。经与受益人联系后，你行得知有关货物系按离岸价格签订合同，因此你行已冒昧更改为"货到即付"，并将该证通知了受益人。现请你代表你行写一封信给开证行通知上述信用证修改一事并要求他们查证。

3. Translate the following letter into English:

你行信用证号……；我行议付编号……，日期……

我行通过我伦敦分行向伦敦劳和银行索偿上述信用证项下的议付款时，得知由于信用证10月31日期满，款已支付但保留追索权。

现在指明根据你行9月10日修改电，货运和信用证有效期已延长到12月31日，我行估计是你行未及时将修改电通知偿付行，也可能是发出的通知中途丢失，现在请你行立即通知伦敦劳和银行撤保。

望今后不再发生类似情况。

# PART III
## TELEGRAM, TELEX AND SWIFT BUSINESS
## 第三部分 电报、电传和 SWIFT 业务

Unit Seven　Telegram & Telex Business
第 7 单元　电报和电传业务
Unit Eight　SWIFT Business
第 8 单元　SWIFT 业务

## Unit Seven  Telegram & Telex Business

## 第7单元  电报和电传业务

**After studying this unit, you will be able to:**
- Understand there are many kinds of messages related to international banking business in cable and telex format before SWIFT came into use
- Recognize the features of them in format and style after learning samples
- Learn how to write cable and telex message
- Master the language skills of this respect
- Evaluate your writing skills by completing the self-test checklists in the unit

## I. Introduction（概述）

Most of the transactions in international banking business were usually to be conducted in detail through airmail letters, telegrams (cables), telexes during the past decades, but with the development of information technology and telecommunication, nowadays most of which are to be done via SWIFT. However, as some kinds of transmission vehicles, telegrams and telexes have more advantages in speed and security than letters and have higher costs compared to SWIFT (details in Unit 8), which as a most reliable communication means has the most advantages in great security and plays a most significant role in international banking business.

## II. Telegrams（电报）

Telegrams or cables are messages sent by telegraph, which once became one of the most effective means of communication because they are much faster than letters, and can better draw the attention of the receiver to the urgent nature of the matter concerned. With the development of communication, telegrams are rarely used nowadays. But the abbreviations and the compounded words used in telegrams are still having effects on SWIFT format. So it is necessary to make a brief introduction to telegrams.

### 1. The kinds of telegrams（电报的种类）

Banking telegrams or cables may be classified into plain language telegrams and code language telegrams. The former are written in any languages using the ordinary alphabets, whereas the latter are in commercial codes, such as Acme and Bentley's. Owing to its complicated procedure of preparation, nowadays the code telegram is not commonly used as the plain telegram. Based on the transmission channels, plain telegram can be classified into such kinds as CABLE, WIRE TELEGRAM, RADIOGRAM, FAXMAIL or PHOTOTELEGRAM, but according to the speed of its transmission, telegrams may be classified into three types: ordinary, urgent and letter telegrams. However, since January 1, 1980, the telegram offices of all countries have stopped accepting letter telegrams. So only the ordinary and urgent telegrams are used widely in the world.

An ordinary telegram can reach the address within 3–4 hours, whereas an urgent telegram will reach its destination within 1–2 hours.

### 2. The charges of telegrams（电报的收费）

The telegrams are to be charged based on the class of telegrams sent, the number of their words used, and the localities destined for, i.e. the distance and speed of the transmission of telegrams. Usually the charges per word in urgent telegram are double than that for an ordinary one inclusive of the word "URGENT". The more the words and the farther the distance, the more expensive, thus in order to save the expenses of the foreign exchange, we should pay more attention to the three Cs, i.e. Courtesy, Conciseness and Clarity when drawing telegrams.

Telegrams are charged as per one unit of a minimum of 7 words including the sender's and the addressee's telegraphic addresses, and the terminal cities. Even if the message has less than 7 words it will be also counted and charged as one unit of 7 words. The cable charges are computed as the standards as follows:

(1) Each word in the message inclusive of the cable address and city located of the addressee and the cable address of the sender with the name of nation excluded.

(2) Each dictionary word or natural word inclusive of ten letters are to be regarded as one "word", and the word less than 20 letters but more than 10 letters can be counted as two "words". e.g. "INRECEIPTOFURLETTER" can be counted as two words.

(3) Two or more than two short phrases can be combined into one cable word but less than 10 letters.

(4) Figures and words can be compounded into one cable word within 10 letters.

e.g. the "words" in telegrams mean not only the natural words, such as "WHERE", "PAID", etc., but also the abbreviations such as "FYI"(for your information), "RYL" (referring to your letter), "IMF" (international monetary fund), etc., and the compounded words such as "ASSOONAS"(as soon as), "INVIEWOF"( in view of), "NEWYORKNC"(New York, N. C.).

## 3. The structure of a telegram（电报的结构）

Generally an English telegram may consist of three parts:

(1) Address of addressee : Cable Address and the City located.

(2) Cable Message (Body of the telegram).

(3) Address of Sender : Cable Address.

e.g.

**An outgoing telegram:**

```
URGENT
CITIBANK N. A. NEW YORK
339 PARK AVE. NEW YORK N. Y. 10022
TEST...FOR NO. AMT
AIRMAILED CREDIT...AMOUNT...FAVORING...ACCOUNT...COVERING (...)
```

> GOODS ASPER CONTRACT… FOB… TO…SHPMTLATEST… CHUNGKUO TEST…
> AIRMAILED CREDIT… FAVORING… ACCOUNT… AMOUNT… RECONTRACT…
> SHIPMENT… VALIDITY… PREADVICE RGDS CHUNGKUO CHANGS

**Notes:**

1. This is a tested simple urgent cable credit with the receiver being Citibank New York and sender being Bank of China, Hunan Branch with its cable address of CHUNGKUO CHANGS, but with the SENDER'S NAME ADDRESS AND TELEPHONE NUMBER… NOT TO BE TRANSMITTED.

2. **TEST** 密押号

3. **Cable Address** 电报挂号

   Cable address usually consists of two or more words or numbers, e.g.

   Cable Address：1234

   Cable Address：JSIMP NANJING

   第一个词是机构代号；第二个词表示城市。不过城市必须是众所周知的，否则须于其后注明国名。

4. 电文译文：

   密押……

   航空邮寄信用证……金额……受益人……账号……包括……货物。合同号……船上交货价……交给……最迟期限……中国（密押）航空邮寄信用证……受益人……账户……金额……重定合同……装运……有效期……提前通知。谨致。

   中国

**An incoming telegram:**

（1）UC10 OT 658

（2）URGENT NEWYORK 21 24 2030

（3）URGENT

（4）CHUNGKUO BEIJING

（5）YOURS 16TH…/…CREDIT TERMS PAYMENT BY MT WE CANNOT OBTAIN OUR PRINCIPALS AUTHORITY TO CHANGE TO TT

（6）CITINYORK

**Notes to the above sample cable:**

（1）the number of the telegram office（电报局编号）.

（2）the classifications（急电）; location of the sender（纽约），numbers of the message（21个字），time of the cable sent（24日20：30）.

（3）the rate of charge（按急电收费）.

（4）the cable address of the addressee[收报人电报挂号，收报地（北京）].

（5）电文译文：你行16日……/……电，信用证条款规定用信汇付款，我行无法征得客户同意，请改成电汇。

（6）the cable address of sender（纽约花旗银行的电挂地址）.

**Attention:**

（1）the heading in telegram including the numbers of message, class and the numbers charged are to be written by the telegram office.

（2）the class of the telegram is to be stated by the sender.

（3）the name and the address of the addressee should be written in detail.

（4）if there is no cable address, the name and address of the addressee and/or the post office number and number of telex etc. are to be written in detail.

（5）the telegram message is to be written in capitalized letter.

## 4. Rules of drafting telegrams（起草电报的规则）

How to draft the English plain language telegrams is a complicated issue. When writing a telegram, in order to save words and reduce the expenses, the methods of simplification of sentences and abbreviations and combination of words and phrases may be used.

（1）When referring to the incoming letter, the name and number of the relative documents such as number of Credit, Contract, Invoice and Bill of Lading are usually placed at the beginning of the message. e.g.

YOUR L/C 3456 UNRECEIVED

你方3456号证未收到。

YOURS 25TH OUR CREDIT…YOU MAY ACCEPT DOCUMENTS

回你行25日电。我行证……可议付。

YOUR L/C…NEGOTIATED TODAY DOCUMENTS COMPLIED WITH USD…OUR CHARGES

你行信用证……单证相符今日议付金额为……美元，我行收费。

YOUR CREDIT…OUR BP…DOCUMENTS NEGOTIATED TERMS COMPLIED WITH USD…OUR CHARGES

你行信用证……我行面函……，全部单据符合条款，已议付……美元，我行收费。

（2）Only key words such as nouns, verbs are to be used in the cable message with the unnecessary structure words such as auxiliary verbs, link-verbs, modal verbs, most pronouns, prepositions and some adjectives, adverbs crossed out, e.g.

WE HAVE NOT RECEIVED YOUR PAYMENT ORDER

可省略为：YOUR PAYMENT ORDER UNRECEIVED

你方支付通知未收到。

其中代词 WE，助动词 HAVE 可以省去，有时代词所有格 YOUR 也可省略。至于介词是否可省略，则依情况而定。如下列例中的介词绝对不能省略。

INVOICE 123 AMOUNT INCREASED BY USD1000

INVOICE 123 AMOUNT INCREASED TO USD1000

前者意思是发票金额增加 1000 美元，而后者是发票金额增加到 1000 美元。两者的含义截然不同。

（3）The v-ing, and v-ed structures in the message can be represented as some tenses and voice.

i. present participle (V–ING) refers to some action in the present and future tense. e.g.

WE ARE OPENING THE RELATIVE LETTER OF CREDIT

可省为：OPENING L/C（正在开证）

WE SHALL SEND YOU OUR CONTROL DOCUMENTS

可省为：SENDING CONTROL DOCUMENTS（将寄控制文件）

ii. past participle (V–ED) can not only be used as adjective, but also refer to some action in past tense and passive voice. e.g.

WE HAVE OPENED THE LETTER OF CREDIT NO123

可省为：L/C123 OPENED（完成时态）

THE PAYMENT WAS EFFECTED TODAY

可省为：PAYMENT EFFECTED TODAY（被动语态）

（4）One word can be used to replace a phrase or short sentence in the cable message. e.g.

| PER | instead of | AS PER | 按照，根据 |
| SUBJECT | instead of | SUBJECT TO | 以……为准 |
| OWING | instead of | OWING TO | 由于，因为 |
| ACCORDING | instead of | ACCORDING TO | 根据，依据 |
| SOONEST | instead of | AS SOON AS POSSIBLE | 尽快，速 |
| CONSIDERING | instead of | IN CONSIDERATION OF | 考虑 |
| ON | instead of | ON CONDITION THAT | 以……条件 |

（5）Short words in the message can be used to replace long words. e.g.

| SOON | instead of | IMMEDIATELY | 立即，马上 |
| PROMPTLY | instead of | IMMEDIATELY | 立即，马上 |
| UNACEPTABL | instead of | UNACCEPTABLE | 不可接受的 |

（6）V–ABLE structure in the message can be used to express "CAN BE DONE". e.g.

| PAYABLE | instead of | CAN BE PAID | 可支付的 |

| | | | |
|---|---|---|---|
| SHIPPABLE | instead of | CAN BE SHIPPED | 可装运的 |
| ACCEPTABLE | instead of | CAN BE ACCEPTED | 可接受的 |
| AGREEABLE | instead of | CAN BE AGREED | 可同意的 |
| CHARGABLE | instead of | CAN BE CHARGED | 可收费的 |

（7）Short phrases in the message can be combined into COMPOUND WORDS. e.g.

| | | | |
|---|---|---|---|
| AMOUNTTO | instead of | AMOUNT TO | 总数达…… |
| CABLEREPLY | instead of | CABLE REPLY | 电复 |
| PLSEXTEND | instead of | PLEASE EXTEND | 请延期 |
| PLSRUSHLC | instead of | PLEASE RUSH L/C | 请速开证 |

（8）Punctuations and some signs or symbols in the message are to be transformed into written words. e.g.

| | | | |
|---|---|---|---|
| COMMA | instead of | ， | （逗号） |
| STOP | instead of | 。 | （句号） |
| PCT/0/0 | instead of | % | （百分比） |
| QUOTE…UNQUOTE | instead of | "" | （引号） |
| AND | instead of | & | （和） |
| PLUS | instead of | + | （加） |
| CNY | instead of | ¥ | （人民币） |
| USD/D | instead of | $ | （美元） |
| YEN | instead of | ¥ | （日元） |
| GBP/ STG | instead of | £ | （英镑） |

（9）Some abbreviations internationally accepted are commonly used in the message. e.g. Examples as stated in the abbreviations table in the appendix II.

## 5. Specimen telegrams（样例电报）

### Sample 1

```
TO: BANK OF CHINA H. O.  BEIJING
DATE: MARCH 21, 2018
TEST…FOR NO AMT
PLS TEST AND RELAY THE FOLLOWING TO NATIONAL BANK OF EGYPT CARIO
EGYPT QUOTE
ATTN: GUARANTEE DEPT
YOUR REF: NO 119/233/GS
YOU ARE KINDLY REQUESTED TO MAKE AMENDMENTS AS FOLLOWS.
```

1. SUBSTITUTE QUOTE CONSEQUENTLY ANY CLAIM… UNTIL WITH AUTHORIZED CERTIFICATE ATTHELATEST UNQUOTE BY QUOTE THIS L/G HOLDGOOD UNTIL THE AUG. 15, 2018 ATTHELATEST UNQUOTE

2. DELETE QUOTE OUR GUARANTEE INYRFAVOR IS VALID FOR 15DAYS AFTER EXPIRYDATE FOR LODGEMENT OF YOUR CLAIM UNQUOTE

3. PLS AMEND ALL THE AMOUNT USD180,000.00 APPEARED IN THE GUARANTEE AND COUNTERGUARANTEE INTO USD18,000.00

4. INSERT QUOTE OURSELVES OR ANOTHER PARTY WHATSOEVER AND DESPITE ANY CONTESTATION BY OUR CLIENT UNQUOTE

5. PLS DELIVER THE GUARANTEE TO THE BENEFICIARY DIRECTLY TKS AND RGDS

UNQUOTE

TKS

CHUNGKUO CHANGS

**Notes:**

1. This is a cable requesting for amendment to the L/G contents.

2. **SUBSTITUTE…BY…** 由……代替……

3. **HOLDGOOD** 保持有效（是 HOLD GOOD 的合成词）

4. **DELETE** vt. 删去

5. **LODGEMENT OF YOUR CLAIM** 提出索赔

6. **INSERT** vt. 加入

**Sample 2**

REYOUR LCNO…FOR USD…OURREF…
THE DOCUMENTS WERE SENT TO YOU ON…BY EXPRESS MAIL BUT YOUR PAYMENT TOUS WAS DELAYED FOR…DAYS STOP PLS LOOKINTO AND COMPENSATE US FOR OUR INTEREST LOSS IN THE AMOUNT OF USD… (INCLUDING USD…AS CHARGES FOR THIS CABLE) AT THE RATE OF…PCT PA BY CREDITING OURACCT WITH…BANK UNDERTLX ADVICE TO US QUOTING OURREF RGDS CHUNGKUO BEIJING

**Notes:**

1. This is a cable inquiry for the reason of delay in payment.

2. **BY EXPRESS MAIL** 快递

3. **AT THE RATE OF…PCT PA** 按年利率…%，其中 PCT 是百分比（%），PA 是

每年（是 PER ANNUAL 的缩写形式）

4. **OURACCT**　我方账户（是 OUR ACCOUNT 的合成词）

### Sample 3

REOUR BP…FOR USD…UNDER L/CNO…
WE NEGOTIATED THE DRAFT WITH RELATIVE DOCUMENTS DRAWN UNDER THE CAPTIONDLC ON…AND REQUESTED YOU TO CREDIT THE PROCEEDS TO OUR ACCT WITH YOU STOP HOWEVER WE HAVENOT RECEIVED ANY CREDIT ADVICE TO THIS EFFECT FROM YOU NOR FROM THE CLEARING BANK UPTODATE STOP SINCE THIS MATTER HAS BEEN LONG OUTSTANDING PLS LOOKINTO WHETHER OR NOT YOU HAVE ALREADY CREDITED/REMITTED THE PROCEEDS ASREQUESTD AND INFORMUS OF THE RESULT SOONEST RGDS CC…

**Notes:**

1. This is a reimbursement tracer by cable.

2. **STOP**　句号

3. **TO THIS EFFECT**　上述内容

4. **CC…**　抄送

### Sample 4

YOUR 9TH CLC…OURREF…UNPAID…STATE WILL PAY ACCORDING INSPECTION RESULT AFTER ARRIVAL GOODS
YOUR REF…OURLCNO…PAYMENT DOCUMENTS USD…REFUSED OWING PACKGLIST INCOMPLETE RGDS CHUNGKUO CHANGS

**Notes:**

1. This is a cable dishonoring documents.

2. **CLC**　托收（是 COLLECTION 的缩写形式）

3. **STATE** *vt.*　声明

4. **PACKGLIST**　装箱单（是 PACKING LIST 的合成词）

### Sample 5

(TEST)…LC…BY…(BANK) CLAIM USD…CHARGES…
PLSCREDIT OUR HO BEIJING ACCOUNT CABLEADUS QUOTING BP…CHUNGKUO NEWYORK

> PLSRLYMSG TO… ATTN LCREIMBURSE DEPT QUOTE LCNO…ISSUED BY…
> CLAIM USD…PLSPAYTO BANK OF TOKYO NEWYORK YOUR CABLEADUS
> QUOTING OURBP…CHUNGKUO
> PLSRLYMSG TO HABIB BANKLTD NEWYORK QUOTE YOUR KARACHI OFFICE
> LC…CLAIM USD…CHARGES…PLSPAYTO OURNEWYORK OFFICE YOUR
> CABLEADUS BP…UNQUOTE

**Notes:**

1. This is a cable claim for reimbursement.

2. **PLSCREDIT** 请贷记（是 PLEASE CREDIT 的合成词）

3. **CABLEADUS** 电告我方（是 CABLE ADVICE TO US 的合成词）

4. **PLSRLYMSG** 请转告电文（是 PLEASE RELAY THE MESSAGE 的合成词）

5. **LCREIMBURSE DEPT** 信用证偿付部（是 L/C REIMBURSING DEPARTMENT 的合成词）

6. **HABIB BANKLTD** 哈比银行（BANKLTD 是 BANK LTD 的合成词）

## 6. Commonly used sentences on banking telegrams（银行电报常用句型）

（1）YOURS14TH WE CONFIRM OURLCNO…SIGNATURE CORRECT
  回复你14日函，我行确认我证签字无误。

（2）REPLY TO YOUETLX DATED…REF…OURLCNO…PLS NEGOTIATE
  现回复你行×日编号×电我行证……金额……请议付。

（3）PLSCABLE AUTHORIZE OURHO TO DEBIT YOURACCT
  请电报授权我总行借记你行账户。

（4）PLSCREDIT HO A/CNO…UNDER CABLEADUS
  请贷记我总行账户……并电告我方。

（5）NEGOTIATED UNDER…(BANK) L/CNO…OURBP…USD…CHARGES…TERM CMPLIEDWTH
  ……银行信用证……项下单据已议付。

（6）OURBP USD…CHARGES…TODAY REIMBURSED THROUGH…(BANK) BY CABLE
  我行面函金额……美元，费用……今日已经……银行电报偿付。

（7）YOURS25TH OURCREDIT…YOU MAY ACCEPT DOCUMENTS
  回你行25日电，我行证……可议付。

（8）YOURCREDIT…DOCUMENTS PRESENTED TODAY B/L ANTEDATED… WHETHER…NEGOTIABLE TELEINSTRUCT

你行证……单据今日提示，提单日期倒填为……可否议付，请电告。

（9）YOURREF...OURLC...RESERVE PLACE ON PAYMENT FF MAY RELEASED

你行案号……我行证号……付款……法郎的保留可以撤销。

（10）UPON RECEIPT PLSCANCEL AND RETURN OUR PAYMENT ADVICE...SF...DATED5TH THIS MONTH

收信后请撤销并退回我行付款通知……瑞士法郎……日期为本月5日。

## III. Telexes（电传）

### 1. Characteristics of telexex（电传的特证）

Telexes have been extensively used in 1990s as a means of communication in international banking business. By this service, messages can be sent to or received from foreign countries through telex equipment, the main unit being a set of teleprinters. In fact, TELEX is the abbreviation of TELEPRINTER EXCHANGE or TELETYPEWRITER EXCHANGE, which refers to the message or information exchanged between teleprinters with the following advantages compared to the telegram:

（1）More convenient in use.

It is operable any time round the clock and possible to receive messages even if the machine is left unattended since the telex equipment works automatically with the messages received at night being ready to be dealt with first thing in the next morning.

（2）Faster in speed.

Once the telex is connected, the message can be transmitted to and appeared on the telex machine of the addressee simultaneously when the sender types it on his telex machine.

（3）Cheaper in cost.

Telex affords quick and effective communication and brings about economical result. Its charges are calculated according to the time engaged in transmission, but not the number of words a message contains in the case of cable. The minimum charge for a telex is fixed on the basis of one minute. Rough calculation has it that four hundred letters or so can be transmitted every minute.

（4）Clearer in expression.

Much more words are used in telex, which can express the meaning more clearly.

### 2. The form and structure of telexes（电传的格式和结构）

The form of telexes is different from that of telegrams and letters, which can usually be shown as follows:

(1) THE HEADING

This part contains the telex number or answering call code of the receiver and the sender, date and test of the message in transmission, name and address of the sender and receiver. e.g.

| | |
|---|---|
| 98187 HNBOC CN | 收电人电传挂号/呼叫号码 |
| 92238 NBEUN UN | 发电人电传挂号/呼叫号码 |
| CAIRO 7/11/18 | 发电地址，交发日期 |
| FROM：NATIONAL BANK OF EGYPT CAIRO | 发电人单位 |
| TO：BANK OF CHINA HUNAN BRANCH CHANGSHA | 收电人单位 |
| TEST 3334… | 该电文密押 |

or

| | |
|---|---|
| 98187 HNBOC CN | 收电人电传挂号 |
| FROM：92238 NBEUN | 发电人电传挂号 |
| CAIRO 7/11/18 | 发电地址，发电日期 |

or

| | |
|---|---|
| 92238 NBEUN UN | 发电人电传挂号 |
| CAIRO 7/11/18 | 发电地址，发电日期 |
| TO：98187 HNBOC CN | 收电人电传挂号 |

or

| | |
|---|---|
| TO：BANK OF CHINA, CHENGDU | 收电人单位 |
| FM：CHAMANBANK, NEW YORK | 发电人单位 |
| MAY 12, 2018 | 发电日期 |

(2) THE BODY OF THE TELEX

This is the main part of a telex message which contains what the sender wants to say in great detail.

(3) ENDING/CLOSE

This is the ending of a telex with complimentary close, the repetition of the answering call number of the sender and receiver and the time used in transmission.

e.g.

| | |
|---|---|
| BEST REGARDS | 敬语结束语 |
| 98107 HNBOC CN | 收电人电传挂号（重复） |
| 92238 NBEUN UN | 发电人电传挂号（重复） |
| 07.11.2018 0419 | 发电日期，发电所花费的时间（4分19秒） |

| | |
|---|---|
| 或 | |
| RGDS/TKS AND RGDS/THANKS/END TKS | 敬语结束语 |
| 98107 HNBOC CN | 收电人电挂 |
| 92238 NBEUN UN | 发电人电挂 |
| 07.11.2018  0234 | 发电日期，发电时间 |

e.g.

An incoming telex

（1）98107 HNBOC CN

（2）92238 NBEUN UN

（3）CAIRO 7/11/18

（4）FM :NATIONAL CAIRO

（5）TO :BANK OF CHINA HUNAN BRANCH CHANGSHA

（6）TEST 3331…

（7）RE YOUR LETR DD…REFNBR BP…UNDER…BANK L/C NO…WE CREDITED YOUR BEIJING ACCT USD… ON DD… FOR YOUR CREDIT STOP RGDS. NATIONAL CAIRO

（8）98187 HNBOC CN

（9）92238 NBEUN UN

（10）07.11.18  0326


**Notes to the above telex:**

（1）98107 is the answer back code of the receiver.

　　HNBOC is the short name of the receiver's bank, whose complete name is BANK OF CHINA HUNAN BRANCH, CN is the telex code of CHINA.

（2）92238 is the answer back code of the sender.

　　NBEUN is the short name of the sender's bank whose complete name is NATIONAL BANK OF EGYPT CAIRO EGYPT, UN is the telex code of EGYPT.

（3）CAIRO is the city of sender's bank located in, 7/11/18 is the date of the telex（2018年11月7日）.

（4）name of the sender's bank（开罗国家银行）.

（5）name of the receiver's bank（中国银行湖南省分行）.

（6）telex test（电传密押）.

（7）电文译文：兹回复你行×月×日函，案号……，……银行信用证号……我行于×月×日贷记你行北京账户……美元。致礼！开罗国家银行。

(8) repetition of the receiver's answer back code.

(9) repetition of the sender's answer back code.

(10) date of telex (2018年11月7日) and time used in transmission (3分26秒).

**Attentions:**

(1) Message in telex is to be written in capitalized letter.

(2) Telex message can contain complete sentences and punctuation marks exclusive of any signs such as ￥, $, currency units and & etc. We can use YEN instead of ￥, CNY instead of ￥, USD instead of $, STG or GBP instead of £ etc.

(3) We usually use "PCT" or "0/0" to replace "%", "PERMILL" to replace "‰". e.g.: 5%/5PCT; 5‰/5PERMILL.

(4) Sometimes in order to save time in transmission, when drafting telex, we can combine the cable sentences and complete sentences with the short forms and simplified words accepted in international customary practice( please see Appendix II), and also with all the punctuation marks and/or structural words omitted.

3. **Rules for simplifying words and phrases in telex messages**（简化电文单词与词组的规则）

(1) Keep all the consonant-letters and the initial vowel-letter of the word by crossing out all other vowels to form an abbreviation. e.g.

   ABT=ABOUT              BTWN=BETWEEN
   ARVD=ARRIVED           RCVD=RECEIVED
   ACTBL=ACCEPTABLE       CFM=CONFIRM
   AGRD=AGREED            FLW=FOLLOW
   UNWRKBL=UNWORKABLE     HV=HAVE

(2) Keep the first syllable and the first consonant of the second syllable to form an abbreviation. e.g.

   DOC=DOCUMENT           ADV=ADVICE
   ADJ=ADJUSTMENT         AVE=AVENUE
   IMP=IMPORT             EXP=EXPORT
   AD=ADVERTISEMENT       CERT=CERTIFICATE
   AIR=AIRMAIL            IMM=IMMEDIATELY

(3) Keep the first and last letter of the word. e.g.

   BK=BANK                FM=FROM
   YR=YOUR                WT=WEIGHT

HD=HAD   FT=FOOT

(4) Keep the first and second syllable to form an abbreviation. e.g.

AVE=avenue   MEMO=memorandum

CONDI=condition   NEGO=negotiation

(5) Keep the initial letter of each word of the phrase. e.g.

ASAP=AS SOON AS POSSIBLE

AF=AS FOLLOWS

USO=UNLESS OTHERWISE SPECIFIED

USC=UNDER SEPARATE COVER

CIF=COST INSURANCE AND FREIGHT

ETA=ESTIMATED TIME OF ARRIVAL

EL=EXPORT LICENCE

RYL=REFERRING TO YOUR LETTER

RYT=REFERRING TO YOUR TELEX

RYC=REFERRING TO YOUR CABLE

FYR=FOR YOUR REFERENCE

FYI=FOR YOUR INFORMATION

IVO=IN VIEW OF

EMP=EUROPEAN MAIN PORTS

IMF=INTERNATIONAL MONETARY FUND

(6) Keep the important consonants and the last letter of the word inclusive of "y" if the last one is "y". e.g.

MSG=MESSAGE   SBJ=SUBJECT

QTY=QUANTITY   FRT=FREIGHT

THKS=THANKS   PCTG=PERCENTAGE

(7) Simplify some commonly used suffixes. e.g.

D=ED   RCVD=RECEIVED

G=ING   SHPG=SHIPPING

MT=MENT   PAYMT=PAYMENT

TN=TION   INSTRCTN=INSTRUCTION

SN=SION   CMSN=COMMISSION

BL=ABLE/IBLE/BLE   SHPBL=SHIPPABLE

R=ER/OR/URE   CSTMR=CUSTOMER

L=AL/IAL   TTL=TOTAL

SPECL=SPECIAL

Z=IZE                   RLZ=REALIZE

...

(8) Remember some technical terms and abbreviations commonly used in international customary practice. e.g.

CIF=COST INSURANCE AND FREIGHT

CFR=COST AND FREIGHT

L/C=LETTER OF CREDIT

D/P=DOCUMENTS AGAINST PAYMENT

D/A=DOCUMENTS AGAINST ACCEPTANCE

BP=BILLS PURCHASED

M/T=MAIL TRANSFER

T/T=TELEGRAPHIC TRANSFER

D/D=DEMAND DRAFT

DZ=DOZEN

OZ=OUNCE

L/T=LONG TON

MT=METRIC TON

F/O=IN FAVOR OF

...

(9) Use one or several letters pronounced alike to replace a word. e.g.

V/W=WE              U=YOU

UR=YOUR             ZS=THIS

GIZ=THESE           HV=HAVE

BIZ=BUSINESS        R=ARE

B=BE                THRO=THROUGH

WK=WEEK             THO=THOUGH

NU=NEW              HZ=HAS

...

## 4. Specimen telexes（样例电传）

### Sample 6

FM: HONGKONG AND SHANGHAI BANKING CORP(HSBC). NEW YORK

TO: BANK OF CHINA BEIJING

```
TEST : …TR. FOLLOWG FOR UR CHENGDU BRANCH

UR REIMBURSEMENT LTR DD…WZ BP…FOR USD…UNPAID AS OPENING
BANK DOES NOT HV AN ACCT WZ US AND V DO NOT HOLD REIMBURSEMENT
AUTHORITY UNDER THEIR DOCUMENTARY CREDITS. PLS INSTRCT ATTN
EXPORTS DEPARTMENT QUOTING OUR REF. RGDS
EXP NY BC
```

**Notes:**

1. This is a telex showing that the reimbursing bank does not hold the reimbursement authority.

2. **CORP.** = corporation

3. **UR** =your

4. **DD** =date

5. **WZ** = with

6. **BP** =bills purchased   押汇，面函

7. **HV** = have

8. **V** = we

## Sample 7

```
98107 HNBOC CN

92238 NBEUN UN

CAIRO 3/11/18

FM : NATIONAL CAIRO

TO : BANK OF CHINA HUNAN BRANCH

TEST 2345 WITH PEKING FOR NO…AMT…

WE REMIND YOU OF OUR 19/10/18 STILL WITHOUT YOUR REPLY READING AS
FOLLOWS QUOTE

OUR TELEX DD 22/9/18  RE L/G NO A/83594

YOUR REF NO LG 18000018…06

WHICH STILL UNANSWERED STOP BENEFICIARIES INSIST CONFISCATE VALUE
SAID GUARANTEE UNLESS ITS VALIDITY IS EXTENDED UP TO 15/11/18 STOP PLS
TLX WZ TEST YOUR APPROVAL. REQUIRED EXTENSION OTHERWISE REMIT TO
OUR ACCT WZ BANK OF NEW YORK THE SUM OF USD 18,000.00 ACRDG TO UR
OBLIGATIONS TOWARDS US UNDER UR COUNTER GUARANTEE IN OUR FAVOR
STOP OUR REF NO A/83594/122  UNQUOTE RGDS
```

```
NATIONAL CAIRO
98107 HNBOC CN
92238 NBEUN UN
3.11.2018  0300
```

**Notes:**

1. This is a telex request for extension of the L/G validity.

2. **L/G = letter of guarantee**   保函

3. **STOP** *n.*   句号

4. **CONFISCATE** *vt.*   没收

5. **ACRDG TO =according to**   根据

6. **COUNTER GUARANTEE**   反担保

### Sample 8

```
TO：…BANK
FM：…BANK
RE：…USD…L/A DD…
IN ACCORDANCE WZ CLAUSE…OF THE LOAN AGREEMENT, THE BORROWER HZ DELIVERD A NOTICE FOR THE…TH DRAWING OF USD…WHICH WILL TAKE PLACE ON…2018.
V CONFM THAT THE BORROWER'S REPRESENTATIONS AND WARRANTS AS SET FORTH IN CLAUSE…OF THE LOAN AGREEMENT REMAIN UNWAIVED AND UNCHANGED. THE FACTS AND CIRCUMSTANCES SUBSISTG ON THE DATE OF HIS NOTICE TO US REMAIN TRUE AND CORRECT AND NO EVENT OF DEFAULT HZ OCCURRD NOR ANY IS PROSPECTIVE.
PLS CNFM BY RETURN TLX THAT U WL ARRANGE UR POSITN OF ZS ADVANCE OF USD…TO OUR ACCT NO…WZ…BK, NEW YORK, VALUE DD…2018. THE INTEREST PERIOD FOR ZS ADVANCE WL B FM…TO…(…DAYS) AND THE INTEREST RATE WL B FIXED ON…2018 AT 11：00A.M. LONDON TIME. V SHL NOTIFY U OF THE APPLICABLE INTEREST RATE IN DUE COURSE.
BEST RGDS
```

**Notes:**

1. This is a telex confirming that the borrower hasn't breached the terms of the agreement.

2. **L/A = LOAN AGREEMENT**   贷款协议

3. **SUBSIST** *vi. vt.*   存在

4. **DEFAULT** *n. vi. & vt.* 违约

5. **POSITN** 头寸

6. **VALUE** *n. vt.* 起息

## Sample 9

NEW YORK NY 78/76 201550
TO: CHUGKUO CHENGDU
FM: BANK OF BARODA NY
RYC 12/20/18 REGARDING UR REIMBURSEMENT CLAIM FOR USD…. UNDER OUR BONBAY OFFICE LC NO. … AND UR REF BP…STOP THE ABOVE CLAIM WAS PAID VIA CHIPS THRU MANTRUST NEW YORK TO SANWA BANK LTD NEW YORK FOR UR HO A/C QUOTING ABV REF ON 11/16/18 STOP KINDLY CONTACT SANWA BANK DRCTLY REGARDING STATUS OF THE FUNDS QUOTING MANTRUST CHIPS SEQUENCE NBR 94937096 CH STOP RGDS
FORENBAR

**Notes:**

1. This is a telex advising that proceeds has been credited to your H.O. through…bank.

2. **BANK OF BARODA NY** 纽约巴罗达银行

3. **RYC = referring to your cable**

4. **BONBAY OFFICE** 孟买分行

5. **CHIPS =Clearing House Inter-bank Payment System** （纽约）银行间电子清算系统

6. **MANTRUST NEW YORK** 纽约汉华实业银行

7. **SANWA BANK LTD** 纽约三和银行

8. **CHIPS SEQUENCE NBR** 清算系统序号

## Sample 10

FM: BANGKOK BANK LTD BANGKOK
TO: CITIBANK N. A. NEW YORK
YOUR REF. … BP NO. … OUR CREDIT…DOCUMENT USD… UNACEPTBL OWING DISCREPANCIES:
AAA: LATE SHIPMENT
BBB: CREDIT EXPIRED STOP
HOLDING DOCS UR DISPOSAL PLS TLX INSTRCT US STOP CREDIT OUR ACCT

USD... COST ZS TLX WZ OUR NEW YORK AGENCY
RGDS

**Notes:**

1. This is a telex advising that the relative documents differ.

2. **BANGKOK BANK**　曼谷银行

3. **CITIBANK N. A.**　花旗银行（N. A. 是 NATIONAL 的缩写，国民银行的标识）

**Sample 11**

DATE: MAY 20, 2018
TO: CITIBANK N. A., NEW YORK
FM: BANK OF CHINA, NINGBO BRANCH
RE: USD2,000,000.00 SHORT TERM BORROWING
PLS BE ADVISED TT INTEREST RATE FOR THE BORROWING IS SET AT 5.6250/0(LIBOR 4.375 PLUS 1.250 PERCENT). INTEREST FOR THE BORROWING PERIOD(MAY 24, 2018 TO NOV. 24, 2018) IS USD50,376.34.
WE'LL REMIT USD2,000,000.00 TO SHENZHEN DEVELOPMENT BANK'S ACCOUNT WZ CHASE MANHATTAN, NEW YORK A/C NO 10-0-230432-2-003 IN FAVOR OF UR BRANCH VALUE MAY 24, 2018.
BEST REGARDS

**Notes:**

1. This is a telex on interbank borrowing.

2. **LIBOR**　伦敦同业银行拆借利率（London Interbank Borrowing Offer Rate 的缩写）

3. **VALUE**　起息

**Sample 12**

DATE:
TO:
FM:
RE: OUR AMENDMENT REF. NO. 12345
RE OUR CREDIT NO. 23456 FOR USD840,520.00 DD 11/09/18. THE CREDIT IS AMENDED AS FOLLOWS:
• EXPIRY DATE OF L/C: 12/19/18
• TIME OF SHIPMENT: BEFORE 11/30/18

OTHER TERMS AND CONDITIONS UNCHANGED

SUBJECT TO UCP 600

PLEASE ADVISE BENEFICIARY ASAP.

THIS IS AN OPERATIVE AMENDMENT NO MAIL CONFIRMATION TO FOLLOW

BEST REGARDS

**Notes:**

1. This is a telex on amendment to the relative L/C clauses.

2. **UCP** 跟单信用证统一惯例（Uniform Customs and Practice for Documentary Credit 的缩写）

3. **ASAP** 尽快（as soon as possible 的缩写）

**Sample 13**

DATE:

TO:

FM:

RE: YOUR LC NO. 12345-099 FOR USD20,042,006.00

　　OUR BP07103 ON 15 NOV 2018

FUNDS NOT YET RECEIVED

PLS FOLLOW OUR SETTLEMENT INSTRUCTIONS IN OUR COVER LETTER AND CABLE CONFIRM US YOUR EXECUTION WE RESERVE RIGHT TO CLAIM ON YOU FOR ANY UNDUE DELAY PAYMENT INTEREST CAUSED AT YOUR END.

REGARDS.

**Notes:**

1. This is a telex on urging payment.

2. **SETTLEMENT INSTRUCTION** 结算通知

3. **COVER LETTER** 说明函

4. **AT YOUR END** 在你处

5. **Commonly used sentences on banking telexes**（银行电传常用句型）

　　（1）WE CONFIRM THE ABOVE DEAL AND WL PAY EURO3,400,300.00 TO UR ACCT WZ CHASE MANHATTAN NEW YORK ON DUE DATE.

　　（2）PLS REMIT USD5,000,000.00 TO OUR ACCOUNT WZ BANK OF CHINA HK ON THAT DATE.

　　（3）WE BUY USD1,000,000.00 AGST RMB7,018,900.00 AT RATE 5.0189 VALUE01/26/18.

（4）AFTER PAYMT, PLS CREDIT OUR USD A/C NO. 123455 WZ U ON VALUE DATE.

（5）WE WL PAY RMB TO BOC GUANGDONG BR AND AUTHORIZE THEM TO CREDIT UR RMB A/C.

（6）PREADVICE OF IRREVOCABLE LC NO. 1234 OPEND ON 5TH MAY, 2007. ACCOUNTEE ABC CO FAVRING CHINA NATIONAL METALS I/E CORPORATION SHENZHEN BR FOR AMT USD35,000.00 COVERING SUNNDRY METALWARES SHIPMET LATEST MAY 2018 VALIDITY 16TH JUNE, 2018 UR CONFIRMATION TO BE ADDED THERETO.

（7）PLS DEBIT OUR A/C NO. 01-2-1-12345 WZ USD…(CABLE CHGS USD… DEDUCTED) VALUE TODAY UNDER OUR L/C NO. OX 12345 AND P/O NO. CP 98765 AND PAY THE SUM TO BANKERS TRUST CO. NEW YORK FOR CREDIT OF ASAHI BANK LTD HEAD OFFICE ACCT NO. 34567 FAVORING ASAHI BANK LTD OSAKA QUOTING THEIR REF. BB300-01-4234 RGS.

（8）PLS PAY VIA CHIPS TO BANK OF CHINA, NEW YORK FOR OUR ACCT (NO. 123456) WZ THEM UNDER THEIR AND YOUR CABLE ADVICE TO US QUOTING OUR BP NO. 4040694.

## IV. Exercises（练习）

1. **Translate the following into cable message：**

   日期：

   我行 BP 号……

   你行信用证号……

   我行已收到你行 10 月 6 日来函及你行贷记通知副本一份，函告你行于同日将……贷记我北京总行账下，偿付应付我行标题下的议付款项。

   我行现需指出，在我行电报发出两周后你行才付款，耽误的时间超出常规。

   请查告迟付原因。

2. **Put the following into Telex message:**

   发文：……香港银行

   日期：

   我行案号：

   我行跟单信用证号：

   你行面函号：

我行已收悉你行……日来函邮寄向我行汇寄的上述跟单信用证单据，为方便偿付此议付款项，请选择下面可供偿付的方式：

（　　）你行借记我行在你北京总行的账户；
（　　）我行贷记你行在我行的账户；
（　　）我行将……款项汇寄至……以偿付你行。
……香港银行谨启

## Unit Eight   SWIFT Business

## 第8单元   SWIFT业务

**After studying this unit, you will be able to:**
- Understand there are many kinds of messages related to international banking business in SWIFT format
- Recognize the features in format and style of SWIFT message, after learning samples in many kinds of business
- Learn how to write SWIFT message
- Master the language skills of this respect
- Evaluate your writing skills by completing the self-test checklists in the unit

# I. Introduction to SWIFT（简介）

SWIFT is the abbreviation of the Society for Worldwide Inter-bank Financial Telecommunication which is a non-profitable worldwide inter-bank organization with its headquarters in Brussels. It was established in 1973 with 240 large European and North American banks in this inter-bank communication network. As a cooperative and automatic worldwide telecommunication system, SWIFT enables member banks to transit among themselves international payments, statements and other transactions relating to international banking in several minutes, so the use of the network is more convenient and reliable than the past methods(letter, telex and cable), and enables banks to offer better services to their customers.

With the increasing development of SWIFT, up to June 2007, there are 8100 SWIFT member banks across 207 countries and districts all over the world. In China, Bank of China took the lead in joining SWIFT in 1983, and its Head Office began using the SWIFT system in 1985, then followed by other Chinese financial institutions. Up to the present there are more than 80 financial institutions conducting international banking business by SWIFT system.

SWIFT is a fully integrated computer transmission system where messages can be transmitted in a standardized format and SWIFT Code, i.e. original BIC(Bank Identifier Code) approved by ISO. SWIFT enables international banks transfer funds at a faster speed. It is less expensive in cost and yet more reliable in security. In fact, banks are able to record their balances on computers and make payment transfer electronically almost at zero additional cost.

## 1. Message types（电文种类）:

All SWIFT messages are formatted and standardized so as to be readily and easily processed by computers. Message types represent different types of banking transactions. Each message type (MT) consists of three digits indicating actual transactions of the same type.

There are 10 message types (MTs). Besides, under each Message Type there is a Common Group( MTn/Category n). Following are the 10 Message Types.

Type 1: CUSTOMER TRANSFERS & CHECKS（客户汇款与支票）
    MT 103– CUSTOMER TRANSFER
    MT 110– ADVICE OF CHECK

Type 2: FINANCIAL INSTITUTION TRANSFERS（金融机构间头寸调拨）
    MT 200– BANK TRANSFER FOR ITS OWN ACCOUNT
    MT 201–BANK TRANSFER FOR ITS OWN ACCOUNT(MULTIPLE)
    MT 210–ADVICE TO RECEIVE

Type 3: MONEY MARKET–FX & LOAN/DEPOSIT CONFIRMATION（货币市场交易）

MT 300-FOREIGN EXCHANGE CONFIRMATION

MT 320-FIXED LOAN/DEPOSIT CONFIRMATION

MT 350-ADVICE OF LOAN/DEPOSIT INTEREST PAYMENT

Type 4: COLLECTION AND CASH LETTERS（托收与光票）

MT 400-ADVICE OF PAYMENT

MT 410-ACKNOWLEDGEMENT

Type 5: SECURITIES MARKETS（证券市场）

Type 6: TREASURY MARKET-PRECIOUS METALS AND SYNDICATIONS（贵金属）

Type 7: DOCUMENTARY CREDITS AND GUARANTEES（跟单信用证和保函）

MT 700/701-ISSUE OF A DOCUMENTARY CREDIT

MT 705-PRE-ADVICE OF A DOCUMENTARY CREDIT

MT 707/708-AMENDMENT TO A DOCUMENTARY CREDIT

MT 730-ACKNOWLEDGEMENT[①]

MT 732-ADVICE OF DISCHARGE[②]

MT 734-ADVICE OF REFUSAL

MT 740-AUTHORISATION TO REIMBURSEMENT[③]

MT 742- REIMBURSEMENT CLAIM[④]

MT 747- AMENDMENT TO AN AUTHORIZATION TO REIMBURSE

MT 750-ADVICE OF DISCREPANCY

Type 8: CREDIT CARDS & TRAVELLERS CHECKS（信用卡与旅行支票）

Type 9: DEBIT, CREDIT AND STATEMENT OF ACCOUNT（现金管理与账务）

MT 900-CONFIRMATION OF DEBIT

MT 910-CONFIRMATION OF CREDIT

MT 950-STATEMENT MESSAGE

Type 10: CABLES AMONG SWIFT SYSTEM（SWIFT 系统电报）

The common group includes the following:

N 90-ADVICE OF CHARGES, INTEREST AND OTHER ADJUSTMENT

N 91-REQUEST FOR PAYMENT OF CHARGES, INTEREST AND OTHER EXPENSES

---

① Acknowledges the receipt of a documentary credit message and may indicate that the message has been forwarded according to instructions. It may also be used to account for the charges or to advise of acceptance or rejection of an amendment of a documentary credit.
② Advises that documents received with discrepancies have been taken up.
③ Requests the receiver to honor claims for reimbursement of payments or negotiations under a documentary credit.
④ Provides a reimbursement claim to the bank authorized to reimburse the sender or its branch for its payment/negotiations.

N 92-REQUEST FOR CANCELLATION

N 95-QUERIES

N 98- PROPRIETARY MESSAGE

N 99-FREE FORMAT

In addition, there are some changes to the message type. From Nov. 18th 2000, MT103 has been officially used as a supplement to MT100, and has substituted it in recent years. This type of message is sent by or on behalf of the financial institution of ordering customer, directly or through a correspondent, to the financial institution of the beneficiary customer.

It is used to convey a fund transfer instruction when the ordering customer or the beneficiary customer, or both, are non-financial institutions from the perspective of the Sender.

This message may only be used for clean payment instructions. It must not be used to advise the remitting bank for a clean payment, e.g. cheque, collection, nor to provide the cover for a transaction whose completion was advised separately, e.g. via an MT400.

## 2. Fields（业务域）

There are different fields subordinated to each Message Type. Each field is preceded by a field tag. The following shows some fields descriptions:

20: Transaction Reference Number

21: Related Reference

32A: Value Date, Currency Code, Amount

50: Ordering Customer

53: Sender's Correspondent (Preferred Option A)

54: Receiver's Correspondent (Preferred Option A)

57: Account with Institution (Preferred Option A)

58: Beneficiary Institution (Preferred Option A)

59: Beneficiary Customer

70: Details of Payment

71A: Details of Charges

72: Sender to Receiver Information

e.g.

    A. MT 103

    20: YOUR REFERENCE

    32A: JUNE 26, 2018 HKD 2,005.00

    50: ABC TRADING CO. LTD

    59: /6000125001AAA TEXTILE INC.

  70: COLL.NO. 833221

  71A: BENEF

  B. MT 202

  20: YOUR REFERENCE

  21: FXDEAL 12345

  32A: OCT 21, 2018 GBP5,000.00

  53B: /002-80332-001/

  57A: BKCHHKHH

  58A: BKCHCHBJ300

## 3. Structure of a SWIFT message（电文结构）

A SWIFT message consists of the following five parts usually termed BLOCKS.

（1）BASIC HEADER BLOCK

（2）APPLICATION HEADER BLOCK

（3）USER HEADER BLOCK

（4）TEXT BLOCK

（5）TRAILER BLOCK

e.g.

### A. An Output Message

| | |
|---|---|
| （1）BASIC HEADER | F 01 BKCHCNBJAXXX 7842 511316 |
| （2）APPLICATION HEADER | O 799 1207 180803 YYCBHKHHAXXX 2733 3757754 180803 1512 N |
| | *YIEN YIEN COMMERCIAL BANK LTD., THE |
| | *HONG KONG BRANCH |
| | *HONG KONG |
| （3）USER HEADER | BANK，PRIORITY 113: |
| | MSG USER REF.108: 033932 |
| （4）TRN | *20:B--2 8-N-04602--01 |
|  NARRATIVE | *79:ADVICE OF MATURITY |
| | YOUR REF. BP9706003720 |
| | BILL AMOUNT USD74,250.00 |
| | OUR REF. B--2 8-N--04 602--01 |
| | DRAFT ACCEPTED TO MATURE ON 180902 |
| | CABLE CHARGES USD33.00 WILL BE DEDUCTED |
| | FROM THE PROCEEDS. |

（5）TRAILER　　　　　　　　　ORDER IS <MAC:><ENC:><CHK:><TNG:><PDE:>
　　　　　　　　　MAC: 7CDF018D
　　　　　　　　　CHK: 87866A5EAAAA
　　　　　　　　　DLM:

**Notes:**

（1）基本报头（BASIC HEADER）

F 为应用程序标示符：用以识别接收或发送电报的应用程序。F 即 FIN(FINANCIAL APPLICATION)，包括全部用户间的业务电报和 FIN 系统电报。01 为应用程序协议数据单元标识符。表示请求使用全部 FIN 系统以及用户间的业务电报。

BKCHCNBJA970 为逻辑终端地址（LOGICAL TERMINAL ADDRESS）由收报行/发电报的 SWIFT 银行识别代码加上终端代码共 12 位字符组成。

7842 为对话序号，一般为 4 位数字。

511316 为电报接收/发送序号，一般为 6 位数字。

（2）应用报头（APPLICATION HEADER）

O 为输入/输出标识码：输出（OUTPUT）标识符为字母 O。

799 为报文类别：由 3 位数组成，表示被输出的电文的业务类型。

1207 为输入时间（INPUT TIME）：表示发报行发报的当地时间。

180803 YYCBHKHHAXXX 2733 375754 为电报输入参号（MIR）：由 28 位字符组成，包括电报输入日期，发报行的逻辑终端标识符与分支序号和发报序号。

180803 为收报行的收报日期（当地时间）。

1512 为收报行收报的当地时间。

N 为电报优先级（PRIORITY）：表示普通电报（NORMAL）。

（3）用户报头（USER HEADER）

银行业务优先级 113 为标识符。

MSG USER REF. 电报用户参号（MUR）

108 为标识符，表示用户设置其专用参号的自由格式字段。

（4）TRN 为业务参考号（TRANSACTION REFERENCE NUMBER）

正文 79 为正文标识符。

（5）报尾（TRAILER）

在 SWIFT-II 电报中，报尾部分做监督控制用，或表示特殊情况下系统对电报的处理，或传达某些特殊的附加的信息，报尾可由用户或系统添加。报尾由 3 个字母代码开始，随后为引导和报尾自身的信息。

MAC—MESSAGE AUTHENTICATION　用于收报行对电报可靠性的核查认证。

ENC—ENCRYPTION　可选项，用于用户间的业务电报，专用密码。

CHK—CHECKSUN　用户终端自动核查、添加，用以证实电报的正确性：无操作、系统、传输等错误。

TNG—TRAINING　测试、练习电报标志，用以区分于有效的正式电报。

PDE—POSSIBLE DUPLICATE EMISSION　发报行因故重发或漏发的电报，提请收报行注意。

DLM—DELAYED MESSAGE　系统对于超过传送监控失效时限的输出电报均添加 DLM 报尾，供收报行做业务处理参考用。

PDM—POSSIBLE DUPLICATE MESSAGE　系统因故再次传送的电报，提请收报行注意避免重复。

**B. An Input Message**

| | | |
|---|---|---|
| （1） | BASIC HEADER | F 01 BKCHCNBJAXXXl055 120333 |
| （2） | APPLICATION HEADER | I 799 BKCHUS33XXXX U 3003 |
| | | *BANK OF CHINA |
| | | *NEW YORK, NY |
| （3） | USER HEADER | BANK PRIORITY 113: |
| | | MSG USER REF.108: E101 |
| （4） | TRN | *20: BP9706003432 |
| | RELATED REFERENCE | 21: 2659/415 |
| | NARRATIVE | *79: RE ABOVE ITEM FOR USD74,544.60 |
| | | WE ARE ADVISED BY THE BENE |
| | | THAT THE APPL HAS TAKEN UP |
| | | DOCS AGAINST PAYMT BUT UP |
| | | TODAY WE STILL HAVE NOT |
| | | RECVD PROCEEDS FM U. PLS |
| | | PAY ATTN TO THE MATTER N |
| | | EFFECT PAYMT TO US ASAP UNDER |
| | | YR SWIFT ADVICE TO US |
| | | QUOTING OUR A.M BP NO.THKS |
| | | FOR YR KIND COOPERATN.THKS. |
| （5） | TRAILER | ORDER IS<MAC:><ENC:><CHK:><TNG:><PDE:> |
| | | MAC: 7A 1950BB |

**Notes:**

（1）基本报头（略）

（2）应用报头

I 为输入/输出标识符（INPUT）的缩写字母"I"。

799 为报文类别。说明被输入电文的业务类型。

BKCHUS33XXXX 为接受地址。由 12 位字符组成的收报行逻辑终端地址代码。

U 为电报优先级，即加急电报（URGENT）的缩写字母"U"。

3 为传送监控。

003 为失效时限，由 3 位数字组成，以 5 分钟的倍数为单位表示：

002=10 分钟　　　　　003=15 分钟

最大时限为 999=3 天

最小时限为 002=1 0 分钟

当电报优先级选择为 U（加急报）时，失效时限的系统设定值为 003（15 分钟），当电报优先级为 N（普通报）时，失效时限定值为 020（100 分钟）。

（3）用户报头（略）

（4）正文 BENE=BENEFICIARY 受益人　APPL=APPLICANT 申请人

（5）报尾（略）

## 4. How to write a SWIFT message

（1）**Writing principles**

A. Being causal and well-founded in business

When you write or edit a SWIFT message, you should have known accurately and thoroughly the business status and all the SWIFT messages between the banks involved, thus avoiding sending void one. e.g. when you write a message disproving the discrepancies, you should make it well founded based on the facts and customary practice.

B. Being concise and to the point in language

A SWIFT message should be expressed to the best in concise and clear language, telling the receiver why we send this SWIFT message and what they are going to do, thus increasing efficiency of dealing with messages.

C. Being clarified in structure and complied in edition

A SWIFT message should be reasonably structured, coherently and logically arranged with its content, style and its punctuation marks complying with the unique requirements of SWIFT message writing.

D. Being complete in information and correct in quotation

When editing, the transaction reference number and content of incoming message should be correctly and completely quoted. In addition, extra information such as drawer/drawee/invoice number in collection business on the parties involved can be provided based on the specific business.

(2) **Sample**

---

Sequence Number: CC3108
Message Type: 799
Sender Institution: XXXXCNBJXXX
     XXX BANK OF CHINA, THE
     CHENGDU
Receiver Institution: IBBLBDDH118
     ISLAMI BANK BANGLADESH LTD
     210-211, NAWABPUR ROAD
     DHAKA
Message Status: I
Message Input Date: 2018-01-08
Message Priority: N
————Message Content : ————
20: Transaction Reference Number
    223352AD17000045
21: Related Reference
    087117011504
79: Narrative
 ATTN: IMPORT SECTION, MR. SMITH
 RE YR MT707 DATED20171223 AND MT707 DATED20180107
 L/C NO.: 087117011504
 PLS BE ADVISED THAT THE L/C AMOUNT 'USD82,320.00' (BEFORE AMENDMENT)PLUS THE INCREASE AMOUNT 'USD350,600.00'(FIRST AMENDMENT) SHOULD BE 'USD432,920.00'I/O'USD433,000.00'. AND THE NEW
 L/C AMOUNT AFTER SECOND AMENDMENT SHOULD BE 'USD570,120.00' I/O'USD570,200.00'
 PLS KINDLY CHECK THIS MATTER AND REPLY US ASAP
 B.RGDS
 ITPC, EXPORT DEPT. MR./MS. XXXXX

## II. Specimen SWIFT Messages（报文样例）

### 1. Business related to L/C (from importer's bank)（进口银行相关的信用证业务）

**（1） Opening relative L/C（letters of credit）开证**

**Sample 1**

| | |
|---|---|
| SEQUENCE OF TOTAL | *27: 1/2 |
| FORM OF DOC. CREDIT | *40A: IRREVOCABLE |
| DOC. CREDIT NUMBER | *20: 89153/2094 |
| DATE OF ISSUE | *31C: 180602 |
| EXPIRY | *31D: DATE: 180803 PLACE: P.R.OF CHINA |
| APPLICANT BANK | *51: AUSTRALIA AND NEW ZEALAND BANKINGGROUP LIMITED A. C.N.005 357 522 INTERNATIONAL OFFICE 7/46 KIPPAX STREET SURRY HILLS NSW 2010 |
| APPLICANT | *50 KOMPLIMENT STUDIOS PTY LTD 6–10 PURKIS STREET CAMPERDOWN NSW 2050 AUSTRALIA |
| BENEFICIARY | *59 PEKING IMPORT AND EXPORT CORP., BEIJING CHINA |
| AMOUNT | *32 B: CURRENCY: AUD, AMOUNT: 50,000.00 |
| AVAILABLE WITH/BY | *41D: ANY BANK IN PEOPLE'S REPUBLIC OF CHINA BY NEGOTIATION |
| DRAFTS AT… | *42 C: DRAFTS AT 90 DAYS AFTER SIGHT |
| DRAWEE | 42--: DRAWN ON AUSTRALIA AND NEW ZEALAND BANKING GROUP LTD 46 KIPPAX STR SURRY HILLS |
| PARTIAL SHIPMENTS | 43P: ALLOWED |
| TRANSSHIPMENTS | 43T: NOT ALLOWED |
| LOADING IN CHARGE | 44A: LOADING ON BOARD IN CHINA |
| FOR TRANSPORT TO… | 44B: SYDNEY AUSTRALIA |
| ADDITIONAL COND. | 47 A: DRAWEE BANKS DISCOUNT OR INTEREST CHARGES AND ACCEPTANCE COMMISSION ARE FOR ACCOUNT OF THE APPLICANT THEREFORE THE BENEFICIARY IS TO RECEIVE PAYMENT FOR TERM DRAFTS AS IF DRAWN AT SIGHT. |

| | |
|---|---|
| DETAILS OF CHARGES | 71 B: ALL OTHER CHARGES OUTSIDE AUSTRALIA ARE FOR ACCOUNT OF THE BENEFICIARY. |
| PRESENTATION PERIOD 48: | |
| CONFIRMATION | *49: WITHOUT |
| INSTRUCTIONS | 78: THE NEGOTIATING BANK IS AUTHORIZED TO FORWARD DOCUMENTS TO AUSTRALIA AND NEW ZEALAND BANKING GROUP LIMITED A.C.N.005 357 522 INTERNATIONAL OFFICE |
| | 7/46 KIPPAX HILLS NSW 2010 BY TWO CONSECUTIVE AIRMAIL PACKAGES MT 701 02 |
| SEQUENCE OF TOTAL | *27: 2/2 |
| DOC. CREDIT NUMBER | *20: 89153/2094 |
| SHIPMENT OF GOODS | 45B: PRINTED CUSHION COVERS AND CHAIRS PADS DES PENCIL FLOWER. DES RACHEL, DES AZTEC AS PER CONTRACT NO. 93H-1004 TERMS ARE CIF. |
| DOCUMENTS REQUIRED | 46B: COMMERCIAL INVOICES +FULL SET OF CLEAN ON BOARD MARINE BILLS OF LADING MADE OUT TO SHIPPERS ORDER AND ENDORSED IN BLANK MARKED FREIGHT PREPAID DATED NO LATER THAN 24 SEPTEMBER 2017 + INSURANCE POLICY OR CERTIFICATE FOR NOT LESS THAN THE CIF VALUE PLUS 10 PERCENT COVERING MARINE AND WAR RISKS. |
| LOGICAL TERMINAL | |
| ISSUE OF A DOCUMENTARY CREDIT | PAGE |
| FUNC | |
| UMR | |
| "ADVISE THROUGH" | 57D: YOUR… |
| | MAC: |
| | CHK: |
| | DLM: |

**Notes:**

1. This is a FIN message on issue of a documentary credit.

2. **SEQUENCE OF TOTAL**　报文页次

   如果该跟单信用证条款能够全部容纳在该 MT700 报文中，那么该项目内就填入"1/1"；如果该证由一份 MT700 报文和一份 MT701 报文组成，那么在 MT700 报文的项目"27"中填入"1/2"，在 MT 701 报文中的"27"中填入"2/2"。

3. **FORM OF DOC. CREDIT**　跟单信用证形式

4. **DATE OF ISSUE**　开证日期

5. **EXPIRY AND PLACE**　到期日及到期地点

6. **APPLICANT BANK**　开证申请人的银行

7. **APPLICANT**　开证申请人

8. **BENEFICIARY**　受益人

9. **AMOUNT&CURRENCY: AUD AMOUNT**　跟单信用证的金额及货币澳元

10. **AVAILABLE WITH/BY**　指定的有关银行及信用证兑付方式，该项列明被授权对该证付款、承兑、议付的银行和兑付方式。

    兑付方式一般用下列词句表示：

    **BY PAYMENT:**　即期付款

    **BY ACCEPTANCE:**　远期承兑

    **BY NEGOTIATION:**　议付

    **BY DEF PAYMENT:**　迟期付款

    **BY MIXED PAYMENT:**　混合付款

11. **DRAFTS AT…**　汇票付款期限

12. **DRAWEE**　汇票的付款人

13. **LOADING IN CHARGE**　装运地点

14. **FOR TRANSPORT TO**　货物发送的最终目的地

15. **ADDITIONAL COND**　附加条款

16. **TERM DRAFTS**　远期汇票

17. **DETAILS OF CHARGES**　费用负担

18. **PRESENTATION PERIOD**　交单期限

19. **CONFIRMATION**　保兑指示

20. **INSTRUCTIONS**　给付款行、承兑行或议付行的指示

21. **DESCRIPTION OF GOODS**　货物描述

22. **DOCUMENTS REQUIRED**　单据要求

# Sample 2

Sequence Number: J66927B

Message Type: 700

Sender Institution: XXXXCNBJXXX

                  BANK OF CHINA, THE

                  FUZHOU

Receiver Institution: ISBKTRIS

                  TURKIYE IS BANKASI A.S.

                  4.LEVENT  1 IS KULELERI KULE

                  ISTANBUL

Message Status: I

Message Input Date: 2018-10-12

Message Priority: N

——————Message Content : ——————

27: Sequence of Total  1/1

40A: Form of Documentary Credit      IRREVOCABLE

20: Documentary Credit Number      LC1800012345678

31C: Date of Issue      181012

40E: Applicable Rules      UCP No. 600 (LATEST VERSION)

31D: Date and Place of Expiry      181115IN TURKEY

50: Applicant      ABC CO., LTD.

                123 WUYIROAD,

                XIA MEN, FUJIAN,

                CHINA

59:Beneficiary      XYZ CO., LTD

                NO:288/8 KONAK IZMIR TURKEY

32B:Currency Code, Amount USD43,200.00

39A:Percentage Credit Amount Tolerance   10/10* [①]

41D:Available With … By ANY BANK BY NEGOTIATION

42C:Drafts at 90 DAYS AFTER SIGHT FOR 100PCT OF INVOICE VALUE

42A:Drawee      XXXXCNBJXXX

43P:Partial Shipments      ALLOWED

---

① =39A 表示信用证金额的浮动比例，47A 第 7 条表示货物数量有 10% 的短溢装。

43T:Transshipment                    ALLOWED
44E:Port of Loading/Airport of Departure        IZMIR PORT OF TURKEY
44F:Port of Discharge/Airport of Destination    XIAMEN PORT OF CHINA
44C: Latest Date of Shipment  181031
45A:Description of Goods and/or Services

    MARBLE BLOCKS

    QUANTITY: 240TONS*①

    UNIT PRICE: USD 180.00/TON

    TOTAL AMOUNT: USD43,200.00

    TRADE TERM: FOB IZMIR PORT OF TURKEY

46A:Documents Required

1. SIGNED COMMERCIAL INVOICE IN 3 ORIGINALS AND 2 COPIES INDICATING L/C NO. AND CONTRACT NO. XYZ-123.

2. FULL SET OF CLEAN ON BOARD OCEAN BILL OF LADING MADE OUT TO ORDER AND BLANK ENDORSED, MARKED 'FREIGHT TO COLLECT', AND NOTIFYING APPLICANT WITH FULL NAME, ADDRESS, TEL N FAX.

3. PACKING LIST/WEIGHT MEMO IN 3 ORIGINALS AND 2 COPIES INDICATING QUANTITY, GROSS AND NET WEIGHT OF EACH PACKAGE.

4. CERTIFICATE OF ORIGIN IN DUPLICATE.

5. BENEFICIARY'S CERTIFIED COPY OF TELEX DISPATCHED TO THE APPLICANT TO THE FOLLOWING E-MAIL: XIEQM AT BESTCHEER.COM WITHIN 21 DAYS AFTER SHIPMENT.
ADVISING L/C NO., NAME OF VESSEL, DATE OF SHIPMENT, NAME OF GOODS, QUANTITY, WEIGHT AND VALUE OF GOODS.

6. CERTIFICATE OF HEAT TREATMENT LABELED WITH IPPC MARK OR NO WOOD DECLARATION ISSUED BY BENEFICIARY.

47A:Additional Conditions

1. A FEE OF USD100.00 OR EQUIVALENT AND RELEVANT CABLE CHARGES WILL BE DEDUCTED FROM THE REIMBURSEMENT FOR EACH PRESENTATION OF DISCREPANT DOCUMENTS UNDER THIS CREDIT .

2. AN EXTRA COPY OF ALL DOCUMENTS IS REQUIRED FOR ISSUING BANK'S FILE. IF SUCH COPY IS NOT PRESENTED, A FEE OF USD10.00

---

① 如果数量单位是pcs（件此计件单位已经很具体了，因此不太可能允许信用证金额浮动，如果允许浮动，则意味着价格有可能变动），而此处为吨，是符合UCP600号的39A条款的。

OR EQUIVALENT WILL BE DEDUCTED FROM THE PROCEEDS.
3. REIMBURSEMENT CHARGES 0.1PCT ( MIN USD50.00, MAX USD200.00 OR EQUIVALENT ) ARE FOR THE ACCOUNT OF BENEFICIARY AND SHOULD BE DEDUCTED FROM THE PROCEEDS.
4. ALL DOCUMENTS MUST BE ISSUED IN ENGLISH.
5. DOCUMENTS PRESENTED WITH DISCREPANCY(IES) WILL BE REJECTED. HOWEVER, IF NO WRITTEN INSTRUCTIONS OF THEIR DISPOSAL ARE RECEIVED BY US BY THE TIME THE APPLICANT HAS ACCEPTED THEM DESPITE THE DISCREPANCY(IES), WE SHALL BE ENTITLED TO RELEASE THE DOCUMENTS TO THE APPLICANT WITHOUT PRIOR NOTICE TO THE PRESENTER AND WE WILL HAVE NO LIABILITY TO THE PRESENTER IN RESPECT OF ANY SUCH RELEASE.
6. PURSUANT TO THE SANCTIONS AND RELEVANT REGULATION OF PEOPLE'S REPUBLIC OF CHINA, UNITED NATIONS, THE EUROPEAN UNION, THE UNITED STATES OF AMERICA, THE UNITED KINGDOM OR ANY OTHER INTERNATIONAL BODY OR JURISDICTION, WE MAY BE UNABLE TO PROCESS ANY DOCUMENTS, SHIPMENTS, GOODS, PAYMENTS AND/OR TRANSACTIONS THAT MAY RELATE, DIRECTLY OR INDIRECTLY, TO ANY SANCTION COUNTRIES, ENTITIES AND INDIVIDUALS, AND AUTHORITIES MAY REQUIRE DISCLOSURE OF SUCH INFORMATION. ACCORDINGLY, WE SHALL NOT BE LIABLE FOR ANY LOSS, DAMAGE OR DELAY ARISING IN CONNECTION WITH THE ABOVE MATTERS.
7. QUANTITY AND CREDIT AMOUNT 10PCT MORE OR LESS ARE ALLOWED.
8. APPLICANT'S TEL:
9. BENEFICIARY'S TEL:

FAX:

71B: Charges

ALL BANKING CHARGES OUTSIDE THE ISSUING BANK AND REIMBURSING CHARGES ARE FOR ACCOUNT OF BENEFICIARY.

48: Period for Presentation

ALL DOCUMENT(S) MUST BE PRESENTED WITHIN 15 DAYS AFTER DATE OF SHIPMENT BUT NOT LATER THAN THE EXPIRY DATE OF CREDIT.

49: Confirmation Instructions  WITHOUT

78: Instructions to the Paying/Accepting/Negotiating Bank

1. WE WILL HONOR UPON RECEIPT OF THE STIPULATED DOCUMENTS WHICH CONSTITUTE A COMPLYING PRESENTATION.
2. THE AMOUNT(S) SO DRAWN MUST BE ENDORSED ON THE REVERSE OF THE ORIGINAL CREDIT.
3. T/T REIMBURSEMENT NOT ALLOWED.
4. ALL DOCUMENTS TO BE SENT DIRECTLY TO XXX BANK, XX BRANCH ATTN: INT'L BUSINESS DEPT. IN ONE LOT VIA COURIER SERVICE BY ADDRESS AS FOLLOWS: detailed address, FUJIAN PROVINCE P. R. CHINA ( PC: 123456)

Operator Name: Jiang Haitao
Checker Name: Chen Wei
Authorizer Name: xxx

**Notes:**

1. This is a documentary letter of credit by SWIFT with simple terms and clauses, issued by XXX Bank, XXX branch to TURKIYE IS BANKASI A.S. ISTANBUL.
2. **UCP No. 600（LATEST VERSION）: Uniform Customs and Practice for Documentary Credit**　跟单信用证统一惯例与实务 600 号（最新版）
3. **Drafts at 90 DAYS AFTER SIGHT FOR 100PCT OF INVOICE VALUE**　90 天远期汇票，汇票金额为发票金额的百分之百
4. **BENEFICIARY'S CERTIFIED COPY**　经收益人证明的副本
5. **IPPC MARK**　国际植物保护公约（International Plant Protection Convention）标记
6. **PURSUANT TO THE SANCTIONS AND RELEVANT REGULATION**　根据相关制裁条款和规定

**Sample 3**

Sequence Number: J1A6E9
Message Type: 700
Sender Institution: XXXXCNBJXXX
　　　　　　　　　XXX BANK OF CHINA, THE
　　　　　　　　　FUZHOU
Receiver Institution: AGRIFRPP822
　　　　　　　　　　CREDIT AGRICOLE

SAINT BRIEUC

Message Status: I

Message Input Date: 2018-09-12

Message Priority: N

——————————Message Content : ——————————

| | |
|---|---|
| 27:Sequence of Total | 1/2 |
| 40A:Form of Documentary Credit | IRREVOCABLE |
| 20:Documentary Credit Number | LC18000012 |
| 31C:Date of Issue | 180912 |
| 40E:Applicable Rules | UCP No. 600 (LATEST VERSION) |
| 31D:Date and Place of Expiry | 181121IN FRANCE |
| 50:Applicant | XYZ CO., LTD |
| | ADD: |
| 59:Beneficiary | ABC CO., LTD |
| | ADD: |

32B:Currency Code, Amount    EUR 374,400.00

39A:Percentage Credit Amount Tolerance  10/10

41D:Available With … By … ADVISING BANK BY NEGOTIATION

42C:Drafts at … AT SIGHT FOR 100PCT OF INVOICE VALUE

42A:Drawee   XXXXCNBJXXX

43P:Partial Shipments   ALLOWED

43T:Transshipment   ALLOWED

44E:Port of Loading/Airport of Departure  ANY EUROPEAN PORTS

44F:Port of Discharge/Airport of Destination
   TIANJIN, CHINA OR SHANGHAI, CHINA OR DALIAN, CHINA

44C:Latest Date of Shipment    181031

46A:Documents Required

   1.FULL SET OF ON BOARD BILLS OF LADING IN 3 ORIGINALS AND 3 COPIES MARKED 'FREIGHT PREPAID' CONSIGNED TO XYZ CO., LTD, ADD: TEL: AND NOTIFY APPLICANT.

   2.SIGNED COMMERCIAL INVOICE IN 3 ORIGINALS SHOWING THE CONTRACT NO.(12345).

   3.PACKING LIST ISSUED AND SIGNED BY BENEFICIARY IN 2 ORIGINALS.

   4.ORIGINAL CERTIFICATE OF HEALTH ISSUED BY AUTHORIZED

INSTITUTION.

5.CERTIFICATE OF ORIGIN IN 1 ORIGINAL ISSUED BY AUTHORIZED INSTITUTION.

6.NON-WOOD PACKING DECLARATION ISSUED AND SIGNED BY BENEFICIARY IN 1 ORIGINAL.

47A: Additional Conditions

1.ALL DOCUMENTS MUST BE ISSUED IN ENGLISH.

2.A FEE OF USD50.00 OR EQUIVALENT AND RELEVANT CABLE CHARGES WILL BE DEDUCTED FROM THE REIMBURSEMENT FOR EACH PRESENTATION OF DISCREPANT DOCUMENTS UNDER THIS CREDIT.

3.AN EXTRA COPY OF ALL DOCUMENTS IS REQUIRED FOR ISSUING BANK'S FILE. IF SUCH COPY IS NOT PRESENTED, A FEE OF USD20.00 WILL BE DEDUCTED FROM THE PROCEEDS.

4.DOCUMENTS PRESENTED WITH DISCREPANCY(IES) WILL BE REJECTED. HOWEVER, IF NO WRITTEN INSTRUCTIONS OF THEIR DISPOSAL ARE RECEIVED BY US BY THE TIME THE APPLICANT HAS ACCEPTED THEM DESPITE THE DISCREPANCY(IES), WE SHALL BE ENTITLED TO RELEASE THE DOCUMENTS TO THE APPLICANT WITHOUT PRIOR NOTICE TO THE PRESENTER AND WE WILL HAVE NO LIABILITY TO THE PRESENTER IN RESPECT OF ANY SUCH RELEASE.

5.PURSUANT TO THE SANCTIONS AND RELEVANT REGULATION OF PEOPLE'S REPUBLIC OF CHINA, UNITED NATIONS, THE EUROPEAN UNION, THE UNITED STATES OF AMERICA, THE UNITED KINGDOM OR ANY OTHER INTERNATIONAL BODY OR JURISDICTION, WE MAY BE UNABLE TO PROCESS ANY DOCUMENTS, SHIPMENTS, GOODS, PAYMENTS AND/OR TRANSACTIONS THAT MAY RELATE, DIRECTLY OR INDIRECTLY, TO ANY SANCTION COUNTRIES, ENTITIES AND INDIVIDUALS, AND AUTHORITIES MAY REQUIRE DISCLOSURE OF SUCH INFORMATION. ACCORDINGLY,WE SHALL NOT BE LIABLE FOR ANY LOSS, DAMAGE OR DELAY ARISING IN CONNECTION WITH THE ABOVE MATTERS.

6.APPLICANT'S TEL:

7.QUANTITY AND CREDIT AMOUNT 10PCT MORE OR LESS ARE ALLOWED.

8.DOCUMENTS ISSUED EARLIER THAN THIS L/C ISSUING DATE ARE NOT ACCEPTABLE.

9.FORWARDER B/L(HOUSE B/L), SHORT FORM B/L, BLANK BACK B/L UNACCEPTABLE.

10.A MISSPELLING OR TYPING ERROR AND ABBREVIATION THAT DOES NOT AFFECT THE MEANING OF A WORD OR THE SENTENCE IN WHICH IT OCCURS DOES NOT MAKE A DOCUMENT DISCREPANT, EXCEPT IN FIGURES AND COMMODITY.

11.A THIRD PARTY DOCUMENT IS ACCEPTABLE EXCEPT INVOICE AND PACKING LIST. INVOICE AND PACKING LIST MUST REMARK THE DETAILS OF PRODUCTS.

71B: Charges

ALL BANKING CHARGES AND INTEREST, IF ANY, OUTSIDE ISSUING BANK INCLUDING REIMBURSING CHARGES ARE FOR ACCOUNT OF THE BENEFICIARY.

48:Period for Presentation

ALL DOCUMENT(S) MUST BE PRESENTED WITHIN 21 DAYS AFTER THE DATE OF SHIPMENT BUT WITHIN THE VALIDITY OF THIS CREDIT.

49:Confirmation Instructions   WITHOUT

78:Instructions to the Paying/Accepting/Negotiating Bank

1.WE WILL HONOUR UPON RECEIPT OF THE STIPULATED DOCUMENTS WHICH CONSTITUTE A COMPLYING PRESENTATION.

2.THE AMOUNT(S) SO DRAWN MUST BE ENDORSED ON THE REVERSE OF THE ORIGINAL CREDIT.

3.T/T REIMBURSEMENT NOT ALLOWED.

4.ALL DOCUMENTS TO BE SENT IN ONE LOT BY DHL DIRECTLY TO

XXX BANK OF CHINA, FUJIAN BRANCH

ADD:

---

Operator Name: Liu Fang

Checker Name: Li Ming

Authorizer Name: Zhang Wei

---

Sequence Number: J1A409

Message Type: 701

Sender Institution: XXXXCNBJXXX

XXXL BANK OF CHINA, THE
GUANGZHOU

Receiver Institution: AGRIFRPP822
CREDIT AGRICOLE
SAINT BRIEUC

Message Status: I

Message Input Date: 2018-09-12

Message Priority: N

————————Message Content : ————————

27:Sequence of Total
　2/2

20:Documentary Credit Number　LC18000014

45B: Description of Goods and/or Services

（1）FROZEN PORK HEADS, WHOLE

　　COUNTRY OF ORIGIN: FRANCE

　　ORDER NO. XXX

　　PLANT NO. SHALL BE FR22093001CE

　　PACKED IN 20 OR 25KGS/CTN, CATCH WEIGHT

　　N.W.:48,000KGS AT PRICE EUR0.95 PER KG

　　TOTAL QTY: 48,000KGS

　　TOTAL AMOUNT: EUR45,600.00

　　TERMS OF PAYMENT: CFR TIANJIN, CHINA

　　DESTINATION: TIANJIN, CHINA

（2）FROZEN PORK BACK BONE

　　COUNTRY OF ORIGIN: FRANCE

　　ORDER NO. YYY

　　PLANT NO. SHALL BE FR22093001CE OR FR35188001CE

　　PACKED IN CARTONS

　　N.W.:72,000KGS AT PRICE EUR0.5 PER KG

　　TOTAL QTY: 72,000KGS

　　TOTAL AMOUNT: EUR36,000.00

　　TERMS OF PAYMENT: CFR TIANJIN, CHINA

　　DESTINATION: TIANJIN, CHINA

(3) FROZEN PORK HOCKS, BONE IN
COUNTRY OF ORIGIN: FRANCE
ORDER NO. ZZZ
PLANT NO. SHALL BE FR22093001CE OR FR35188001CE
PACKED IN 20 OR 25KGS/CTN, CATCH WEIGHT
N.W.: 48,000KGS AT PRICE EUR1.7 PER KG
TOTAL QTY:48,000KGS
TOTAL AMOUNT: EUR81,600.00
TERMS OF PAYMENT: CFR SHANGHAI, CHINA
DESTINATION:SHANGHAI, CHINA

(4) FROZEN PORK HIND FEET
COUNTRY OF ORIGIN: FRANCE
ORDER NO. SSS
PLANT NO. SHALL BE FR22093001CE OR FR35188001CE
PACKING BY NEW CARTON EACH TO CONTAIN 10KGS NET WEIGHT
N.W.: 48,000KGS AT PRICE EUR1.75 PER KG
TOTAL QTY:48,000KGS
TOTAL AMOUNT: EUR84,000.00
TERMS OF PAYMENT: CFR SHANGHAI, CHINA
DESTINATION: SHANGHAI, CHINA

(5) FROZEN PORK FRONT FEET, TOES ON, NAILS OFF
COUNTRY OF ORIGIN: FRANCE
ORDER NO. RRR
PLANT NO. SHALL BE FR22093001CE OR FR35188001CE
PACKING BY NEW CARTON EACH TO CONTAIN 10KGS NET WEIGHT
N.W.: 24,000KGS AT PRICE EUR2.55PER KG
TOTAL QTY:24,000KGS
TOTAL AMOUNT: EUR61,200.00
TERMS OF PAYMENT: CFR DALIAN, CHINA
DESTINATION: DALIAN, CHINA

(6) FROZEN PORK SPARE RIBS
COUNTRY OF ORIGIN: FRANCE
ORDER NO. KKK
PLANT NO. SHALL BE FR22093001CE OR FR35188001CE

PACKING BY NEW CARTON EACH TO CONTAIN 10KGS NET WEIGHT
N.W.: 24,000KGS AT PRICE EUR2.75 PER KG
TOTAL QTY: 24,000KGS
TOTAL AMOUNT: EUR66,000.00
TERMS OF PAYMENT: CFR DALIAN, CHINA
DESTINATION: DALIAN, CHINA

---

Operator Name: Liu Fang

Checker Name: Li Ming

Authorizer Name: Zhang Wei

**Notes:**

1. This is a documentary letter of credit by SWIFT in sequence of total with 2 pages, which is an L/C with more complex terms and clauses inclusive of description of goods in more detail, issued by XXX Bank of China, XXX branch to CREDIT AGRICOLE SAINT BRIEUC in France.

2. **Drafts at … AT SIGHT FOR 100PCT OF INVOICE VALUE** 见票即付的即期汇票，金额为发票金额的百分之百。

3. **FORWARDER B/L (HOUSE B/L)** 运输行签发的提单（FORWARDER B/L），业务中习惯又将其称为（HOUSE B/L），二者是一个概念，都是代货单。首先，代货单不是物权凭证，只是货物收据；其次，运输行在管辖货物时对货物负责，货物在运输途中发生风险它不负责任；最后，运输行本身信用不如实际承运人，资力也较小。所以银行不会接受此类单据。

4. **SHORT FORM B/L, BLANK BACK B/L** 简式提单，空白提单

5. **DHL** 敦豪快递公司（Dalsey, Hillblom and Lynn），一家创立于美国、目前为德国邮政集团100%持股的国际快递货运公司，是目前世界上最大的航空快递货运公司之一。

6. **PACKED IN 20 OR 25KGS/CTN, CATCH WEIGHT N.W.: 48,000KGS AT PRICE EUR0.95 PER KG**
货物包装按每纸板箱装20或25公斤，实际重量（不受规则限制）净重48,000公斤，单价为每公斤0.95欧元。

7. **FROZEN PORK BACK BONE** 冻猪蹄膀

8. **FROZEN PORK HOCKS, BONE IN** 冻猪肘子

9. **FROZEN PORK HIND FEET** 冻猪后腿

10. **FROZEN PORK FRONT FEET, TOES ON, NAILS OFF** 冻猪前腿，留趾去甲

## 11. FROZEN PORK SPARE RIBS 冻猪小排

### Sample 4

---

Sequence Number: GDDE98

Message Type: 700

Sender Institution: XXXXCNBJXXX

        XXX BANK OF CHINA, THE

        FUZHOU

Receiver Institution: OCBCHKHH

        OVERSEA-CHINESE BANKING CORPORATION

        9 QUEEN'S ROAD, CENTRAL  FLOOR 9

        HONG KONG

Message Status: I

Message Input Date: 2018-11-21

Message Priority: N

——————Message Content : ——————

27:Sequence of Total    1/3

40A:Form of Documentary Credit    IRREVOCABLE

20:Documentary Credit Number    LC18000012

31C:Date of Issue    181121

40E:Applicable Rules    UCP NO. 600

31D:Date and Place of Expiry    180106HONGKONG

50:Applicant

      ABC CO., LTD.

        ADD:…, FUZHOU

59:Beneficiary

      XYZ CO., LTD.

        ADD:…, HONGKONG

32B:Currency Code, Amount    USD  4,455,000.00

39A:Percentage Credit Amount Tolerance    10/10

41D:Available With … By …    ANY BANK  BY NEGOTIATION

42C:Drafts at …    AT 20181228 FOR 100PCT OF INVOICE VALUE

42A:Drawee    XXXXCNBJ123

43P:Partial Shipments         PROHIBITED
43T:Transshipment              PROHIBITED
44E:Port of Loading/Airport of Departure        RUWAIS, UAE
44F:Port of Discharge/Airport of Destination    QUANZHOU, CHINA
44C:Latest Date of Shipment                     181123
45A:Description of Goods and/or Services
  DESCRIPTION
  FULLY REFRIGERATED PROPANE
  TOTAL AMOUNT: USD4,455,000.00
  QUANTITY: 11,000.00MTS
  PRICE TERM: DES, ONE SAFE PORT, ONE SAFE BERTH, QUANZHOU,CHINA
46A:Documents Required
  1. MANUALLY SIGNED AND STAMPED COMMERCIAL INVOICE BASED ON B/L IN 1 ORIGINAL AND 1 COPY INDICATING L/C NO., L/C ISSUING BANK, ISSUING DATE AND CONTRACT NO. 123456.
  2. FULL SET OF CLEAN ON BOARD OCEAN BILLS OF LADING MADE OUT TO ORDER AND BLANK ENDORSED, MARKED 'FREIGHT PAYABLE AS PER CHARTER PARTY.
71B:Charges
  +ALL BANKING CHARGES INCURRED AT ISSUING BANK ARE FOR APPLICANT'S ACCOUNT. ALL BANKING CHARGES INCURRED AT BENEFICIARY'S BANK ARE FOR BENEFICIARY'S ACCOUNT.
48:Period for Presentation
  +ALL DOCUMENT(S) MUST BE PRESENTED WITHIN THE VALIDITY OR THE CREDIT.
49:Confirmation Instructions    WITHOUT
78:Instructions to the Paying/Accepting/Negotiating Bank
  +WE WILL HONOUR UPON RECEIPT OF THE STIPULATED DOCUMENTS WHICH CONSTITUTE A COMPLYING PRESENTATION.
  +THE AMOUNT(S) SO DRAWN MUST BE ENDORSED ON THE REVERSE OF THE ORIGINAL CREDIT.
  +T/T REIMBURSEMENT NOT ALLOWED.
  +ALL DOCUMENTS TO BE SENT DIRECTLY TO XXX BANK OF CHINA XXX BRANCH  ATTN: INT'L BUSINESS DEPT.

IN ONE LOT VIA COURIER SERVICE BY ADDRESS AS FOLLOWS:

ADD: P. R. CHINA

ATTN: INT'L CLEARING CENTER, TEL:

Operator Name: Li Ming

Checker Name: Wen Xin

Authorizer Name: Zhou Ping

Sequence Number: GDDF62

Message Type: 701

Sender Institution: XXXXCNBJXXX

   XXX BANK OF CHINA, THE

   XXXXXX

Receiver Institution: OCBCHKHH

   OVERSEA-CHINESE BANKING CORPORATION

   9 QUEEN'S ROAD, CENTRAL FLOOR 9

   HONG KONG

Message Status: I

Message Input Date: 2018-11-21

Message Priority: N

——————Message Content : ——————

27:Sequence of Total

 2/3

20:Documentary Credit Number LC18000012

47B:Additional Conditions

1. AN EXTRA COPY OF ALL DOCUMENTS IS REQUIRED FOR ISSUING BANK'S FILE, OTHERWISE USD20.00 WILL BE DEDUCTED FM THE PROCEEDS.
2. DOCUMENTS PRESENTED WITH DISCREPANCY(IES) WILL BE REJECTED. HOWEVER, IF NO WRITTEN INSTRUCTIONS OF THEIR DISPOSAL ARE RECEIVED BY US BY THE TIME THE APPLICANT HAS ACCEPTED THEM DESPITE THE DISCREPANCY(IES), WE SHALL BE ENTITLED TO RELEASE THE DOCUMENTS TO THE APPLICANT WITHOUT PRIOR NOTICE TO THE PRESENTER AND WE WILL HAVE NO LIABILITY TO THE PRESENTER IN

RESPECT OF ANY SUCH RELEASE.

3. A FEE OF USD100.00 WILL BE DEDUCTED FROM THE REIMBURSEMENT FOR EACH PRESENTATION OF DISCREPANT DOCUMENTS UNDER THIS CREDIT.

4. DRAFTS DRAWN HEREUNDER MUST BEAR ISSUING BANK'S NAME, THE CREDIT NO. AND DATE OF DRAFTS.

5. UNLESS OTHERWISE STATED, ALL DOCUMENTS REQUIRED TO BE PRESENTED SHALL BE IN ENGLISH.

6. BOTH QUANTITY AND CREDIT AMOUNT 10PCT MORE OR LESS ARE ALLOWED.

7. ACCEPTANCE OF ANY DISCREPANCIES IN ANY DOCUMENTS PRESENTED SHALL NOT IMPLY OR CONSTITUTE ANY AMENDMENT OF THE TERMS OF THIS LETTER OF CREDIT NOR OBLIGE US TO ACCEPT THE SAME FOR ANY FUTURE DRAWINGS.

8. UNLESS OTHERWISE STIPULATED, ALL DOCUMENTS EXCEPT DRAFTS AND INVOICE, MUST NOT SHOW CONTRACT NO. AND ITS DATE, INVOICE NO. AND ITS DATE, CARGO VALUE, UNIT PRICE, PRICE TERM, INVOICE AMOUNT, PAYMENT TERMS OF THIS CREDIT, WORDS OF 'APPLICANT' AND 'BENEFICIARY', NAME AND ADDRESS OF APPLICANT, ANY L/C NO., ANY L/C DATE, NAME OF ANY BANK, ANY BANK REFERENCE AND/OR STAMPS.

9. ADDITIONS, CORRECTIONS, ERASURES, AMENDMENTS ON ANY DOCUMENTS MUST BE DULY STAMPED AND INITIALED BY THE PARTY/AUTHORITY ISSUING THE DOCUMENT.

10. WITH THE EXCEPTION OF DESCRIPTION OF GOODS, PRICE, SIZE DELIVERY TERMS, QUANTITY AND QUALITY, TYPING ERRORS THAT DOES NOT AFFECT THE MEANING OF A WORD OR THE SENTENCE IN WHICH IT OCCURS, IF ANY, ARE NOT TO BE CONSIDERED DISCREPANCIES.

11. IF PAYMENT DUE DATE FALLS ON A SATURDAY OR A NEW YORK BANKING HOLIDAY OTHER THAN A MONDAY, PAYMENT WILL BE EFFECTED ON THE PRECEDING NEW YORK BANKING DAY. IF PAYMENT DUE DATE FALLS ON A SUNDAY OR A NEW YORK BANKING HOLIDAY, PAYMENT WILL BE EFFECTED ON THE FOLLOWING NEW YORK BANKING DAY.

12. DOCUMENTS SHOWING SHIPMENT DATE PRIOR TO L/C ISSUANCE DATE ARE ACCEPTABLE.

13. DOCUMENTS SHOWING ISSUING DATE PRIOR TO L/C ISSUANCE DATE ARE

ACCEPTABLE.

14. PRODUCT DESCRIPTION SHOWING 'REFRIGERATED PROPANE' OR 'PROPANE' ALSO ACCEPTABLE.
15. BENEFICIARY'S TEL:
16. IN THE EVENT THAT THE ORIGINAL BILLS OF LADING ARE NOT AVAILABLE AT THE TIME OF PRESENTATION, PAYMENT WILL BE MADE AGAINST PRESENTATION OF DRAFTS AND COMMERCIAL INVOICE MENTIONED IN FIELD 46A AND LETTER OF INDEMNITY ISSUED BY BENEFICIARY IN THE FOLLOWING FORMAT:

---

Operator Name: Li Ming

Checker Name: Wen Xin

Authorizer Name: Zhou ping

---

Sequence Number: GDDF98

Message Type: 701

Sender Institution: XXXXCNBJXXX
     XXX BANK OF CHINA, THE
     XXXXXX

Receiver Institution: OCBCHKHH
     OVERSEA-CHINESE BANKING CORPORATION
     9 QUEEN'S ROAD, CENTRAL FLOOR 9
     HONG KONG

Message Status: I

Message Input Date: 2018-11-21

Message Priority: N

——————Message Content : ——————

27:Sequence of Total  3/3

20:Documentary Credit Number  LC18000012

47B:Additional Conditions
  QUOTE-
  LETTER OF INDEMNITY
  DATE:
  TO : L/C APPLICANT

DEAR SIRS,
WE REFER TO A CARGO OF… METRIC TON OF … SHIPPED ON BOARD THE VESSEL '…' PURSUANT TO THE BILLS OF LADING DATED…

ALTHOUGH WE HAVE SOLD AND TRANSFERRED TITLE OF SAID CARGO TO YOU, WE HAVE BEEN UNABLE TO PROVIDE YOU WITH THE ORIGINAL BILLS OF LADING STIPULATED UNDER THE L/C NO. ISSUED BY (INSERT THE NAME OF L/C ISSUING BANK) COVERING THE SAID SALE.

IN CONSIDERATION OF YOUR PAYMENT OF THE FULL INVOICE PRICE OF USD … AT THE DUE DATE WITHOUT HAVING THE AFORESAID DOCUMENTS, WE HEREBY EXPRESSLY WARRANT THAT WE HAVE MARKETABLE TITLE, FREE AND CLEAR OF ANY LIEN OR ENCUMBRANCE ON SUCH MATERIAL AND THAT WE HAVE FULL RIGHT AND AUTHORITY TO TRANSFER SUCH TITLE AND EFFECT DELIVERY OF SUCH MATERIAL TO YOU.

WE FURTHER AGREE TO MAKE ALL REASONABLE EFFORTS TO OBTAIN AND SURRENDER TO YOU AS SOON AS POSSIBLE THE ORIGINAL BILLS OF LADING TO PROTECT, INDEMNIFY AND SAVE YOU HARMLESS FROM AND AGAINST ANY AND ALL DAMAGES, COSTS AND EXPENSES (INCLUDING REASONABLE ATTORNEY'S FEES) WHICH YOU MAY SUFFER BY REASON OF THE ORIGINAL BILLS OF LADING REMAINING OUTSTANDING, OR BREACH OF THE WARRANTIES GIVEN ABOVE INCLUDING BUT NOT LIMITED TO ANY CLAIMS AND DEMANDS WHICH MAY BE MADE BY A HOLDER OR TRANSFEREE OF INTEREST IN OR LIEN ON THE CARGO OR PROCEEDS THEREOF.

OUR OBLIGATION TO INDEMNIFY YOU IS, OF COURSE, SUBJECT TO THE CONDITION THAT YOU SHALL GIVE US NOTICE OF ASSERTION OF ANY CLAIM (S) AND FULL OPPORTUNITY TO CONDUCT THE DEFENCE THEREOF AND THAT YOU SHALL NOT SETTLE ANY SUCH CLAIM (S) WITHOUT OUR APPROVAL.

THIS LETTER OF INDEMNITY SHALL BE GOVERNED BY AND CONSTRUED IN ACCORDANCE WITH THE LAWS OF ENGLAND AND EACH AND EVERY PERSON LIABLE UNDER THIS IDEMNITY SHALL AT YOUR REQUEST SUBMIT TO THE

JURISDICTION OF THE HIGH COURT OF JUSTICE OF ENGLAND.

THIS INDEMNITY SHALL BE AUTOMATICALLY CANCELLED AND BECOME NULL AND VOID BY 20180130 OR UPON OUR TENDERING THE ORIGINAL BILLS OF LADING TO YOU, WHICHEVER IS EARLIER.

YOURS FAITHFULLY,
FOR AND ON BEHALF OF STARGAS LIMITED
(AUTHORIZED SIGNATURE)
UNQUOTE-

---

Operator Name: Li Ming

Checker Name: Wen Xin

Authorizer Name: Zhou Ping

**Notes:**

1. This is a documentary letter of credit by SWIFT in sequence of total with 3 pages, which is an L/C with more complex terms and more additional conditions, issued by XXX Bank of China, XXXXXX branch to OVERSEA-CHINESE BANKING CORPORATION at 9 QUEEN'S ROAD, CENTRAL FLOOR 9, HONG KONG.

2. **DES**　目的港船上交货［This is the short form of Delivered Ex Ship, which, as a trade term requires the seller to deliver goods to a buyer at an agreed port of arrival. The seller remains responsible for the goods until they are delivered. "目的港船上交货（……指定目的港）"是指在指定的目的港，货物在船上交给买方处置，但不办理货物进口清关手续，卖方即完成交货。卖方必须承担货物运至指定的目的港卸货前的一切风险和费用。只有当货物经由海运或内河运输或多式联运在目的港船上交货时，才能使用该术语。］

3. **ONE SAFE PORT, ONE SAFE BERTH**　安全港口；安全泊位

4. **CHARTER PARTY**　租船合约［一般地，班轮提单中，运费有 freight prepaid（运费已付）或 freight collected（运费到付），集装箱装运的货物一般走班轮；而在租船提单中，一般运费会用：freight payable as per charter party（运费按租约）；一般大宗散货会专门租船装运，就会涉及租船提单；信用证中提单条款怎么规定，与商务合同的内容有关。］

5. **VIA COURIER SERVICE**　快递服务

6. **ERASURES**　涂改

7. **LETTER OF INDEMNITY** 担保函

8. **FREE AND CLEAR OF ANY LIEN OR ENCUMBRANCE ON SUCH MATERIAL** 该货物产权明晰，且没有任何留置权或权利负担或障碍［encumbrance 一词是指物权上的负担（不影响权利的转让，但是会随着权利而转让给受让人，这也是限制物权的一般特性）］

9. **EFFECT DELIVERY** 交货

10. **ATTORNEY'S FEES** 律师诉讼费

11. **THE ORIGINAL BILLS OF LADING REMAINING OUTSTANDING** 提单正本依然未达

12. **BREACH OF THE WARRANTIES** 担保违约

13. **TRANSFEREE** 受让人

14. **LIEN ON THE CARGO OR PROCEEDS** 货物或货款的留置权

15. **THIS LETTER OF INDEMNITY SHALL BE GOVERNED BY AND CONSTRUED IN ACCORDANCE WITH THE LAWS OF ENGLAND** 该担保函应受英国法律制约，并按英国法解释

（2）Amending relative L/C 修改信用证

**Sample 5**

Sequence Number: J0B123

Message Type: 707

Sender Institution: XXXXCNBJXXX

                      BANK OF CHINA, THE

                      HEFEI

Receiver Institution: CRESCHZZ80A

                      CREDIT SUISSE

                      ZURICH

Message Status: I

Message Input Date: 2018-09-04

Message Priority: N

———————Message Content : ———————

20:Sender's Reference   LC1800024

21:Receiver's Reference   SGAX 132-153496

31C:Date of Issue      180322

30:Date of Amendment    180904

26E:Number of Amendment    1

59:Beneficiary (before this amendment)

    ABC TRADING AG

  ADD: …, SWITZERLAND

32B:Increase of Documentary Credit Amount    USD1,579,503.46

34B:New Documentary Credit Amount After Amendment    USD16,070,766.62

79:Narrative

  THE AMENDMENT FEE USD35.00 OR EQUIVALENT IS FOR ACCOUNT OF BENEFICIARY, IT WILL BE DEDUCTED FROM PROCEEDS UPON PAYMENT.

  ALL OTHER TERMS AND CONDITIONS REMAIN UNCHANGED

72:Sender to Receiver Information

  /TELEBEN/PLS ADVISE US WHETHER THE BEN ACCEPT THIS AMENDMENT OR NOT. THIS AMENDMENT IS SUBJECT TO UCP600.

---

Operator Name: Xia Hong

Checker Name: Liang Ping

Authorizer Name: Li Ming

**Notes:**

1. This is a SWIFT of amendment to relative Letter of Credit by increasing the amount from USD1,579,503.46 to USD16,070,766.62 addressed to CREDIT SUISSE ZURICH by BANK OF CHINA, THE XXX.

2. **THE AMENDMENT FEE USD35.00 OR EQUIVALENT IS FOR ACCOUNT OF BENEFICIARY.**　35美元或等额的相关信用证修改费由受益人承担。

3. **THIS AMENDMENT IS SUBJECT TO UCP600.**　该修改通知书受跟单信用证统一惯例第600号条款的限制。

4. **CREDIT SUISSE ZURICH**　苏黎世瑞士信贷（银行）

# Sample 6

Sequence Number: J2D0514

Message Type: 707

Sender Institution: XXXXCNBJXXX

BANK OF CHINA, THE
XXX

Receiver Institution: CITIHKHX
CITIBANK N. A.
CITIBANK TOWER CITIBANK PLAZA 3 GA
RDEN ROAD
HONG KONG

Message Status: I

Message Input Date: 2018-09-19

Message Priority: N

————Message Content : ————

20:Sender's Reference LC18000136

21:Receiver's Reference 5596715547

31C:Date of Issue 180913

30:Date of Amendment 180919

26E:Number of Amendment 1

59:Beneficiary (before this amendment)
XYZ CO. LIMITED

79:Narrative

1. UNDER FIELD 48,

   'ALL DOCUMENTS TO BE PRESENTED WITHIN 15 DAYS AFTER L/C ISSUING DATE BUT WITHIN THE VALIDITY OF THE CREDIT.' IS AMENDED AS:

   'ALL DOCUMENTS TO BE PRESENTED WITHIN 15 DAYS AFTER SHIPMENT DATE BUT WITHIN THE VALIDITY OF THE CREDIT.'

2. UNDER FIELD 71B,

   ADD: 'ACCEPTANCE COMMISSION AND STAMP DUTY (IF ANY) IN ISSUING BANK ARE FOR ACCOUNT OF APPLICANT'

3. ALL OTHER TERMS AND CONDITIONS REMAIN UNCHANGED.

72:Sender to Receiver Information

   /TELEBEN/PLS ADVISE US WHETHER THE BEN ACCEPT THIS AMENDMENT OR NOT. THIS AMENDMENT IS SUBJECT TO UCP600.

Operator Name: Zhu Qian

Checker Name: Fan Wei

Authorizer Name: Wang Fang

**Notes:**

1. This is a SWIFT of amendment to relative Letter of Credit by correcting and adding some content of the relative clauses stipulated in letter of credit by BANK OF CHINA, THE XXX to CITIBANK N. A. CITIBANK TOWER CITIBANK PLAZA 3 GA RDEN ROAD HONG KONG.
2. **ACCEPTANCE COMMISSION AND STAMP DUTY (IF ANY)** 承兑佣金和印花税（如果有）
3. **BEN: beneficiary** 受益人

**Sample 7**

---

Sequence Number: C9FE907

Message Type: 799

Sender Institution: XXXXCNBJXXX
                BANK OF CHINA, XXX BRANCH
                XXX

Receiver Institution: ICBCTWTP
                  MEGA INTERNATIONAL COMMERCIAL BANK
                  100 CHIN LIN ROAD FLOOR 9
                  TAIPEI

Message Status: I

Message Input Date: 2018-11-29

Message Priority: N

————Message Content : ————

20:Transaction Reference Number  LC18000167

21:Related Reference  NONE

79:Narrative
    RE:OUR L/C NO. LC18000167
    AMOUNT: CNY47,043,951.00.
    PLS CONVERT THE CURRENCY AND AMOUNT OF THE A/M L/C TO USD7,475,000.00 BEFORE ADVISING IT TO BENEFICIARY.
    PLS ADD THE FOLLOWING CLAUSE TO FIELD 47A OF THE L/C:

QUOTE

AT THE SAME TIME OF FORWARDING DOCUMENTS TO THE ISSUING BANK, THE PRESENTING/NEGOTIATING BANK MUST SWIFT ADVISE THE REIMBURSING BANK (ICBCTWTP007) OF THE DETAILS ABOUT THE SHIPMENT, INCLUDING L/C NO., AMOUNT CLAIMED, DESCRIPTION OF GOODS, PORT OF LOADING, PORT OF DISCHARGE AND SO ON.

UNQUOTE

WE CONFIRM THAT YOU ARE AUTHORIZED BY US TO MAKE SUCH CONVERSION INDICATED AS ABOVE AND TAKE ANY OTHER ACTION NECESSARY AS THE CASE MAY BE. ALL YOUR BANKING CHARGES ARE FOR ACCOUNT OF THE APPLICANT.

B.RGDS.

ITPC, IMPORT DEPT. MR./MS.XXXXX

**Notes:**

1. This is a SWIFT sent by the issuing bank (BANK OF CHINA, XXX BRANCH XXX) to the advising bank (MEGA INTERNATIONAL COMMERCIAL BANK100 CHIN LIN ROAD FLOOR 9, TAIPEI), authorizing them to change the currency from CHY to US dollar stipulated in L/C and add some relative clauses to the FIELD 47A of the L/C quoted as stated.
2. **MEGA INTERNATIONAL COMMERCIAL BANK** 兆丰国际商业银行，兆丰商银，或兆丰银行，是我国台湾地区大型商业银行之一，总行设于台北市。
3. A/M : above-mentioned 上述提到的

### Sample 8

Sequence Number: C7FE112

Message Type: 799

Sender Institution: XXXXCNBJXXX

                BANK OF CHINA, XXX XXX CHINA

Receiver Institution: MIDLGB22

                HSBC BANK PL/C MANCHESTER TRADE

SERVICE CENTRE
PO BOX 322, 3 FL. 4 HARDMAN
SQUARE MANCHESTER M60 1PX

Message Status: O

Message Input Date: 180104

Message Output Date: 180104

MUR: 108:0018634817

Message Priority: N

——————Message Content : ——————

20:Transaction Reference Number
　　　LC18000003

79:Narrative
　ATTN:L/C DEPT.
　RE OUR L/C NO. LC18000003 DD180103,
　APPLICANT: ABC CO., LTD.
　BENEFICIARY: XYZ CO., LIMITED
　TOTAL AMOUNT: USD1,004,003.00

　PLS CORRECT THE A/M L/C AS BELOW:
1.EXPIRY DATE AND PLACE SHOULD BE READ AS
　180831HONGKONG.
2.IN FIELD 45A:'PACKING:1.1MT PER BAG'
　SHOULD BE READ AS 'PACKING:2.5MT PER BAG'.

PLEASE TREAT THIS MESSAGE AS A CORRECTION ONLY
I/O AN AMENDMENT AND ADVISE IT TO THE BENEFICIARY
ACCORDINGLY. PLEASE DO NOT CHARGE FOR THIS
CORRECTION EITHER TO THE BENEFICIARY OR TO US.

SORRY FOR THE INCONVENIENCE CAUSED.
B.RGDS.
ITPC, IMPORT DEPT. MR./MS.XXXXX

**Notes:**

1. This is a SWIFT Amendment to L/C concerning two clauses of expiry date and packing list.
2. **PACKING:1.1MT PER BAG** 包装：每包 1.1 公吨（MT=metric ton）。

### （3）Making payment  付款

### Sample 9

---

Sequence Number: BCB517

Message Type: 799

Sender Institution: XXXXCNBJXXX
        BANK OF CHINA, XXX BRANCH,
        XXX, CHINA

Receiver Institution: MIDLGB22
        HSBC BANK PL/C MANCHESTER TRADE
        SERVICE CENTRE
        PO BOX 322, 3 FL. 4 HARDMAN
        SQUARE MANCHESTER M60 1PX

Message Status: O

Message Input Date: 180104

Message Output Date: 180104

MUR: 108:0013634817

Message Priority: N

——————Message Content :——————

20:Transaction Reference Number  14EL00034679

79:Narrative
    REFER TO YOUR REF NO. 14EL00034679 FOR USD1,004,003.00
    DRAWN UNDER OUR L/C NO. LC18000011.
    PLS BE INFORMED THAT WE WILL REIMBURSE YOU DIRECTLY.
    AS THE ROUTE OF PAYMENT GIVEN ON YOUR
    COVER SCHEDULE IS CONFUSING AND NOT APPLICABLE,
    WE CAN'T MAKE PAYMENT ACCORDINGLY. IN THIS REGARD
    PLS GIVE US YR CLEAR PAYMENT INSTRUCTIONS BY MT799 ASAP SO THAT
    PAYMENT CAN BE EFFECTED WITHOUT DELAY
    YOUR EARLY REPLY WOULD BE HIGHLY APPRECIATED.

B.RGDS.

ITPC, IMPORT DEPT. MR./MS.XXXXX

**Notes:**

1. This is a message sent by the issuing bank to the presenting bank or the negotiating bank asking the clear payment instruction as the payment route is not clearly expressed in the incoming cover letter.
2. **ROUTE OF PAYMENT** 付款路径
3. **COVER SCHEDULE** 面函
4. **ASAP: as soon as possible** 尽快

## Sample 10

Sequence Number: B8A678

Message Type: 799

Sender Institution: XXXXCNBJXXX

     BANK OF CHINA, THE

     XXX

Receiver Institution: DEUTDEDE

     DEUTSCHE BANK AG

     LINDENALLEE 29–45

     ESSEN

Message Status: I

Message Input Date: 2018–03–05

Message Priority: N

————Message Content : ————

20:Transaction Reference Number  LC180000019

21:Related Reference  123456XC60078

79:Narrative

  RE OUR MT756 DD180305 CONCERNING YR REF.

  NO. 123456XC60078 FOR EUR390,000.00

  DRAWN UNDER OUR L/C NO. LC18000019

  PLS BE ADVISED THAT THE DISCREPANCY

  FEE EUR37.00 WAS DEDUCTED DUE TO THE

FOLLOWING DISCREPANCIES:

1. TOTAL CONTRACT VALUE SHOWN ON INVOICE AND P/L CONFLICTS WITH THAT STIPULATED IN THE L/C.

2. ITEM NO. SHOWN ON P/L DIFFERS FROM THAT ON INVOICE.

B.RGDS.

ITPC, IMPORT DEPT. MR./MS.XXXXX

---

**Notes:**

1. This is a message sent by the issuing bank to the presenting bank or the negotiating bank advising some affairs concerning discrepancies in the documents presented and some deductions related to.

2. **DEUTSCHE BANK AG**  德意志银行（AG：股份公司）

3. **P/L : packing list**  装箱单

## Sample 11

---

Sequence Number: B8A388

Message Type: 799

Sender Institution: XXXXCNBJXXX

                BANK OF CHINA, THE

                XXX

Receiver Institution: HSBCTWTPCBS

                HONGKONG AND SHANGHAI BANKING CORP.

                TAIPEI

Message Status: I

Message Input Date: 2018-01-25

Message Priority: N

——————— Message Content : ———————

20:Transaction Reference Number   LC18000079

21:Related Reference   NOAHBK201694

79:Narrative

    RE YR MT799 DD JAN 24, 2018

    ALSO RE YR PRESENTATION WITH REF. NOAHBK201194

    FOR USD5,000,000.00 DRAWN UNDER OUR L/C NO.: 18000079.

PLS FIND BREAKDOWN OF CHARGES WE DEDUCTED AS FOLLOWS:
PAYMENT CHGS USD200.00,
CABLE CHGS 55.00 AND
DISCREPANCY FEE USD50.00 DED.

B.RGDS.
ITPC, IMPORT DEPT. MR./MS.XXXXX

---

**Notes:**

1. This is a SWIFT message sent by the issuing bank to the presenting bank or the negotiating bank replying to an inquiry on the breakdown of charges deducted by the issuing bank.
2. **HONGKONG AND SHANGHAI BANKING CORP** 汇丰银行
3. **YR: your** 你方
4. **DRAWN UNDER OUR L/C NO.: LC18000079** 我行第18000079号信用证下的汇票（金额）
5. **BREAKDOWN OF CHARGES WE DEDUCTED** 我行扣费明细
6. **CABLE CHGS: cable charges** 电报费

## Sample 12

---

Sequence Number: B75626

Message Type: 799

Sender Institution: XXXXCNBJXXX
　　　　　　　　　BANK OF CHINA, THE
　　　　　　　　　XXX

Receiver Institution: HSBCHKHHHKH
　　　　　　　　　　HONGKONG AND SHANGHAI BANKING CORPO
　　　　　　　　　　HONGKONGBANK BUILDING  SUITE 123 1
　　　　　　　　　　QUEEN'S ROAD CENTRAL
　　　　　　　　　　HONG KONG

Message Status: I

Message Input Date: 2018-01-04

Message Priority: N

————Message Content :————

20:Transaction Reference Number  LC18000027

21:Related Reference   BACTST538930

79:Narrative

RE YR DOCS FOR USD4,058,228.06 UNDER OUR L/C NO. 18000027

YR REF:BACTST538930

PLS BE ADVISED THAT WE HAVE INSTRUCTED ABOCHKHH TO REMIT THE PROCEEDS TO YOU AS PER YR PAYMENT INSTRUCTION VALUE ON 20180104.

B.RGDS.

ITPC, IMPORT DEPT. MR./MS.XXXXX

### Notes:

1. This is an advice message sent by the issuing bank to the presenting bank or the negotiating bank that the payment has been made by their corresponding bank and the value date is to be on Jan. 4th, 2018.
2. **REMIT THE PROCEEDS TO YOU**   货款已经汇入你行
3. **VALUE** *vt.*   起息

### Sample 13

Sequence Number: C55514

Message Type: 799

Sender Institution: XXXXCNBJXXX

               BANK OF CHINA, THE

               XXX

Receiver Institution: SCBLAEAD

               STANDARD CHARTERED BANK

               STANDARD CHARTERED BANK BLDG. AL M

               ANKHOOL ROAD

               DUBAI

Message Status: I

Message Input Date: 2018-09-06

Message Priority: N

────────── Message Content : ──────────

20:Transaction Reference Number  LC18000009

21:Related Reference    123150851363-JL

79:Narrative

    RE YOUR PRESENTATION WITH REF. 123150851363-JL

    UNDER OUR L/C NO. 18000009 TOTAL AMOUNT:USD17,728.19.

    PLS BE INFORMED THAT WE WILL REIMBURSE YOU DIRECTLY.

    IN THIS REGARD, PLS REPLY TO US WITH YOUR PAYMENT

    INSTRUCTION SO THAT WE CAN EFFECT PAYMENT ACCORDINGLY.

    B.RGDS.

    ITPC, IMPORT DEPT. MR./MS.XXXXX

---

**Notes:**

1. This is a SWIFT message sent by the issuing bank to the presenting bank or the negotiating bank advising that the reimbursement can be made by the issuing bank directly upon receipt of their payment instruction.
2. **EFFECT PAYMENT**　付款
3. **STANDARD CHARTERED BANK**　渣打银行

## Sample 14

---

Sequence Number: BC01AE

Message Type: 799

Sender Institution: XXXXCNBJXXX

                BANK OF CHINA, THE

                XXX

Receiver Institution: GEBABEBB

                FORTIS BANK S.A./N.V. BRUSSELS (FOR

                MONTAGNE DU PARC 3

                BRUSSELS

Message Status: I

Message Input Date: 2018-03-28

Message Priority: N

————Message Content :————

20:Transaction Reference Number   LC18000009

21:Related Reference   FOBECHX664018002

79:Narrative

    ATTN:L/C EXPORT DEPT.

    REFER TO YOUR MT799 DATED 180327 CONCERNING

    YOUR PRESENTATION WITH REF NO. FOBECHX664018002

    DRAWN UNDER OUR L/C NO. 18000009

    THE APPLICANT ASSERTED THAT THEY HAD PAID EUR18,500.00 FOR THE BILL DIRECTLY TO THE BENEFICIARY BY T/T ON JAN 31, 2018.

    PLS CONTACT THE BENEFICIARY TO CONFIRM THIS AND REPLY TO US BY MT799. AFTER RECEIVING YOUR CONFIRMATION MESSAGE, WE WILL CLOSE OUR FILES ACCORDINGLY.

    YR SOONEST REPLY WILL BE HIGHLY APPRECIATED.

    B.RGDS.

    ITPC, IMPORT DEPT. MR./MS.XXXXX

**Notes:**

1. This is a SWIFT message sent by the issuing bank to the L/C Export Dept. of the presenting bank or the negotiating bank, advising that the payment has been made directly to beneficiary by T/T, but now awaiting their confirmation.
2. **FORTIS BANK S.A./N.V.**　富通银行责任有限公司

### Sample 15

Sequence Number: C03697

Message Type: 799

Sender Institution: XXXXCNBJXXX

          BANK OF CHINA, THE

          XXX

Receiver Institution: OURBTWTP

          TA CHONG BANK LTD.

          NO. 21, LANE 583, RUEIGUANG ROAD NE

          IHU DISTRICT FLOOR 7

          TAIPEI

Message Status: I

Message Input Date: 2018-06-13

Message Priority: N

————Message Content : ————

20:Transaction Reference Number LC18000026

21:Related Reference 019BE62122260001

79:Narrative

  RE: BILL AMOUNT: CNY 1,979,280.77

  UNDER OUR L/C NO.: 18000026

  DRAFT TENOR: 360 DAYS AFTER B/L DATE

  THE MATURITY DATE 180611 FELL ON OUR NATIONAL PUBLIC HOLIDAY,

  SO PAYMENT SHOULD BE POSTPONED TO 180613 ACCORDINGLY.

  WE CONFIRM THAT WE HAVE PAID THE PROCEEDS OF CNY1,977,974.27 AS PER

  YOUR INSTRUCTIONS WITH THE BREAKDOWN OF CHARGES DED AS FOLLOWS:

  1. PAYMENT CHGS CNY1000.00

  2. DISCREPANCY FEE CNY306.5

   PLEASE CHECK YOUR ACCOUNT.


B.RGDS.

ITPC, IMPORT DEPT. MR./MS.XXXXX

---

**Notes:**

1. This is a SWIFT message sent by the issuing bank to the L/C Export Dept. of the presenting bank or the negotiating bank, informing them that the payment has been postponed due to the maturity date being a public holiday instead of a business day.
2. **DRAFT TENOR: 360 DAYS AFTER B/L DATE**　汇票期限：提单日后 360 天。
3. **THE BREAKDOWN OF CHARGES DEDUCTED**　扣费明细
4. **CHGS: charges**　业务费
5. **DED: deducted**　扣除


（4）**Making acceptance**　承兑

**Sample 16**

---

Sequence Number: IC2901

Message Type: 799

Sender Institution: XXXXCNBJXXX

    BANK OF CHINA, THE

    XXX

Receiver Institution: EWBKUS66

    EAST-WEST BANK

    135 N. LOS ANGLES AVE

    PASADENA, CA

Message Status: I

Message Input Date: 2018-08-01

Message Priority: N

————Message Content : ————

20:Transaction Reference Number  LC18000225

21:Related Reference  17EBN84964 YZHAN

79:Narrative

  RE:BILL AMOUNT: USD 247,060.20

  UNDER OUR LC NO.: 18000098

  DRAFT TENOR: 90 DAYS AFTER SIGHT

  THE A/M BILL HAS BEEN ACCEPTED TO BE MATURE ON 181026 NOTWITHSTANDING THE FOLLOWING DISCREPANCY:

  BL:LACK OF ON BOARD DATE.

  WE WILL REMIT THE A/M AMOUNT TO YOU ACCORDING TO YOUR INSTRUCTION DEDUCTING OUR CHARGES.

  HOWEVER, IF THE MATURITY DATE FALLS ON OUR NATIONAL PUBLIC DATE, PAYMENT WILL BE POSTPONED ACCORDINGLY.

  B.RGDS

---

Operator Name: Li Ming

Checker Name: Wu wei

Authorizer Name: Zhu Jun

**Notes:**

1. This is a SWIFT sent by the issuing bank to the paying bank informing them that the relative time draft has been accepted in spite of discrepancy in B/L and will be paid on maturity, which is an abnormal acceptance as there is a discrepancy in relative document.

2. **LACK OF ON BOARD DATE**: lack of shipment date　缺装船日

3. **THE A/M AMOUNT**: the above-mentioned amount　上述金额

## Sample 17

Sequence Number: C7C067

Message Type: 799

Sender Institution: XXXXCNBJXXX
　　　　　　　　　BANK OF CHINA, XXX BRANCH
　　　　　　　　　XXX

Receiver Institution: ICBCTWTP007
　　　　　　　　　　MEGA INTERNATIONAL COMMERCIAL BANK
　　　　　　　　　　100 CHI LIN ROAD
　　　　　　　　　　TAIPEI

Message Status: I

Message Input Date: 2018-10-23

Message Priority: N

————Message Content:————

20:Transaction Reference Number　LC18000188

21:Related Reference　AAAHLA307129

79:Narrative

　PLS RELAY THE FOLLOWING ACCEPTANCE MESSAGE ON OUR BEHALF BY MT799 TO THE PRESENTING/NEGOTIATING BANK, I.E.CHINA CONSTRUCTION BANK, HONG KONG (SWIFT CODE: PCBCHKHH):

　QUOTE

　PLS BE NOTIFIED THAT DOCUMENTS FOR USD6,653,815.00 WITH YOUR REF NO. ECUC18/01162 UNDER OUR L/C NO. 18000188 HAVE BEEN ACCEPTED.

WE, BANK OF CHINA INNER MONGOLIA BRANCH, AS ISSUING BANK WILL EFFECT PAYMENT FOR THE ABOVE AMOUNT AT MATURITY 190421.

UNQUOTE

MEANWHILE, WE UNDERTAKE TO MAKE PAYMENT TO YOU ONE

BANKING DAY BEFORE THE MATURITY DATE IN CNY FOR AN AMOUNT THAT IS SUFFICIENT TO COVER THE ABOVE-MENTIONED AMOUNT IN USD. THE EXCHANGE RATE WILL BE DETERMINED ON OR BEFORE 2 BANKING DAYS PRIOR TO THE MATURITY DATE.

B.RGDS.
ITPC, IMPORT DEPT. MR./MS.XXXXX

**Notes:**

1. This is a SWIFT sent by the issuing bank to the first advising bank, asking them to relay the relative acceptance SWIFT message with the quotations to the presenting or the negotiating bank that the relative time draft has been accepted and will be paid on banking day before the maturity date.
2. **RELAY** 传达
3. **ACCEPTANCE MESSAGE** 承兑电文
4. **QUOTE … UNQUOTE: "…"** 引号的英文表达式
5. **EFFECT PAYMENT: make payment** 付款
6. **CNY** 人民币元
7. **EXCHANGE RATE** 汇率

## Sample 18

Sequence Number: BE520U

Message Type: 799

Sender Institution: XXXXCNBJXXX
     BANK OF CHINA, THE
     XXX

Receiver Institution: NBADHKHH
     NATIONAL BANK OF ABU DHABI
     HONG KONG

Message Status: I

Message Input Date: 2018-05-10

Message Priority: N

──────Message Content :──────

20:Transaction Reference Number　　LC18000056
21:Related Reference　　　　　　　NBADHKGBD180132
79:Narrative

　　ATTN:TRADE FINANCE DEPT
　　RE YR MT799 DATED 180502
　　CONCERNING YR BILL REF NBAD/HKG/BD/180132
　　FOR CNY51,012,660.48
　　DRAWN UNDER OUR L/C NO.18000056

　　KINDLY BE ADVISED THAT WE SENT OUR
　　ACCEPTANCE TO YR BANK ON 180422.
　　THE A/M BILL HAS BEEN ACCEPTED TO
　　BE MATURE ON 190415 AND WE WILL
　　REMIT THE A/M AMOUNT TO YOU ACCORDING
　　TO YOUR INSTRUCTION.

　　HOWEVER, IF THE MATURITY DATE FALLS
　　ON OUR NATIONAL PUBLIC HOLIDAY,
　　PAYMENT WILL BE POSTPONED ACCORDINGLY.

　　B.RGDS.
　　ITPC, IMPORT DEPT. MR./MS.XXXXX

**Notes:**

1. This is a SWIFT sent by the issuing bank to the presenting bank or the negotiating bank, informing them that the relative time draft has been accepted and will be paid on maturity only if it is a banking business date.
2. **NATIONAL BANK OF ABU DHABI**　阿布达比国民银行
3. **PAYMENT WILL BE POSTPONED ACCORDINGLY**　付款相应延期

**Sample 19**

Sequence Number: CD2SP2

Message Type: 799

Sender Institution: XXXXCNBJXXX
                BANK OF CHINA, THE
                XXX

Receiver Institution: PNBPUS3NNYC
                WELLS FARGO BANK. N. A. NEW YORK NY
                NEW YORK, NY

Message Status: I

Message Input Date: 2018-01-24

Message Priority: N

————Message Content : ————

20:Transaction Reference Number      LC18000007

21:Related Reference                98619416

79:Narrative

    RE YR MT799 DD180118, PLS BE ADVISED THAT

    WE HAVE CONFIRMED THE ACCEPTANCE TO RHBBMYKL

    VIA SWIFT MT799 AS FOLLOWS:

    PLS QUOTE:

    20:Transaction Reference Number

      LC18000007

    21:Related Reference

      TCXC803918PJA

79:Narrative

    RE:BILL AMOUNT: USD 715,439.09

    UNDER OUR L/C NO.: 18000007

    DRAFT TENOR: 90 DAYS AFTER B/L DATE

    THE A/M BILL HAS BEEN ACCEPTED TO

    BE MATURE ON 180331.

    WE WILL REMIT THE A/M AMOUNT TO YOU ACCORDING

    TO YOUR INSTRUCTION DEDUCTING OUR CHARGES.

    HOWEVER, IF THE MATURITY DATE FALLS

    ON OUR NATIONAL PUBLIC HOLIDAY,

    PAYMENT WILL BE POSTPONED ACCORDINGLY.

B.RGDS
UNQUOTE.

B.RGDS.
ITPC, IMPORT DEPT. MR./MS.XXXXX

**Notes:**

1. This is a SWIFT reply sent by the issuing bank to the third party bank which expedite the acceptance of the relative draft, confirming that the draft has been accepted by quoting the acceptance message to prove the fact.

2. **DRAFT TENOR: 90 DAYS AFTER B/L DATE**　汇票期限：提单日后 90 天

## （5）Dealing with discrepancies in documents　单据差异的处理

### Sample 20

Sequence Number: C7E414

Message Type: 799

Sender Institution: XXXXCNBJXXX
　　　　　　　　　BANK OF CHINA, THE
　　　　　　　　　XXX

Receiver Institution: NDEADKKK
　　　　　　　　　　NORDEA BANK DENMARK A/S
　　　　　　　　　　STRANDGADE 3
　　　　　　　　　　COPENHAGEN

Message Status: I

Message Input Date: 2018-10-25

Message Priority: N

————Message Content :————

20:Transaction Reference Number　LC18000024

21:Related Reference　L/CN181681

79:Narrative

　　++++++++++++++++++++++++++++++++++++++++++++++

　　URGENT　　　URGENT　　　URGENT

　　++++++++++++++++++++++++++++++++++++++++++++++

ATTENTION: L/C DEPARTMENT

RE OUR MT799 DATED 181023
UNDER OUR L/C NO.: 18000024
DRAFT TENOR: 90 DAYS AFTER B/L DATE
BENEFICIARY: CARGILL INTERNATIONAL TRADING PTE LTD.
APPLICANT: XYZ CO., LTD.
PLS BE ADVISED THE DRAFT AND INVOICE VALUE IS USD3,736,365.86. BUT IN YOUR COVER LETTER, THE AMOUNT IS USD3,736,365.89.
PLEASE INVESTIGATE IT AND CONFIRM THE CORRECT AMOUNT BY AUTHENTICATED SWIFT ASAP. IF NO REPLY RECEIVED, WE WILL REMIT USD3,736,365.86 ACCORDING TO YOUR INSTRUCTION DEDUCTING OUR CHARGES AT MATURITY.
THANKS FOR YOUR COOPERATION.

B.RGDS.
ITPC, IMPORT DEPT. MR./MS.XXXXX

### Notes:

1. This is a SWIFT message sent by the importer's bank to the presenting bank or the negotiating bank, informing them that there exists discrepancies in relative documents, i.e. amount in cover letter is different from that in invoice and draft.
2. **NORDEA BANK DENMARK A/S** 北欧银行（丹麦第二大银行，是瑞典Nordea银行集团的附属公司，北欧最大的金融服务提供商）
3. **THE COVER LETTER** 说明函或面函
4. **ASAP: as soon as possible** 尽快

### Sample 21

Sequence Number: B77A65
Message Type: 799
Sender Institution:XXXXCNBJXXX
                BANK OF CHINA, THE

XXX

Receiver Institution: KREDBEBB

KBC BANK NV

HAVENLAAN 2 B

BRUSSELS

Message Status: I

Message Input Date: 2018-01-06

Message Priority: N

————Message Content : ————

20:Transaction Reference Number   LC18000036

21:Related Reference   09160418928440JO

79:Narrative

RE: OUR MT734 DD181219 AND MT799 DD181228.

UNDER YOUR REF. NO.:09160418928440JO

OUR REF. NO.: LC18000036

L/C NO.:LC18000036 FOR EUR23,400.00

CONCERNING DISCREPANCIES OF A/M DOCUMENTS,

AT THE REQUEST OF APPLICANT, WE TODAY

RETURNED THE DOCUMENTS TO YOU BY DHL

(DHL NO. 5432791221) TO THE ADDRESS ON YOUR COVER SHEET.

THE POST FEE EUR63.00 IS FOR ACCOUNT OF BENEFICIARY.

PLEASE REMIT THE TOTAL AMOUNT

TO WELLS FARGO BANK N. A.(PNBPUS3NNYC)

BY T/T FOR CREDIT OF BANK OF CHINA HEAD OFFICE

(XXXXCNBJ)F/O HUNAN BR. QUOTING OUR REF: LC12000036

B.RGDS.

ITPC, IMPORT DEPT. MR./MS.XXXXX

**Notes:**

1. This is a SWIFT message sent by the importer's bank to the presenting bank or the negotiating bank, informing them that relative documents have been returned because of discrepancies.

2. **KBC BANK NV**　比利时联合银行

3. **DHL** Deutsche Post DHL 旗下的快递公司，DHL Express 敦豪航空货运公司（由

Dalsey、Hillblom 和 Lynn 三位创始人姓氏的首写字母组成）

4. **WELLS FARGO BANK N. A.** 国富银行（美国国民银行）

5. **F/O**：**in favor of** 以……为受益人

## Sample 22

Sequence Number: BC01AE

Message Type: 799

Sender Institution: XXXXCNBJXXX
                BANK OF CHINA, THE
                XXX

Receiver Institution: GEBABEBB
                  FORTIS BANK S. A./N. V. BRUSSELS (FOR
                  MONTAGNE DU PARC 3
                  BRUSSELS

Message Status: I

Message Input Date: 2018-03-28

Message Priority: N

————Message Content : ————

20:Transaction Reference Number      LC18000015

21:Related Reference                FOBECHX664018002

79:Narrative

    L/C NO. 18000015

    OUR REF. LC18000015

    TOTAL AMOUNT: USD4,900,000.00

    RE YR MT799 DD180326,

PLS BE ADVISED THAT WE SENT YOU A MT734 DD180321, AND REFUSED THE DOCUMENTS WITH DISCREPANCIES AS BELOW:

+L/C EXPIRED.

+LATE SHIPMENT.

+LATE PRESENTATION.

WE ARE HOLDING THE DOCUMENTS UNTIL WE RECEIVE

A WAIVER FROM THE APPLICANT AND AGREE TO ACCEPT IT,

OR RECEIVE FURTHER INSTRUCTION FROM YOUR GOOD BANK

PRIOR TO OUR AGREEING TO ACCEPT APPLICANT'S
WAIVER OF A/M DISCS.
PLS CHECK YOUR FILE.

B.RGDS.
ITPC, IMPORT DEPT. MR./MS.XXXXX

**Notes:**

1. This is a SWIFT message sent by the issuing bank to the presenting bank or the negotiating bank, informing them that the documents are dishonored due to the discrepancies existed thereon and they are awaiting for further instruction from the presenting bank or the negotiating bank.

2. **A WAIVER FROM THE APPLICANT** 申请人放弃单据不符点（一般来说，如果提交单据有不符点，开证行将向开证申请人征求意见是否放弃不符点。如果开证申请人同意接受不符点，开证行可放单付款；也可以在放单前等待交单行的进一步指示。开证行对于不符点单据的处理方式属于免责声明）

3. **A/M DISCS**：above-mentioned discrepancies　上述不符点

（6）**Delaying payment by the holidays**　假期付款延期

**Sample 23**

Sequence Number: B757B9
Message Type: 799
Sender Institution: XXXXCNBJXXX
　　　　　　　　　BANK OF CHINA, XXX BRANCH
　　　　　　　　　XXX, CHINA
Receiver Institution: ANZBNZ22102
　　　　　　　　　ANZ NATIONAL BANK LIMITED (FORMERLY
　　　　　　　　　CORNER QUEEN AND VICTORIA STREETS
　　　　　　　　　AUCKLAND
Message Status: I
Message Input Date: 2018-12-31
Message Priority: N
──────Message Content：──────

20:Transaction Reference Number    LC18000035

21:Related Reference    LX2661801166

79:Narrative

    REFER TO YR MT799 DD181231

    YR REF. NO.:LX2661801166

    OUR REF. NO.: LC18000035

    L/C NO.: 18000035

    WE HAVE RECEIVED YR COMPLYING DOCS

    FOR USD105,230.00 ON DEC 26, 2018.

    PLS NOTE THAT THE DAYS FROM JAN 1, 2019

    TO JAN 3, 2019 ARE OUR NATIONAL

    PUBLIC HOLIDAYS. SO WE WILL EFFECT PAYMENT ON 010419.

    B.RGDS.

    ITPC, IMPORT DEPT. MR./MS.XXXXX

---

**Notes:**

1. This is a SWIFT message sent by the issuing bank to the presenting bank explaining that the payment has to be postponed because of public holiday.
2. **YR COMPLYING DOCS.** 你方相符（符合信用证条款的）单据

### Sample 24

---

Sequence Number: B97EBD

Message Type: 799

Sender Institution: XXXXCNBJXXX

                      BANK OF CHINA, THE

                      XXX

Receiver Institution: BPPBCHGG

                      BNP PARIBAS (SUISSE) SA

                      2 PLACE DE HOLLANDE

                      GENEVA

Message Status: I

Message Input Date: 2018-02-08

Message Priority: N

——————Message Content : ——————

20:Transaction Reference Number     LC18000012

21:Related Reference     LCEX41066068

79:Narrative

RE:YOUR PRESENTATION WITH

REF. NO. LCEX41066068 FOR USD 3,149,279.82

UNDER OUR L/C NO.: 18000012

PLS BE INFORMED THAT WE RECEIVED A/M DOCS ON FEB. 04, 2018.

SINCE THE MATURITY DATE FALLS ON OUR NATIONAL PUBLIC

HOLIDAY, PAYMENT WILL BE POSTPONED ACCORDINGLY.

WE HAVE INSTRUCTED CHASHKHH TO MAKE PAYMENT OF USD3,149,154.82

(BILL AMOUNT LESS OUR REIM. CHG.USD100.00 AND

CABLE CHG.USD25.00) TO YOU VALUE ON FEB. 15, 2018.

AS PER YR PAYMENT INSTRUCTION AND OUR OBLIGATION OF PAYMENT

UNDER A/M L/C IS RELEASED.

B.RGDS.

ITPC, IMPORT DEPT. MR./MS.XXXXX

## Notes:

1. This is a SWIFT message sent by the issuing bank to the presenting bank advising that the payment has to be postponed because of public holiday and also arranged to be effected by the reimbursing bank.
2. **BNP PARIBAS (SUISSE) SA**     法国巴黎银行瑞士银行
3. **REIM.CHG: reimbursing charges**     偿付费
4. **VALUE ON FEB. 15, 2018.**     2018年2月15日开始起息

(7) **Arguing on banking charges**　关于银行收费的争议

Sample 25

Sequence Number: CA2S88

Message Type: 799

Sender Institution: XXXXCNBJXXX
　　　　　　　　　BANK OF CHINA, THE
　　　　　　　　　XXX

Receiver Institution: BCITFRPP
　　　　　　　　　　BANCA INTESA FRANCE
　　　　　　　　　　23 RUE LINOIS
　　　　　　　　　　PARIS

Message Status: I

Message Input Date: 2018-12-04

Message Priority: N

————Message Content :————

20:Transaction Reference Number  LC18000076

21:Related Reference　BRAE2872

79:Narrative

　　REFER TO YOUR REF:BRAE2892

　　DOC AMOUNT: EUR210,503.10

　　DRAWN UNDER OUR L/C NO. 18000076

　　PLS BE ADVISED THAT WE CAN NOT ACT AS PER YOUR INSTRUCTION ON THE COVER SCHEDULE CONCERNING YOUR AMENDMENT ADVISING COMMISSIONS.

　　ACCORDING TO THE STIPULATION IN FIELD 71B OF A/M L/C, THE AMENDMENT ADVISING COMMISSIONS SHOULD BE BORNE BY THE BENEFICIARY.

　　WE WILL EFFECT THE PAYMENT OF EUR210,375.00 DEDUCTING OUR CHARGES ( IF ANY ) ON DUE DATE.

　　B.RGDS.
　　ITPC, IMPORT DEPT. MR./MS.XXXXX

**Notes:**

1. This is a SWIFT message sent by the issuing bank to the advising bank informing them that the relative amendment advising commission to be charged is not reasonable based on the stipulations in the L/C.
2. **BANCA INTESA FRANCE** 意大利联合商业银行法国分行（意大利联合商业银行是欧洲最大的银行集团之一，是意大利第二大银行集团，2005年设立分行3970家，其中意大利3106家，国外分行864家，在中国北京、上海和香港设有分行和代表处）
3. **ON THE COVER SCHEDULE** 面函上的交单列表［通常，交单行（或议付行）在交单面函时（即议付行邮寄单据时）贴在邮袋表面的交单列表］
4. **AMENDMENT ADVISING COMMISSIONS** 修改通知佣金
5. **BE BORNE BY THE BENEFICIARY** 由受益人承担
6. **ON DUE DATE** 到期日

## Sample 26

Sequence Number: FA2B56

Message Type: 7xx

Sender Institution: BCITFRPP

                      BANCA INTESA FRANCE

                      23 RUE LINOIS

                      PARIS

Receiver Institution: XXXXCNBJXXX

                      BANK OF CHINA, THE

                      XXX

Message Status: O

Message Input Date: 2018-12-04

Message Priority: N

————Message Content : ————

20:Transaction Reference Number    LC18000038

21:Related Reference    BRAE2872

79:Narrative

    RE YOUR MT799 DD. 04.12.2018, BE ADVISED THAT

    AS PER YOUR MT707 DD. 10.07.2018 'THE BANKING

    CHARGES FOR THIS AMENDMENT ARE FOR THE ACCOUNT

OF THE APPLICANT'.

PLEASE CHECK YOUR RECORDS AND EFFECT THE PAYMENT
FOR THE TOTAL AMOUNT OF EUR 210,503.10 AT SIGHT,
BY CREDITING OUR ACCOUNT NR. 100100004831 HELD
WITH BCITITMM, QUOTING OUR REF.

RGDS
BCITFRPP

**Notes:**

1. This is a SWIFT message reply sent by the advising bank to the issuing bank expressing their disagreement on amendment advising commission based on the relative stipulations in the L/C that banking charges for the amendment are for the applicant's account.

## Sample 27

Sequence Number: CA5059
Message Type: 799
Sender Institution: XXXXCNBJXXX
　　　　　　　　　BANK OF CHINA, THE
　　　　　　　　　XXX
Receiver Institution: BCITFRPP
　　　　　　　　　BANCA INTESA FRANCE
　　　　　　　　　23 RUE LINOIS
　　　　　　　　　PARIS
Message Status: I
Message Input Date: 2018-12-05
Message Priority: N
　　　　——Message Content : ——
20:Transaction Reference Number　LC18000078
21:Related Reference BRAE2892
79:Narrative
　　RE YOUR MT799 DD 20181204, PLEASE NOTE

THAT AS PER OUR MT707 DD 20180710, 'THE BANKING
CHARGES FOR THIS AMENDMENT ARE FOR THE ACCOUNT OF
APPLICANT' MEANS THE APPLICANT SHOULD BEAR THE
AMENDMENT CHARGES OCCURRED IN THE ISSUING BANK,
I/O THE AMENDMENT ADVISING COMMISSIONS.

THE A/M L/C FIELD 71B CLEARLY STIPULATES THAT, THE
AMENDMENT ADVISING CHARGES YOU CLAIMED SHOULE BE
BORNE BY THE BENEFICIARY.
THEREFORE, WE WILL EFFECT THE PAYMENT FOR THE TOTAL
AMOUNT OF EUR210,375.00 DEDUCTING OUR CHARGES ( IF ANY )
ONLY ON DUE DATE.

B.RGDS.
ITPC, IMPORT DEPT. MR./MS.XXXXX

### Notes:

1. This is a reply message sent by the issuing bank to the advising bank emphasizing the fact that the relative amendment advising commission to be borne by the beneficiary based on the charges stipulations in the L/C field 71B.
2. **I/O: instead of** 而不是

## Sample 28

Sequence Number: 835123
Message Type: 799
Sender Institution: CITISGSG
     CITIBANK, N. A.
     300 TAMPINES AVENUE 5  TAMPINES JUN
     CTION HEX 06–00
     SINGAPORE
Receiver Institution: XXXXCNBJXXX
     BANK OF CHINA, THE
     XXX

Message Status: O

Message Input Date: 180529

Message Output Date: 180529

MUR: 108: 30529GEU43329SPD

Message Priority: N

──────Message Content : ──────

20:Transaction Reference Number     6949608193/DC

21:Related Reference     BP18000046

79:Narrative

    //TOP URGENT//

    ATTN:L/C EXPORT DEPT.

    RE YOUR BILL REF NO. BP18000046 FOR

    USD86,292.00 DRAWN UNDER OUR L/C NO. 5949601088

    AS PER THE L/C AMENDMENT DATED 26 FEB 2018, AMENDMENT

    CHARGES SHOULD BE FOR ACCOUNT OF BENEFICIARY.

    AS WE OMITTED TO DEDUCT AMENDMENT CHARGES

    USD148.26 WHEN WE MADE PAYMENT TO YOUR GOOD BANK

    ON 02 APRIL 2018.

    THEREFORE , WE SHALL APPRECIATE YOUR KIND ASSISTANCE TO

    RETURN THE AMOUNT OF USD148.26 TO OUR ACCOUNT 10991581

    WITH CITIBANK NA NEW YORK QUOTING

    OUR REF. 6949608193 AS SOON AS POSSIBLES.

    THANKS IN ADVANCE FOR YOUR KIND COOPERATION IN

    THIS MATTER.

    B.RGDS.

    ITPC, IMPORT DEPT. MR./MS.XXXXX

**Notes:**

1. This is a message sent by the issuing bank to the presenting or negotiating bank asking them to return the amendment charges amounting to US$148.26 omitted to be deducted.

2. **TOP URGENT** 加急报文

3. **CITIBANK NA NEW YORK** 纽约花旗银行

## (8) Querying the clauses stipulated by L/C  信用证条款的疑问

### Sample 29

Sequence Number: CA26SD2

Message Type: 799

Sender Institution: XXXXCNBJXXX
　　　　　　　　　BANK OF CHINA,THE
　　　　　　　　　XXX

Receiver Institution: ANZBSGSX XXXXXXXX

Message Status: I

Message Input Date: 181203

Message Output Date: 181203

MUR: 108: 0018634817

Message Priority: N

――――――Message Content : ――――――

20:Transaction Reference Number　　LC18000026

21:Related reference NONREF

79:Narrative

　　ATTN:L/C ADVISING DEPT.

　　RE OUR MT700 DD181129,

　　L/C NO.: 18000026 FOR CNY184,701,720.00,

　　BENEFICIARY:TRAFIGURA AG
　　　　　　　　ZURICHSTRASSE 31,6002 LUCERNE
　　　　　　　　SWITZERLAND

APPLICANT DECLARE THAT THE BENEFICIARY HAS NOT RECEIVED THE L/C. PLS CONFIRM US BY AUTHENTICATED SWIFT WHETHER AND WHEN YOU ADVISED THE L/C TO THE BENEFICIARY.

B.RGDS.

ITPC, IMPORT DEPT. MR./MS.XXXXX

**Notes:**

1. This is a SWIFT message sent by the issuing bank to the advising bank inquiring why the relative L/C has not been received by the beneficiary.

2. **ATTN:L/C ADVISING DEPT.**　经办人部门：信用证通知部

3. **AG**　德语股份公司的缩写

4. **AUTHENTICATED SWIFT**　加密报文

5. **B.RGDS**　礼貌用语（Best Regards 的缩写）

## Sample 30

Sequence Number: CA2602

Message Type: 799

Sender Institution: XXXXCNBJXXX

    BANK OF CHINA, THE

    XXX

Receiver Institution: ANZBSGSX

    XXXXXXXX

Message Status: I

Message Input Date: 181203

Message Output Date: 181203

MUR: 108:0018634836

Message Priority: N

————Message Content : ————

20:Transaction Reference Number  LC18000025

21:Related reference      NONREF

79:Narrative

  ATTN:L/C ADVISING DEPT.

  OUR L/C NO.: 18000025

  TOTAL AMOUNT CNY184,701,720.00,

  BENEFICIARY:TRAFIGURA AG

  RE YR MT799 DD181202，PLS BE ADVISED THAT THE EXPIRY PLACE SHOULD BE READ AS SINGAPORE. PLS KINDLY ADVISE TO THE BENEFICIARY. SORRY FOR ANY INCONVENIENCE CAUSED.

  B.RGDS.

  ITPC, IMPORT DEPT. MR./MS.XXXXX

**Notes:**

1. This is a reply sent by the issuing bank to the advising bank explaining the query about the discrepancies on the expiry place.

2. **RE YR MT799 DD181202 : Referring to your MT799 dated on Dec. 2, 2018.** 关于你方2018年12月2日799报文。

## Sample 31

---

Sequence Number: C54BS6

Message Type: 799

Sender Institution: XXXXCNBJXXX
     BANK OF CHINA, THE
     XXX

Receiver Institution: CITIHKHX
     CITIBANK N. A.
     CITIBANK TOWER CITIBANK PLAZA 3 GA
     RDEN ROAD
     HONG KONG

Message Status: I

Message Input Date: 2018-09-06

Message Priority: N

————Message Content : ————

20:Transaction Reference Number　LC18000026

21:Related Reference　　5594706433

79:Narrative
  ATTN:L/C ADVISING DEPT
  OUR L/C NO. 18000026
  TOTAL AMOUNT:USD3,900,000.00
  RE YR MT799 DD180905,
  PLS BE INFORMED THAT THE BENE'S
  CORRECT NAME SHOULD BE READ AS:
  'BOYA GROUP (HK) LIMITED' I/O ORIGINALLY STATED.

  B.RGDS.

ITPC, IMPORT DEPT. MR./MS.XXXXX

**Notes:**

1. This is a reply sent by the issuing bank to the advising bank informing them the correct name of beneficiary.

2. **I/O : instead of** 替代

## 2. Business related to L/C (from exporter's bank)（出口银行的信用证相关业务）

### （1）Querying some terms on L/C before advising  通知前对信用证条款的疑问

**Sample 32**

Sequence Number: CAABSG

Message Type: 799

Sender Institution: XXXXCNBJXXX
     BANK OF CHINA, THE
     XXX

Receiver Institution: SHBKKRSE
     SHINHAN BANK
     120, 2-GA, TAEPYUNG-RO, CHUNG-GU
     SEOUL

Message Status: I

Message Input Date: 2018-12-12

Message Priority: N

————Message Content : ————

20:Transaction Reference Number LC18000201

21:Related Reference M88AG1812NU00025

79:Narrative

 ATTN: TRADE BUSINESS DEPARTMENT
 REFER TO YOUR L/C NO. 18000201 DATED 181209
 WE HEREBY ACKNOWLEDGE RECEIPT OF THE SAID L/C.
 IT'S REQUIRED BY THE SAID L/C THAT 'T/T
 REIMBURSEMENT NOT ALLOWED' AND 'IN REIMBURSEMENT
 THE DRAFTS ARE TO BE FORWARDED TO THE DRAWEE BANK
 -SHBKHKHXXXX'. BUT THE ADDRESS OF SHBKHKHXXXX

IS NOT MENTIONED IN THE L/C. THEREFORE, PLS KINDLY INFORM US THE DETAILED ADDRESS OF SHBKHKHXXXX BY REPLYING SWIFT AS SOON AS POSSIBLE.

B.RGDS.

ITPC, EXPORT DEPT. MR./MS.XXXXX

## Notes:

1. This is a SWIFT message sent by the advising bank to the issuing bank acknowledging receipt of the relative L/C and inquiring detailed address of the reimbursing bank.
2. **SHINHAN BANK** 新韩银行，新韩金融集团全资控股的银行，是韩国最大的商业银行之一，目前共设 1000 多家分行，在 9 个国家设有海外分行。
3. **T/T REIMBURSEMENT NOT ALLOWED** 不允许电汇偿付
4. **DRAWEE BANK** 受票银行，即偿付行

## Sample 33

Sequence Number: B706G8

Message Type: 799

Sender Institution: XXXXCNBJXXX

BANK OF CHINA, THE

XXX

Receiver Institution: SCBLBDDX

STANDARD CHARTERED BANK

ALICO BUILDING 18-20 MOTIJHEEL COM-MERCIAL AREA

DHAKA

Message Status: I

Message Input Date: 2018-12-26

Message Priority: N

————Message Content : ————

20:Transaction Reference Number  LC18000056

21:Related Reference  248612021567

79:Narrative

ATTN: L/C DEPARTMENT.

REFER TO YOUR L/C NO. 18000056
OUR REF NO. LC18000056 FOR USD52,963.50

WE HEREBY ACKNOWLEDGE RECEIPT OF ABOVE-MENTIONED
L/C, BUT WE ARE CONFUSED ABOUT THE FOLLOWING CLAUSES:
IN FIELD 46A ITEM 2 IT'S REQUIRED TO PRESENT
'CERTIFICATE OF ORIGIN IN TWO COPIES…', MEANWHILE ITEM 5 OF FIELD
47A REQUIRES 'ORIGINAL CERTIFICATE OF ORIGIN MUST BE
SENT TO APPLICANT BY COURIER WITHIN 5 DAYS AFTER SHIPMENT'.

ACCORDING TO SUB.ARTICLE 17E OF UCP600, THE PHRASE
'IN TWO COPIES' MEANS AT LEAST ONE ORIGINAL. SO IT
CONFLICTS WITH THE REQUIREMENT STATED IN FIELD 47A.
PLEASE CLARIFY THIS MATTER AND REPLY US ASAP.

B.RGDS.
ITPC, EXPORT DEPT. MR./MS.XXXXX

**Notes:**
1. This is a SWIFT message sent by the advising bank to the issuing bank acknowledging receipt of the relative L/C and asking them to make clear the relative clauses stipulated by the L/C as it conflicts with each other thereon.
2. **CERTIFICATE OF ORIGIN** 原产地证明书
3. **ORIGINAL** 正本
4. **BY COURIER** 由快递公司传递

### Sample 34

Sequence Number: CA6769
Message Type: 799
Sender Institution: XXXXCNBJXXX
　　　　　　　　 BANK OF CHINA, THE
　　　　　　　　 XXX
Receiver Institution: UOVBSGSG

UNITED OVERSEAS BANK LIMITED
UOB PLAZA  80 RAFFLES PLACE
SINGAPORE

Message Status: I

Message Input Date: 2018-01-13

Message Priority: N

————————Message Content : ————————

20:Transaction Reference Number   LC18000021

21:Related Reference   1CML/C564678

79:Narrative

 ATTN:IMPORT DEPT

 REFER TO YOUR L/C NO. 1CML/C564678

 DATED 181231 AMOUNT: SGD44,500.00

 BENEFICIARY: YANBIAN BAOLIXIANG BEEKEEPING CO., LTD

 APPLICANT: WINTER HONEY TRADING CO.

 PLS VERIFY THE AUTHENTICITY OF THE ABOVE-MENTIONED

 LETTER OF CREDIT BY MT799 TO US

 B.RGDS.

 ITPC, EXPORT DEPT. MR./MS.XXXXX

**Notes:**

1. This is a SWIFT message sent by the advising bank to the issuing bank acknowledging receipt of the relative L/C and asking them to verify it as it can't be authenticated.

2. **SGD : Singapore dollar**   新加坡元

（2）**Making amendment to relative L/C**   关于信用证的修改通知

## Sample 35

Sequence Number: S9C3T9

Message Type: 799

Sender Institution: XXXXCNBJXXX

   BANK OF CHINA, XXX BRANCH

XXX, CHINA

Receiver Institution: ANZBNZ22102

ANZ NATIONAL BANK LIMITED (FORMERLY
CORNER QUEEN AND VICTORIA STREETS
AUCKLAND

Message Status: I

Message Input Date: 2018-02-20

Message Priority: N

————Message Content :————

20:Transaction Reference Number   LC18000022

21:Related Reference IMP/18/001

79:Narrative

　　WE TRANSMIT THE MT707 MESSAGE ISSUED
　　BY TDBMMNUB TO YOU
　　AS FOLLOWED

　　QUOTE
　　20:Sender's Reference  IMP/18/001
　　31C:Date of Issue    180102
　　30:Date of Amendment  180208
　　26E:Number of Amendment   1
　　59:Beneficiary (before this amendment)
　　FONTERRA LIMITED, PRIVATE
　　BAG 92032, 9 PRINCESS ST,
　　AUCKLAND, NEW ZEALAND
　　79:Narrative
　　WE HEREBY AMEND OUR L/C AS FOLLOWS:
　　+PLEASE AMEND REQUIRED TRANSPORTATION DOCUMENT
　　IN FIELD 46A AS FOLLOWS:
　　'+FULL SET OF MULTIMODAL TRANSPORT DOCUMENT MADE
　　OUT TO ORDER AND BLANK ENDORSED MARKED 'FREIGHT
　　PREPAID' NOTIFYING APU COMPANY' I/O PREVIOUS.

　　ALL OTHER TERMS AND CONDITIONS SHALL REMAIN

UNCHANGED.

BEST REGARDS,
TRADE FINANCE SETTLEMENT UNIT
UNQUOTE

B.RGDS.
ITPC, EXPORT DEPT. MR./MS.XXXXX

**Notes:**

1. This is a SWIFT message sent by the advising bank to the exporter's bank transiting the amendment to L/C by the issuing bank, which is an advice further to the previous one.
2. **ANZ NATIONAL BANK LIMITED** 澳新国民银行
3. **MODIFY** 修改
4. **I/O :instead of** 替代

## Sample 36

Sequence Number: CS3109

Message Type: 799

Sender Institution: XXXXCNBJXXX
                   BANK OF CHINA, THE
                   XXX

Receiver Institution: IBBLBDDH118
                     ISLAMI BANK BANGLADESH LTD
                     210-211, NAWABPUR ROAD
                     DHAKA

Message Status: I

Message Input Date: 2018-01-08

Message Priority: N

————Message Content : ————

20:Transaction Reference Number   LC18000066

21:Related Reference   087117011607

79:Narrative

ATTN: IMPORT DEPT.

REFER TO YOUR MT707 DATED171223 AND 180107
UNDER L/C NO.:087117011607.

PLS BE ADVISED THAT THE L/C AMOUNT 'USD82,320.00'
(BEFORE AMENDMENT) PLUS THE INCREASED AMOUNT
'USD350,600.00' IN FIRST AMENDMENT SHOULD BE
'USD432,920.00' I/O 'USD433,000.00'IN FIRST AMENDMENT. AND THE NEW
L/C AMOUNT AFTER THE SECOND AMENDMENT SHOULD BE
'USD570,120.00' I/O 'USD570,200.00'.

PLS KINDLY CHECK THIS MATTER AND REPLY TO US
AS SOON AS POSSIBLE.

B.RGDS.

ITPC, EXPORT DEPT. MR./MS.XXXXX

**Notes:**

1. This is a SWIFT message sent by the advising bank to the issuing bank comparing the revised clauses with that in the old L/C after receipt of the amendment to L/C and confirming its correctness through comparison and check-up.
2. **ISLAMI BANK BANGLADESH LTD** 孟加拉伊斯兰银行
3. **DHAKA** 达卡，孟加拉首都

**Sample 37**

Sequence Number: CC67G9

Message Type: 799

Sender Institution: XXXXCNBJXXX
                BANK OF CHINA, THE
                XXX

Receiver Institution: CZNBKRSE
                KOOKMIN BANK, BUSAN BRANCH
                15-1 JUNGANG-DONG 2(1)-GA
                BUSAN KOREA

Message Status: I

Message Input Date: 2019-01-10

Message Priority: N

————Message Content : ————

20:Transaction Reference Number　　LC18000201

21:Related Reference　　M07D01812NU00040

79:Narrative

　　REFER TO YOUR MT707 DATED 190108, AMENDMENT NUMBER 1.

　　PLS BE ADVISED THAT THE BENEFICIARY HAS ACCEPTED THE ABOVE-MENTIONED AMENDMENT.

　　B.RGDS.

　　ITPC, EXPORT DEPT. MR./MS.XXXXX

**Notes:**

1. This is a reply message sent by the advising bank to the issuing bank informing them that the amendment to L/C has been accepted by the beneficiary.

2. **KOOKMIN BANK, BUSAN BRANCH**　韩国国民银行釜山分行

（3）**Claiming Reimbursement By BP**　押汇索偿

**Sample 38**

Sequence Number: CD9SD6

Message Type: 799

Sender Institution: XXXXCNBJXXX

　　　　　　　　　AGRICULTURAL BANK OF CHINA, THE

　　　　　　　　　XXX

Receiver Institution: IBKOKRSE

　　　　　　　　　INDUSTRIAL BANK OF KOREA

　　　　　　　　　50, UL/CHIRO 2-GA, CHUNG-GU

　　　　　　　　　SEOUL

Message Status: I

Message Input Date: 2018-02-07

Message Priority: N

————— Message Content : —————

20:Transaction Reference Number    241297BP18000001

21:Related Reference    M04GP311NU00071

79:Narrative

    ATTN: IMPORT L/C DEPT.

    REFER TO OUR REF NO. BP18000032

    DATED 20180127

    FOR USD48,635.00

    UNDER YOUR L/C NO. M04GP311NU00071.

    AS OF TODAY, THE CAPTIONED BILL REMAINS

    UNPAID/UNACCEPTED, PLEASE URGENTLY MAKE

    PAYMENT/ACCEPTANCE TO US OR ADVISE REASON(S) FOR

    NONE-PAYMENT/NON-ACCEPTANCE BY SWIFT.

    B.RGDS.

    ITPC, EXPORT DEPT. MR./MS.XXXXX

### Notes:

1. This is an automatic standardized SWIFT message sent by the negotiating bank to the issuing bank urging them to make payment or acceptance and give reasons for non-payment or non-acceptance.
2. **INDUSTRIAL BANK OF KOREA**    韩国工业银行
3. **AS OF TODAY**    截至今天
4. **BP: bills purchased**    押汇

### Sample 39

Sequence Number: CC0P89

Message Type: 999

Sender Institution: XXXXCNBJXXX

                    BANK OF CHINA, THE

                    XXX

Sender Institution: ISLDSAJE

                    ISLAMIC DEVELOPMENT BANK

                    JEDDAH

Message Status: I

Message Input Date: 2018-01-06

Message Priority: N

————Message Content : ————

20:Transaction Reference Number   BP17000101

21:Related Reference   OFSZ/2BD162/1

79:Narrative

+++++++TOP URGENT+++++++++++++++TOP URGENT+++++++
REFER TO YOUR REF. OFSZ/2BD162/1
UNDER L/C NO. 036017010007
OUR REF NO. 228912BP17000101 FOR USD1,270,695.00
APPLICANT: BANGLADESH POWER DEVELOPMENT BOARD
BENEFICIARY: M/S. CHINA CHENGDA ENGINEERING CO.
PLS BE INFORMED THAT WE RECEIVED YOUR GOOD BANK'S
MT799 AUTHORIZING US TO CLAIM REIMBURSEMENT FROM
THE REIMBURSING BANK SINTGB2L ON 171226.
AND WE HAVE SENT REIMBURSEMENT CLAIM TO
SINTGB2L BY MAIL ON 171227 AS PER YOUR
INSTRUCTIONS. BUT AS OF TODAY, WE STILL HAVE NOT
RECEIVED THE PAYMENT FROM SINTGB2L. SINCE THE BANK
WHICH YOU AUTHORIZED TO HONOUR OUR CLAIM HAS NOT PAID US,
PLS URGENTLY PAY US BY YOURSELVES AS SOON AS POSSIBLE.
PLS PAY THE PROCEEDS BY T/T TO OUR HEAD OFFICE (SWIFT CODE: XXXX
CNBJ) ACCOUNT WITH WELLS FARGO BANK NA (SWIFT:
PNBPUS3NNYC) QUOTING OUR REF NO. 228912BP17000101
UNDER YOUR ADVICE TO US. FOR THE CREDIT TO 58A:ABOCCNBJ220.
YR PROMPT REPLY WOULD BE HIGHLY APPRECIATED.
B.RGDS.
ITPC, EXPORT DEPT. MR./MS.XXXXX

**Notes:**

1. This is a top urgent SWIFT message sent by the negotiating bank to the issuing bank urging them directly to make payment as the authorized reimbursing bank cannot effect due payment after claiming reimbursement from them.

2. **ISLAMIC DEVELOPMENT BANK** 伊斯兰开发银行（IDB）

3. **JEDDAH** 吉达，沙特阿拉伯的地名

4. **CLAIM REIMBURSEMENT FROM THE REIMBURSING BANK** 向偿付行索偿

5. **HONOUR OUR CLAIM** 承付我行的索偿

6. **T/T**：**telegraphic transfer** 电汇

7. **HEAD OFFICE** 总部（H.O.）

## Sample 40

Sequence Number: CBSQ56

Message Type: 799

Sender Institution: XXXXCNBJXXX

     BANK OF CHINA, THE

     XXX

Receiver Institution: CITIUS33

     CITIBANK N. A.

     111 WALL STREET

     NEW YORK, NY

Message Status: I

Message Input Date: 2018-12-30

Message Priority: N

————Message Content :————

20:Transaction Reference Number BP18000056

21:Related Reference NONREF

79:Narrative

  ATTN: L/C REIMBURSEMENT DEPT.

  OUR REF NO.: BP18000056 FOR USD21,480.00

  UNDER L/C NO.: L/C-831-671511 ISSUED BY HSBCHKHH

  WE HEREBY CLAIM REIMBURSEMENT FROM YOUR GOOD BANK

  AS INSTRUCTED BY THE L/C. THE AMOUNT CLAIMED IS USD21,480.00

  AND DUE ON 181231. THE FOLLOWING INFORMATION IS PROVIDED TO YOU

  AS REQUIRED BY THE L/C:

    PORT OF LOADING: SHANGHAI, CHINA

PORT OF DISCHARGE: INCHEON, KOREA
PLEASE CREDIT TO OUR HEAD OFFICE (ABOCCNBJ) ACCOUNT WITH
YOU (CITIUS33), FOR FURTHER CREDIT TO US (58A:ABOCCNBJ180),
QUOTING OUR REF NO. UNDER YOUR SWIFT ADVISE TO US.
YOUR PROMPT ACTION IS HIGHLY APPRECIATED.
B.RGDS.
ITPC, EXPORT DEPT. MR./MS.XXXXX

---

**Notes:**

1. This is a SWIFT message sent by the negotiating bank to the reimbursing bank asking them to credit the amount into the relative account of their H. O. with the reimbursing bank as instructed by the L/C.
2. **YOUR GOOD BANK** 贵行（对对方银行的尊称）
3. **PORT OF DISCHARGE: INCHEON, KOREA** 卸货港：韩国仁川

## Sample 41

---

Sequence Number: C09P98

Message Type: 799

Sender Institution: XXXXCNBJXXX
               BANK OF CHINA, THE
               XXX

Receiver Institution: CZNBKRSE
               KOOKMIN BANK, BUSAN BRANCH
               15-1 JUNGANG-DONG 2(1)-GA
               BUSAN KOREA

Message Status: I

Message Input Date: 2018-06-19

Message Priority: N

————Message Content : ————

20:Transaction Reference Number  BP18000021

21:Related Reference  M10HB1805NU00064

79:Narrative
   +++URGENT+++URGENT+++URGENT+++

REFER TO YOUR MT799 DD 11JUN2018.

PLS BE ADVISED THAT OUR REIMBURSEMENT CLAIM WAS REFUSED BY THE REIMBURSING BANK BECAUSE THEY ONLY ACCEPT AUTHENTICATED MESSAGE. HOWEVER, WE DO NOT HAVE RMA WITH CZNBVNVX. THEREFORE, PLS LOOK INTO THE MATTER AND AUTHORISE CZNBVNVX TO REIMBURSE US OR YOU EFFECT PAYMENT TO US BY YOURSELF DIRECTLY ASAP. AS FOLLOWS:

PLS REMIT THE PROCEEDS TO OUR H. O.(XXXXCNBJ) ACCOUNT WITH JPMORGAN CHASE BANK N. A. NEW YORK (CHASUS33) QUOTING OUR REF NO. UNDER ADVICE TO US.

LOOKING FORWARD TO YOUR IMMEDIATE REPLY.

B.RGDS.

ITPC, EXPORT DEPT. MR./MS.XXXXX

---

**Notes:**

1. This is an urgent SWIFT message sent by the negotiating bank to the issuing bank asking them to authorize the reimbursing bank to reimburse them without delay as there is no agency relationship between the two banks, otherwise asking the issuing bank to effect payment directly.
2. **PLS BE ADVISED** 兹通知
3. **AN AUTHENTICATED MESSAGE** 一份加密报文
4. **RMA：relation of message authenticated** 报文密押关系
5. **EFFECT PAYMENT** 付款
6. **PROCEEDS** 货款
7. **JPMORGAN CHASE BANK N. A.** JP摩根大通银行（N. A.是national的缩写，表示美国国民银行的代码）

## Sample 42

---

Sequence Number: CB5687

Message Type: 799

Sender Institution: XXXXCNBJXXX

        BANK OF CHINA, THE

        XXX

Receiver Institution: ICICINBBCTS
             ICICI BANK LIMITED

Message Status: I

Message Input Date: 2019-01-30

Message Priority: N

————Message Content : ————

20:Transaction Reference Number   BP18000221

21:Related Reference    0544ML/C00100714

79:Narrative

    RE YOUR MT752 DATED181125, WE HAVE CLAIMED REIMBURSEMENT FROM ICICHKHHREM ON 190129. HOWEVER, WE HAVE RECEIVED A MT799 TODAY FROM ICICHKHHREM STATING 'WE WISH TO INFORM YOU THAT WE ARE UNABLE TO ACT ON YOUR CLAIM AS THE ISSUING BANK HAS NOT GIVEN US THEIR AUTHORISATION'. PLS URGENTLY LOOK INTO THE MATTER AND AUTHORIZE ICICHKHHREM TO REIMBURSE US AS SOON AS POSSIBLE.

    B.RGDS.

    ITPC, EXPORT DEPT. MR./MS.XXXXX

### Notes:

1. This is a SWIFT message sent by the negotiating bank to the issuing bank asking them to authorize the reimbursing bank soonest to effect payment as the reimbursing bank has not got any authorization from the issuing bank to make payment.

2. **ICICI BANK LIMITED** 印度工业信贷投资银行［它是印度第二大银行，也是印度最大的私营银行，规模仅次于印度国家银行（SBI）］

## Sample 43

Sequence Number: C3SPM6

Message Type: 799

Sender Institution: XXXXCNBJXXX
             BANK OF CHINA, THE

XXX

Receiver Institution: IBKOUS33

INDUSTRIAL BANK OF KOREA, NEW YORK

1250 BROADWAY FLOOR 37

NEW YORK, NY

Message Status: I

Message Input Date: 2018-07-29

Message Priority: N

————Message Content:————

20:Transaction Reference Number   BP18000035

21:Related Reference   M04N6307NU00018

79:Narrative

++++++++++++++++TOP URGENT++++++++++++++++

L/C NO.:M04N6307NU00018

ISSUING BANK:IBKOKRSE

USANCE BILLS PAYABLE AT SIGHT BASIS AS PER L/C TERMS.

OUR REF NO.: BP18000035

FOR USD50,800.00.

AS PER AUTHORISATION OF IBKOKRSE, WE CLAIMED

REIMBURSEMENT FROM YOU ON 180722.

HOWEVER, UP TO NOW, WE HAVE NOT RECEIVED YOUR

REIMBURSEMENT. KINDLY INVESTIGATE THIS MATTER

AND EFFECT PAYMENT AS SOON AS POSSIBLE OR ADVISE

US THE REASON OF NON-PAYMENT.

YOUR IMMEDIATE REPLY WILL BE HIGHLY APPRECIATED.

B.RGDS.

ITPC, EXPORT DEPT. MR./MS.XXXXX

## Notes:

1. This is a top urgent SWIFT message sent by the negotiating bank to the reimbursing bank asking them the reason why the payment has not been made on due date.
2. **INDUSTRIAL BANK OF KOREA**  韩国工业银行

## (4) Disagreeing on the BP Claims Dishonored  押汇索偿退票的异议
## Sample 44

Sequence Number: C5ZHK6

Message Type: 799

Sender Institution: XXXXCNBJXXX
     BANK OF CHINA, THE
     XXX

Receiver Institution: CZNBKRSE
     KOOKMIN BANK, BUSAN BRANCH
     15-1 JUNGANG-DONG 2(1)-GA
     BUSAN KOREA

Message Status: I

Message Input Date: 2018-08-12

Message Priority: N

————Message Content : ————

20:Transaction Reference Number BP18000021

21:Related Reference M07K51806NS00040

79:Narrative

  ATTN: JEONGJA-DONG BRANCH/MANAGE

  REFER TO YOUR MT734 DATED 180809

  PLS BE ADVISED THAT WE CAN NOT AGREE WITH YOU
  ON THE DISCREPANCY. THE B/L PRESENTED STRICTLY
  COMPLIED WITH UCP600 ARTICLE 20 AND THE L/C TERMS.
  ADDITIONALLY, AS PER ISBP745 PARA E4 :'HOUSE BILLS
  OF LADING ARE NOT ACCEPTABLE' HAS NO MEANING IN THE
  CONTEXT OF THE TITLE, FORMAT, CONTENT OR SIGNING OF
  A BILL OF LADING. IN THE ABSENCE OF OTHER SPECIFIC
  REQUIREMENTS, SUCH A STIPULATION IS TO BE DISREGARDED.
  IN FACT, THERE IS NO DISCREPANCY IN THE PRESENTATION.
  PLS RE-CONSIDER THE DISCREPANCY AND PAY US ASAP
  WITHOUT ANY DEDUCTION OF DISCREPANCY FEE.
  WE RESERVE OUR RIGHT TO CLAIM INTEREST FOR DELAYED PAYMENT

B.RGDS.

ITPC, EXPORT DEPT. MR./MS.XXXXX

**Notes:**

1. This is a SWIFT message sent by the presenting bank or the negotiating bank to the issuing bank expressing their disagreement on the discrepancy based on relative terms of L/C, UCP600 and ISBP745 etc. and asking payment without delay or charging interest due to delayed payment.

2. **COMPLIED WITH** 符合

3. **ISBP745: International Standard Banking Practice for the Examination of Documents Under Documentary Credits** 《关于审核跟单信用证项下单据的国际标准实务》，简称 ISBP，于 2002 年首次经国际商会银行委员会通过（第 645 号出版物）。ISBP745 是 ISBP645 号出版物的首次修订本，于 2013 年正式启用。

4. **HOUSE BILLS OF LADING** 无船承运人提单；代理行提单（非物权凭证）

**Sample 45**

Sequence Number: B4567T

Message Type: 799

Sender Institution: XXXXCNBJXXX

     BANK OF CHINA, THE

     XXX

Receiver Institution: HABBPKKATIC

     HABIB BANK LIMITED

     KARACHI

Message Status: I

Message Input Date: 2018-12-13

Message Priority: N

————Message Content :————

20:Transaction Reference Number  BP18000089

21:Related Reference  0007L/C32301/2018

79:Narrative

  ATTN: L/C DEPARTMENT.

  REFER TO YOUR MT734 DD181211,

L/C NO. 0007L/C32301/2018
AND OUR REF NO. BP18000089,
FOR USD51,000
WE DO NOT ACCEPT YR DISCREPANCIES FOR FOLLOWING REASONS:
+FOR 'L/C EXPIRED': AS TO YOUR L/C, THE DATE OF
EXPIRY IS 181130, THE PLACE OF EXPIRY IS CHINA.
THE BENEFICIARY PRESENTED DOCS TO US ON 20181130, OUR
COVER SCHEDULE DATE IS 20181205, ACCORDING TO UCP600
ARTICLE 14 CLAUSE B, THE PRESENTATION WAS IN VALIDITY PERIOD.
+FOR 'LATE PRESENTATION': AS PER L/C FIELD 48A,
'DOCUMENTS MUST BE PRESENTED WITHIN 21 DAYS
AFTER DATE OF ISSUANCE OF TRANSPORT DOCUMENT BUT
WITHIN THE VALIDITY OF THE CREDIT.' THE DATE OF ISSUANCE
OF B/L IS 20181113, AND THE EXPIRY DATE OF THE L/C IS 181130,
SO THE LAST VALID DAY FOR PRESENTATION WAS ON 20181130
THE PRESENTATION MADE ON 20181130 DIDN'T CONSTITUTE
A LATE PRESENTATION.
THE DOCS ARE FULLY IN COMPLIANCE WITH THE TERMS AND
CONDITIONS OF THE CREDIT. PLS CONFIRM US YOUR ACCEPTANCE
OF THE DOCS AND REMIT THE PROCEEDS ON DUE DATE
WITHOUT ANY DEDUCTION OF DISCREPANCY FEE.
YOUR EARLY REPLY WILL BE HIGHLY APPRECIATED.
B.RGDS.
ITPC, EXPORT DEPT. MR./MS.XXXXX

---

### Notes:

1. This is a SWIFT message sent by the presenting bank or the negotiating bank to the issuing bank expressing their disagreement on the discrepancy on the delayed presentation according to the terms of UCP600 the relative L/C, and asking them acceptance and payment on maturity.

2. **HABIB BANK LIMITED** 哈比卜银行（巴基斯坦第一家商业银行，成立于1947年；也是巴基斯坦最大的私人银行，拥有国内外分行1700多家）

3. **KARACHI** 卡拉奇

4. **ARE FULLY IN COMPLIANCE WITH TERMS** （单据提交）完全符合（信用证）条款和条件

# Sample 46

Sequence Number: CS7B2Q

Message Type: 799

Sender Institution:  XXXXCNBJXXX

     BANK OF CHINA, THE

     XXX

Receiver Institution: UNILPKKA

     UNITED BANK LIMITED

     STATE LIVE BUILDING 1 II CHUNDRIGA

     R ROAD

     KARACHI

Message Status: I

Message Input Date: 2018-12-24

Message Priority: N

————Message Content : ————

20:Transaction Reference Number  BP18000077

21:Related Reference  0071IL/C011952

79:Narrative

  REFER TO YOUR MT734 DATED 20181220

  OUR REF NO. BP18000077

  L/C NO. 0071IL/C011952.

  PLS BE INFORMED WE CAN NOT AGREE WITH YOU ON THE

  DISCREPANCY: 'HEALTH CERT. IN ONE COPY I/O ORIGINAL'.

  PLS NOTICE THAT THE ARTICLE 5 IN FIELD 47A

  STIPULATES 'ORIGINAL HEALTH CERT. SHOULD BE

  SENT DIRECTLY TO THE APPLICANT', BUT IN FIELD 46A

  IT REQUIRED 'HEALTH CERT. IN ONE COPY' WHICH

  SHOULD BE INTERPRETED AS THE REQUIREMENT OF

  AN ORIGINAL HEALTH CERT. ACCORDING TO UCP600.

  THERE IS A CONFLICT BETWEEN THESE TWO ARTICLES.

  HOWEVER, THE BENEFICIARY CONFIRMED THAT THEY HAD

  MADE AN AGREEMENT WITH THE APPLICANT TO SEND

THE ORIGINAL HEALTH CERT. OUTSIDE THE L/C.
SINCE THE L/C CLEARLY INSTRUCTED THE ORIGINAL
HEALTH CERT. TO BE SENT DIRECTLY TO THE APPLICANT,
IT'S OBVIOUS THAT YOU HAVE MADE A MISTAKE WITH THE
CLAUSE IN FIELD 46A:'HEALTH CERT. IN ONE COPY'.
AND AS PER ISBP745 'PRELIMINARY CONSIDERATIONS'
PARA V, 'AN ISSUING BANK SHOULD ENSURE THAT
ANY CREDIT OR AMENDMENT IT ISSUED IS NOT
AMBIGUOUS OR CONFLICTING IN ITS TERMS AND
CONDITIONS', THE RISK OF AMBIGUITY IN YR L/C
SHOULD BE TAKEN BY YOURSELVES.
SO WE KINDLY ASK YOU TO HONOUR THE PAYMENT
AS SOON AS POSSIBLE WITHOUT ANY DISCREPANCY
FEE DEDUCTED.
B.RGDS.
ITPC, EXPORT DEPT. MR./MS.XXXXX

**Notes:**

1. This is a SWIFT message sent by the presenting bank or the negotiating bank to the issuing bank expressing their disagreement on the discrepancy on term about "HEALTH CERTIFICATE in copy instead of in original" according to the term of relative L/C and clauses in ISBP745, which are conflicting and ambiguous, thus asking them to effect payment ASAP.
2. **HEALTH CERT : health certificate** 健康证
3. **COPY** 副本
4. **ORIGINAL** 正本
5. **I/O: instead of** 替代
6. **BE INTERPRETED AS** 可以解释或理解为
7. **ARTICLES** 条款
8. **AMBIGUOUS** 模棱两可，模糊不清

# Sample 47

Sequence Number: C857K9

Message Type: 799

Sender Institution: XXXXCNBJXXX
        BANK OF CHINA, THE
        XXX

Receiver Institution: CITIIE2XTRD
        CITIBANK IRELAND FINANCIAL SERVICES
        DUBLIN

Message Status: I

Message Input Date: 2018-10-31

Message Priority: N

————Message Content :————

20:Transaction Reference Number   BP18000165

21:Related Reference   6131606541

79:Narrative

    REFER TO YOUR MT799 DATED181030
    DOCUMENTS VALUE USD112,320.00
    L/C NO. SB/L/C0190/2018
    ISSUED BY SKYE BANK PL/C.
    PLS BE ADVISED THAT WE CAN NOT AGREE ON YOUR DISCREPANCY.
    WE PRESENTED INVOICES AND PACKING LISTS BOTH IN
    5 ORIGINALS AND 1 COPY. ALTHOUGH THE 5 ORIGINALS
    ARE MADE OF CARBON PAPERS AND IN DIFFERENT COLORS
    (THE FIRST ORIGINAL BLACK, THE OTHERS BLUE),
    THEY ALL APPARENTLY BEAR ORIGINAL BLUE STAMP
    OF THE ISSUER, I.E. THE BENEFICIARY SICHUAN
    LOMON TITANIUM INDUSTRY CO., LTD.
    THEREFORE, AS PER ARTICLE 17 B OF UCP600, THE INVOICES AND
    PACKING LISTS ARE IN COMPLY WITH L/C CLAUSE 46A(3),
    (4) AND THIS PRESENTATION IS COMPLIANT.
    THE DISCREPANCY YOU HAVE MENTIONED IS NULL AND
    VOID.
    WE KINDLY ASK YOU TO EFFECT THE PAYMENT WITHOUT
    DISCREPANCY CHARGE DEDUCTED.
    B.RGDS.

ITPC, EXPORT DEPT. MR./MS.XXXXX

**Notes:**

1. This is a SWIFT message sent by the presenting bank or the negotiating bank to the reimbursing bank expressing their disagreement on the discrepancy on original and duplicate documents presented (inclusive of invoice and packing list ) and its copies by stating the facts based on the relative clauses stipulated in the L/C, thus asking them to effect payment ASAP.
2. **CITIBANK IRELAND FINANCIAL SERVICES**　花旗银行爱尔兰金融服务公司
3. **DUBLIN**　都柏林（爱尔兰首都）
4. **SKYE BANK PL/C**　斯凯银行（尼日利亚最大的金融机构之一）
5. **INVOICES AND PACKING LISTS**　发票和装箱单
6. **CARBON PAPERS**　复写纸
7. **BEAR ORIGINAL BLUE STAMP**　盖有正本蓝色章印
8. **ISSUER**　出票人或票据签发人
9. **I.E.: that is.**　即（I. E. 为 id est 的缩写）

## Sample 48

Sequence Number: C8T0A8

Message Type: 799

Sender Institution: XXXXCNBJXXX
　　　　　　　　　　BANK OF CHINA, THE
　　　　　　　　　　XXX

Receiver Institution: ICBCTWTP017
　　　　　　　　　　 MEGA INTERNATIONAL COMMERCIAL BANK
　　　　　　　　　　 42 HSU CHANG STREET
　　　　　　　　　　 TAIPEI

Message Status: I

Message Input Date: 2018-10-09

Message Priority: N

──────Message Content : ──────

20:Transaction Reference Number　BP1800035

21:Related Reference　F3AASD20226/1

79:Narrative
REFER TO OUR REF. NO. BP18000035, FOR USD.262,656.00
AND BP18000035, FOR USD.131,328.00
UNDER YOUR CREDIT NO. F3AASD20226/1.
YOU DEDUCTED THE DISC.CHGS USD90 FROM EACH OF ABOVE-
MENTIONED BILL FOR DISC:
ISSUE DATE OF THE DRAFT BEFORE B/L DATE.
WE DO NOT AGREE WITH YOU UPON THE DISCREPANCIES
DUE TO THAT UCP600 AND ISBP DO NOT REQUIRE
THAT DRAFT SHALL BE ISSUED LATER THAN THE B/L DATE,
NEITHER DOES THE L/C.
THEREFORE, THE DISCREPANCY FEE (USD180 IN TOTAL) DEDUCTED
WAS NOT REASONABLE AND PLS KINDLY REMIT
USD180 TO US AS SOON AS POSSIBLE.
B.RGDS.
ITPC, EXPORT DEPT. MR./MS.XXXXX

**Notes:**

1. This is a SWIFT message sent by the presenting bank or the negotiating bank to the issuing bank expressing their disagreement on the discrepancy on dates of draft based on the terms of UCP600, ISBP and the L/C, thus asking them to return the discrepancies fee ASAP.

2. **MEGA INTERNATIONAL COMMERCIAL BANK**　兆丰国际商业银行，中国台湾地区大型商业银行之一，总部设在台北

3. **DISC.CHGS: discrepancy charges**　不符点收费

### Sample 49

Sequence Number: C12345
Message Type: 799
Sender Institution: XXXXCNBJXXX
　　　　　　　　　BANK OF CHINA, THE
　　　　　　　　　XXX
Receiver Institution: CENAIDJA

BANK CENTRAL ASIA
WISMA BCA I FLOOR 12 JL. JEND. SUD
IRMAN KAV. 22-23
JAKARTA

Message Status: I

Message Input Date: 2018-08-21

Message Priority: N

————Message Content : ————

20:Transaction Reference Number  BP18000015

21:Related Reference  014ITXX037556

79:Narrative

   ATTN: L/C IMPORT DEPARTMENT.
   REFER TO YOUR MT734 DATED180821
   OUR REF NO. BP18000015
   DOCUMENTS AMOUNT: USD43,000.
   PLS BE ADVISED THAT WE CAN NOT AGREE ON
   YOUR DISCREPANCY.
   AS PER THE OPINION OF THE ICC BANKING COMMISSION
   ON DOCUMENT 470/TA.770 REV2,
   'WHEN A CREDIT INDICATES THAT SHIPMENT IS TO BE
   EFFECTED FROM 'ANY CHINESE PORT' (OR TO 'ANY
   CHINESE PORT' ), IT IS RECOGNISED THAT IN THE
   CONTEXT OF EXAMINATION OF ARTICLE 14(a), THIS
   WOULD INCLUDE HONG KONG BEING SHOWN AS THE PORT
   OF LOADING (OR PORT OF DISCHARGE)'.
   THE L/C STATES THAT PORT OF LOADING SHOULD BE
   ANY CHINESE PORT, AND THE B/L PRESENTED SHOWS
   'HONG KONG' AS PORT OF LOADING.
   THEREFORE, THIS IS NOT A DISCREPANCY. PLS EFFECT
   PAYMENT WITHOUT DEDUCTION OF ANY DISCREPANCY CHARGES.
   B.RGDS.
   ITPC, EXPORT DEPT. MR./MS.XXXXX

**Notes:**

1. This is a SWIFT message sent by the presenting bank or the negotiating bank to the issuing bank expressing their disagreement on the discrepancy on port of loading stipulated in the shipping document based on the opinions of the ICC Banking Commission, thus asking them to effect payment ASAP.
2. **ICC: International Chamber of Commerce** 国际商会
3. **Banking Commission** 银行委员会
4. **PORT OF LOADING** 装货港

## Sample 50

Sequence Number: C6B5ST

Message Type: 799

Sender Institution: XXXXCNBJXXX

                BANK OF CHINA, THE

                XXX

Receiver Institution: CNRBINBBFFC

                CANARA BANK

                PLOT NO. 1 CO, FLOOR 2 SECTOR 34

                CHANDIGARH

Message Status: I

Message Input Date: 2018-10-08

Message Priority: N

————Message Content : ————

20:Transaction Reference Number BP18000067

21:Related Reference 1800FL/C234-21

79:Narrative

    REFER TO YOUR MT750 WITH REF NO.:1800FL/C234-21 DATED181001

    AND OUR REF NO.: BP18000067 FOR USD69,000.00.

    PLS BE ADVISED THAT WE CAN NOT AGREE ON

    YOUR DISCREPANCIES BASED ON THE FOLLOWING REASONS:

    WE HAVE RECEIVED YOUR AMENDMENT NO.1 ON 20 AUG, 2018 WHICH

    POSTPONED THE L/C EXPIRY DATE, LATEST SHIPMENT DATE AND

AMENDMENT NO.2 ON 6 SEP, 2018 WHICH ALLOWED PARTIAL SHIPMENT (IN FIELD 43P). THE DOCUMENTS PRESENTED BY THE BENEFICIARY WERE STRICTLY AS PER THE AMENDED L/C. ACCORDING TO UCP600 ART 10(C), IT IS A COMPLYING PRESENTATION. THEREFORE, THE DISCREPANCY YOU MENTIONED IS NULL AND VOID. WE KINDLY ASK YOU TO RE-EXAMINE THE PRESENTATION AND EFFECT PAYMENT TO US AS SOON AS POSSIBLE WITH NO DEDUCTION OF ANY DISCREPANCY FEE.
B.RGDS.
ITPC, EXPORT DEPT. MR./MS.XXXXX

**Notes:**

1. This is a SWIFT message sent by the presenting bank or the negotiating bank to the issuing bank expressing their disagreement on the discrepancy on the amendment to L/C, thus asking them to effect payment ASAP.
2. **CANARA BANK** 卡纳拉银行（一家印度银行，总部位于印度卡纳塔克邦班加罗尔）
3. **CHANDIGARH** 昌迪加尔，印度北部城市
4. **ALLOWED PARTIAL SHIPMENT** 允许分批装运
5. **NULL AND VOID** 无效

## Sample 51

Sequence Number: CSBM49

Message Type: 799

Sender Institution: XXXXCNBJXXX
　　　　　　　　　BANK OF CHINA, THE
　　　　　　　　　XXX

Receiver Institution: CZNBKRSE
　　　　　　　　　　KOOKMIN BANK, BUSAN BRANCH
　　　　　　　　　　15-1 JUNGANG-DONG 2(1)-GA
　　　　　　　　　　BUSAN KOREA

Message Status: I

Message Input Date: 2018-12-30

Message Priority: N

————Message Content : ————

20:Transaction Reference Number BP18000065

21:Related Reference  M07021310ZX00221

79:Narrative

  +++URGENT+++URGENT+++URGENT+++

 FOURTH TRACER

OUR REF NO. BP18000065

L/C NO. M07021310ZX00221

 FOR AMOUNT USD127,260.00.

PLS BE NOTICED THAT THIS IS THE FOURTH TRACER

AND WE HAVE NOT YET RECEIVED ANY RESPONSE FROM

YOU. WE WOULD LIKE TO EMPHASIZE THAT

THE DISCREPANCIES IN YOUR MT734 DATED181220

ARE NULL AND VOID AND THE PRESENTATION

IS COMPLIANT.

PLS INFORM US THE STATUS OF THE DOCS AND

EFFECT PAYMENT WITHOUT ANY DELAY.

PLS CAREFULLY CONSIDER YOUR GOOD REPUTATION AND

IMMEDIATELY FULFILL YOUR RESPONSIBILITY.

WE RESERVE OUR RIGHT TO CLAIM

INTEREST FOR DELAYED PAYMENT AND WE WILL SEEK

FOR LEGAL SOLUTION.

B.RGDS.

ITPC, EXPORT DEPT. MR./MS.XXXXX

---

**Notes:**

1. This is a top urgent SWIFT message and also a further tracer sent by the negotiating bank to the issuing bank emphasizing their disagreement on the discrepancies thus urging them to effect payment ASAP otherwise charging interest for delayed payment.

2. **FULFILL YOUR RESPONSIBILITY**　履行职责

## （5）Asking the issuing bank to return documents　要求开证行退单

### Sample 52

Sequence Number: 634423

Message Type: 799

Sender Institution: XXXXCNBJXXX
　　　　　　　　　BANK OF CHINA, THE
　　　　　　　　　XXX

Receiver Institution: BBVAESMM
　　　　　　　　　　BANCO BILBAO VIZCAYA ARGENTARIA S.A
　　　　　　　　　　CALLE CLARA DEL REY 26
　　　　　　　　　　MADRID

Message Status: I

Message Input Date: 2018-06-21

Message Priority: N

──────Message Content : ──────

20:Transaction Reference Number　BP18000056

21:Related Reference　6252010100121786

79:Narrative

　　RE YR MT799 DATED20180620

　　CONCERNING OUR DOCUMENTS WITH REF NO. BP18000056

　　UNDER YR L/C NO. 6252010100121786.

　　PLS NOTE THAT THE BENEFICIARY REFUSES THE

　　APPLICANT'S REQUEST IN THE A/M MT799

　　(THE NEW MATURITY WILL BE 25 DEC. 2018 INSTEAD OF 22 AUG, 2018

　　AND THE NEW AMOUNT WILL BE USD98,933.04 INSTEAD

　　OF USD128,612.95)

　　PLS RETURN THE A/M DOCUMENTS TO US AS SOON AS POSSIBLE.

　　YOUR COOPERATION WILL BE HIGHLY APPRECIATED.

　　B.RGDS.

　　ITPC, EXPORT DEPT. MR./MS.XXXXX

### Notes:

1. This is a SWIFT message sent by the negotiating bank to the issuing bank asking them

to return the documents as beneficiary disagree with applicant's request on unit price or payment.

2. **BANCO BILBAO VIZCAYA ARGENTARIA S. A.** 比尔巴鄂比斯开银行，西班牙第二大银行

3. **MADRID** 马德里

## Sample 53

Sequence Number: C06S1H

Message Type: 799

Sender Institution: XXXXCNBJXXX

                BANK OF CHINA, THE

                XXX

Receiver Institution: SCBL/CNSXSHA

                STANDARD CHARTERED BANK

                SHANGHAI

Message Status: I

Message Input Date: 2018-06-09

Message Priority: N

————Message Content : ————

20:Transaction Reference Number  BP18000056

21:Related Reference  333153120411-S

79:Narrative

    ATTN:L/C DEPT.

    RE YOUR MT734 DATED 180530

    OUR REF NO. BP18000056 FOR USD85,000

    AS PER BENEFICIARY'S INSTRUCTION, PLS SEND BACK

    THE FORMER CERTIFICATE OF ORIGIN (1 ORIGINAL

    PLUS TWO COPIES) TO THE FOLLOWING ADDRESS BY

    COURIER:

    ABC CO., LTD

    ADD: …, BEIJING, CHINA

    TEL:…, ATTN:LI MING.

    YR POSTAGE CHGS ARE FOR ACCOUNT OF BENEFICIARY.

            B.RGDS.
            ITPC, EXPORT DEPT. MR./MS.XXXXX

---

**Notes:**

1. This is a SWIFT message sent by the negotiating bank to the issuing bank asking them to return the documents to the beneficiary.
2. **YR POSTAGE CHGS**　你方邮寄费
3. **ARE FOR ACCOUNT OF BENEFICIARY**　由受益人负担

## Sample 54

---

Sequence Number: C0S298

Message Type: 799

Sender Institution: XXXXCNBJXXX
                    BANK OF CHINA, THE
                    XXX

Receiver Institution: SCBL/CNSXSHA
                      STANDARD CHARTERED BANK
                      SHANGHAI

Message Status: I

Message Input Date: 2018-06-24

Message Priority: N

————Message Content : ————

20:Transaction Reference Number　BP18000056

21:Related Reference　333153120411-S

79:Narrative

　　ATTN:L/C DEPT.

　　URGENT

　　RE YR MT734 DATED 180530, OUR MT799 DATED 180609

　　OUR REF NO. BP18000056 FOR USD85,000.

　　IN OUR MT799, WE HAVE REQUESTED YOU TO RETURN

　　THE FORMER CERTIFICATE OF ORIGIN (1 ORIGINAL PLUS

　　TWO COPIES). HOWEVER, THE BENEFICIARY STILL HAS NOT

　　RECEIVED THE DOCUMENTS YET. PLS KINDLY ADVISE

US THE COURIER RECEIPT NO., OR IF YOU HAVE
NOT SENT THE A/M C/O, PLS INFORM US THE CURRENT
STATUS OF THE A/M C/O.
THE A/M DOCUMENT IS OF GREAT IMPORTANCE TO THE
BENEFICIARY, YR KIND AND IMMEDIATE COOPERATION
WILL BE HIGHLY APPRECIATED.
PLS ACKNOWLEDGE THIS MESSAGE BY MT799.
B.RGDS.
ITPC, EXPORT DEPT. MR./MS.XXXXX

**Notes:**

1. This is a SWIFT message sent by the negotiating bank to the issuing bank asking them the status of the relative documents, i.e. whether or not the documents has been returned as the beneficiary has not yet received.
2. **STANDARD CHARTERED BANK**　渣打银行
3. **C/O: Certificate of Origin**　原产地证明书

## Sample 55

Sequence Number: BZW323

Message Type: 799

Sender Institution: XXXXCNBJXXX
　　　　　　　　　BANK OF CHINA, THE
　　　　　　　　　XXX

Receiver Institution: AFKBTRIS
　　　　　　　　　　TURKIYE FINANS KATILIM BANKASI A.S.
　　　　　　　　　　ADNAN KAHVECI CAD. NO: 139, KARTAL
　　　　　　　　　　YAKACIK MEVKII HURRIYET MAH.
　　　　　　　　　　ISTANBUL

Message Status: I

Message Input Date: 2018-04-12

Message Priority: N

————Message Content : ————

20:Transaction Reference Number　BP18000025

21:Related Reference    035CM20180025
79:Narrative
   ATTN FOREIGN TRANSACTIONS/OPERATIONS DEPT
   RE YR MT799 DD20804 CONCERNING L/C NO.
   035CM2080025 (CHGS USD00.00)
   PLS BE ADVISED THAT WE HAVE CONTACTED THE BENE. AND
   CHGS USD00 SHOULD BE BORNE BY THE APPLICANT
   (ABC CO., LTD).
   B.RGDS.
   ITPC, EXPORT DEPT. MR./MS.XXXXX

### Notes:

1. This is a SWIFT message sent by the negotiating bank to the issuing bank stating that the relative charges of exchanging documents is to be borne by applicant I/O beneficiary.
2. **TURKIYE FINANS KATILIM BANKASI A.S.**　土耳其金融银行
3. **ISTANBUL**　伊斯坦布尔（土耳其西北部港市）
4. **ATTN: attention**　由……经办
5. **BENE: beneficiary**　受益人
6. **BE BORNE BY**　由谁承担

（6）**Changing the relative BP terms**　变更相关押汇条款

### Sample 56

Sequence Number: B29876

Message Type: 799

Sender Institution:　XXXXCNBJXXX
                  BANK OF CHINA, THE
                  XXX

Receiver Institution: NATXFRPP
                  NATIXIS
                  30 AVENUE PIERRE MENDES FRANCE
                  FRANCE

Message Status: I

Message Input Date: 2018-09-17

Message Priority: N

———— Message Content : ————

20:Transaction Reference Number  BP18000038

21:Related Reference  C1X572326430056

79:Narrative

    ATTN:IMPORT DC DEPT

    RE OUR BILLS REF BP18000038 UNDER YR L/C NO. C1X572326430056.

    AS INSTRUCTED BY THE BENE, SINCE THE APPLICANT HAS

    PREPAID USD1,518.74 AND ENJOYED A DISCOUNT OF

    USD129.76, THE FINAL SETTLEMENT AMOUNT SHOULD BE

    USD11,327.66 (CLAIMED AMOUNT USD12,976.20 LESS

    USD1,648.50).

    PLS CONTACT THE APPLICANT AND EFFECT PAYMENT TO

    US.

    B.RGDS.

    ITPC, EXPORT DEPT. MR./MS.XXXXX

---

**Notes:**

1. This is a SWIFT message sent by the negotiating bank to the issuing bank informing them that the bill amount due has been changed and asking them to urge the applicant to make payment.
2. **NATIXIS**　法国外贸银行，也称那提西银行（Natixis）或者法国 Natixis 银行，是法国 BPCE 集团旗下的投资银行
3. **CLAIMED AMOUNT**　索偿金额

**Sample 57**

---

Sequence Number: AHB589

Message Type: 799

Sender Institution: XXXXCNBJXXX

                  BANK OF CHINA, THE

                  XXX

Receiver Institution: SBININBBFXD

                    STATE BANK OF INDIA

## KOLKATA (CAL/CUTTA)

Message Status: I

Message Input Date: 2018-07-31

Message Priority: N

————Message Content : ————

20:Transaction Reference Number   BP18000021

21:Related Reference   8850218IR0000428

79:Narrative

   +++URGENT+++

   ATTN:MANAGER L/C DEPT

   RE OUR PRESENTATION FOR USD160,000.00 UNDER

   YOUR L/C NO. 8850218IR0000428

   OUR REF. NO. BP1800002110 DATE JULY 27, 2018

   DHL REF NO. 4932567430.

   DUE TO OUR OVERSIGHT, THERE ARE SOME TYPING ERRORS

   ON THE DRAFT AND BANK COVERING LETTER OF THE A/M.

   PRESENTATION. WE HAVE SENT THE CORRECTED DRAFTS AND BANK

   COVERING LETTER BY DHL ON JULY 31, 2018 TO REPLACE THE

   PREVIOUS ONES.

   WE APOLOGIZE FOR THAT AND APPRECIATE YOUR UNDERSTANDING

   AND COOPERATION. IF THERE IS ANY PROBLEM, PLS ALWAYS

   QUOTE OUR REF NO. BP180000211.

   B.RGDS.

   ITPC, EXPORT DEPT. MR./MS.XXXXX

---

**Notes:**

1. This is a SWIFT message sent by the negotiating bank to the issuing bank apologizing that there are some typing errors on relative documents owing to oversight and then sending the new ones to replace the error ones.
2. **COVERING LETTER**   面函
3. **DHL**   敦豪快递
4. **QUOTE**   引用

## 3. Export business related to OC (outward collection)（出口托收业务）

### （1）Exchanging and/or returning documents by OC　替换或退回出口托收的相关单据

**Sample 58**

---

Sequence Number: 649872

Message Type: 499

Sender Institution: XXXXCNBJXXX
　　　　　　　　　BANK OF CHINA, THE
　　　　　　　　　XXX

Receiver Institution: CDMAMAMC700
　　　　　　　　　　CREDIT DU MAROC
　　　　　　　　　　TRADE CENTER EXPANSION KM 7,300 RO
　　　　　　　　　　UTE DE RABAT AIN SEBAA
　　　　　　　　　　CASABLANCA

Message Status: I

Message Input Date: 2018-11-16

Message Priority: N

————Message Content : ————

20:Transaction Reference Number　OC18000016

21:Related Reference NON

79:Narrative

　　ATTN:IMPORT DEPT.
　　RE OUR DOCUMENTARY COLLECTION
　　REF. NO. OC18000016
　　DD 20181103
　　FOR USD17,109.00
　　AT THE DRAWER'S REQUEST, THE AMOUNT
　　OF A/M COLLECTION HAVE BEEN CHANGED TO
　　USD18,944.00. WE HAVE MAILED THE NEW DRAFTS
　　IN 2 COPIES AND INVOICE IN 8 COPIES TO REPLACE
　　THE ORIGINAL DRAFTS AND INVOICE ON 20181111.
　　(DHL NO. 9123404220)
　　SO PLS CONFIRM US THE ORIGINAL DRAFTS AND
　　INV. ARE INVALID BY SWIFT AS SOON AS POSSIBLE.

PLS AVOID DUPLICATION.

B.RGDS.

ITPC, EXPORT DEPT. MR./MS.XXXXX

**Notes:**

1. This is a SWIFT message sent by the remitting bank to the collecting bank asking them to exchange the relative documents as requested by the drawer（our client）.

2. **CREDIT DU MAROC**　摩洛哥开证银行

3. **CASABLANCA**　卡萨布兰卡是摩洛哥第一大城市，得名于西班牙语，意即"白色的房子"

4. **DOCUMENTARY COLLECTION**　跟单托收

5. **DRAWER**　出票人

6. **INV: invoice**　发票

## Sample 59

Sequence Number: C88964

Message Type: 499

Sender Institution: XXXXCNBJXXX
　　　　　　　　　BANK OF CHINA, THE
　　　　　　　　　XXX

Receiver Institution: ZKBKCHZZ
　　　　　　　　　　ZUERCHER KANTONALBANK
　　　　　　　　　　9 BAHNHOFSTRASSE
　　　　　　　　　　ZURICH

Message Status: I

Message Input Date: 2018-10-28

Message Priority: N

————Message Content:————

20:Transaction Reference Number OC18000056

79:Narrative

　　ATTN:IMPORT COLLECTION DEPT.

　　RE OUR COLLECTION DOCS WITH REF. OC18000056

　　FOR USD296,250.00 ON D/P SIGHT BASIS WITH DHL NO.:4146742504.

AT THE DRAWER'S REQUEST, PLEASE RETURN THE A/M
COLLECTION DOCS TO US AT THE FOLLOWING ADDRESS:
'BANK OF CHINA LIMITED, CHONGQING BRANCH
ADD: …, CHONGQING, CHINA, 400000
SWIFT CODE:XXXXCNBJ678'.
PLS INFORM US THE NAME OF THE COURIER SERVICE AND
THE COURIER RECEIPT NO.
ALL YOUR CHARGES WILL BE BORNE BY THE DRAWER.
SORRY FOR ANY TROUBLE INCURRED. YOUR TIMELY
RESPONSE WILL BE HIGHLY APPRECIATED.
B.RGDS.
ITPC, EXPORT DEPT. MR./MS.XXXXX

**Notes:**

1. This is a SWIFT message sent by the remitting bank to the collecting bank asking them to return the relative documents as requested by the drawer (our client).
2. **ZUERCHER KANTONALBANK** 瑞士苏黎世银行
3. **ZURICH** 苏黎世
4. **D/P SIGHT: documents against payment at sight** 即期付款交单
5. **RECEIPT** 收据

**Sample 60**

Sequence Number: C0520Y

Message Type: 499

Sender Institution: XXXXCNBJXXX
               BANK OF CHINA, THE
               XXX

Receiver Institution: SABBSARI
                SAUDI BRITISH BANK, THE
                AL-AMIR ABDUL AZIZ IBN MOSSAAD IBN
                JALAWI STREET
                RIYADH

Message Status: I

Message Input Date: 2018-06-14

Message Priority: N

————Message Content : ————

20:Transaction Reference Number  OC18000026

79:Narrative

    ATTN:SERVICE CENTRE, IMPORT BILLS DEPT.,

    SALAH AL DIN AYOUBI STREET, RIYADH, SAUDI ARABIA

    TEL:966-1-2257225 FAX:966-1-4706943.

    RE OUR REF NO. OC18000026

    AMOUNT:USD34,410.00

    DRAWER NAME: XXX CO., LTD

    ADD:…YUNNAN CHINA

    DRAWEE NAME: ABC CO., LTD.

    ADD: …, NASSER SQUARE DUBAI, U.A.E

    PLEASE BE ADVISED THAT WE SENT THE A/M DOCS TO

    YOUR BANK IN ERROR ON 180607 AND YOU RECEIVED

    THE DOCS ON 2018-06-12. PLEASE KINDLY SEND

    ALL DOCS BACK TO THE FOLLOWING ADDRESS:

    BANK OF CHINA, YUNNAN BRANCH

    ATTN: INT'L CLEARING CENTER.

    ADD: …, KUNMING, 650000 YUNNAN

    PLEASE ADVISE US THE POSTAGE CHARGES AND THE

    REMITTING ROUTE SO THAT WE CAN REMIT TO YOU.

    WE ARE LOOKING FORWARD TO RECEIVING YOUR EARLIEST

    REPLY.

    B.RGDS.

    ITPC, EXPORT DEPT. MR./MS.XXXXX

---

**Notes:**

1. This is a SWIFT message sent by the remitting bank to the collecting bank asking them to return the relative documents forwarded in error.

2. **SAUDI BRITISH BANK**　沙特英国银行，是一家沙特联合股份公司，也是汇丰集团联营公司。它在伦敦设有分公司。它提供投资银行、商业银行、私人银行、伊斯兰银行服务，受沙特阿拉伯货币局和监事会监管。

3. **RIYADH**　利雅得（沙特阿拉伯首都）
4. **POSTAGE CHARGES**　邮寄费
5. **REMITTING ROUTE**　汇款路径

## Sample 61

Sequence Number: CXSHG9

Message Type: 499

Sender Institution: XXXXCNBJXXX

　　　　　　　　　BANK OF CHINA, THE

　　　　　　　　　XXX

Receiver Institution: ASCBVNVX

　　　　　　　　　　ASIA COMMERCIAL BANK

　　　　　　　　　　442, NGUYEN THI MINH KHAI STREET DISTRICT 3

　　　　　　　　　　HO CHI MINH CITY

Message Status: I

Message Input Date: 2018-02-13

Message Priority: N

──────Message Content : ──────

20:Transaction Reference Number　OC18000089

79:Narrative

　　ATTN:IMPORT COLLECTION DEPT.

　　RE OUR COLLECTION DOCS WITH REF NO. OC14000089

　　AMOUNT:USD47,300.00

　　DRAWER: ABC TRADING CO., LTD

　　DRAWEE: XYZ COMPANY

　　PLEASE BE INFORMED THAT WE SENT THE A/M DOCS TO YOUR GOOD BANK BY MISTAKE ON 20180208 WITH THE DHL NO. 7624344685, AND THE DOCS HAVE BEEN RECEIVED AND SIGNED BY YOUR BANK ON 180211.

　　PLEASE KINDLY CHECK YOUR RECEIPT AND

SEND ALL DOCS TO THE FOLLOWING ADDRESS:
ABC BANK, XXX BRANCH,
ADD: ..., HANOI, VIETNAM.
ALL THE EXPENSES (INCLUDING THE POSTAGE CHARGE
AND THE COMMISSION CHARGE) ARISING THEREFROM
WILL BE BORNE BY THE DRAWER.
PLEASE ADVISE US THE COST BREAKDOWN AND THE
REMITTING ROUTE BY SWIFT SO THAT WE CAN REMIT THE
A/M FEES TO YOU.
YR COOPERATION WILL BE HIGHLY APPRECIATED AND
WE ARE ANXIOUSLY WAITING FOR YOUR RESPONSE.
B.RGDS.
ITPC, EXPORT DEPT. MR./MS.XXXXX

**Notes:**

1. This is a SWIFT message sent by the remitting bank to the collecting bank asking them to transmit the relative documents forwarded by mistake to the correct address.
2. **ASIA COMMERCIAL BAN** 亚洲商业银行，是越南规模最大的私营银行，其总部位于胡志明市
3. **HO CHI MINH CITY** 胡志明市
4. **VIETCOMBANK :Bank of Foreign Trade of Vietnam** 越南对外贸易银行
5. **COST BREAKDOWN** 费用明细

## Sample 62

Sequence Number: CF5678

Message Type: 499

Sender Institution: XXXXCNBJXXX
　　　　　　　　　BANK OF CHINA, THE
　　　　　　　　　XXX

Receiver Institution: SABBSARI
　　　　　　　　　SAUDI BRITISH BANK, THE
　　　　　　　　　AL-AMIR ABDUL AZIZ IBN MOSSAAD IBN JALAWI STREET

RIYADH

Message Status: I

Message Input Date: 2018-07-02

Message Priority: N

————Message Content : ————

20:Transaction Reference Number  OC18000089

21:Related Reference CPM/TDS

79:Narrative

+++TOP URGENT+++TOP URGENT+++.
ATTN:THE SAUDI BRITISH BANK(SABB) TRADE
SERVICE CENTRE, IMPORT BILLS DEPT.,
SALAH AL DIN AYOUBI STREET, RIYADH, SAUDI ARABIA
TEL:…  FAX:…
RE OUR MT499 DD180624
YR REF NO. CPM/TDS
OUR REF NO. OC18000089
AMOUNT:USD34,410.00
DRAWER: ABC TRADING CO., LTD
ADD:…, YUNNAN, CHINA
DRAWEE: XYZ TRADING CO., LTD.
ADD: … DUBAI, U.A.E.
AS OF TODAY, WE STILL HAVEN'T RECEIVED YOUR
REPLY TO EITHER OUR MT499 DD180624 OR THE A/M
DOCUMENTS. SINCE THE GOODS HAVE BEEN
DETAINED AT THE PORT OF DISCHARGE FOR A LONG TIME,
OUR CLIENT IS SO ANXIOUS ABOUT THE GOODS AND
DOCUMENTS. PLEASE KINDLY RETURN THE A/M DOCS
TO US AND TELL US THE EXPRESS NO. SO
THAT WE COULD TRACK THE STATUS OF THE DOCS.
PLEASE ADVISE US THE POSTAGE CHARGES AND THE
REMITTING ROUTE SO THAT WE CAN REMIT TO YOU.
WE ARE LOOKING FORWARD TO YOUR PROMPT RESPONSE.
B.RGDS.
ITPC, EXPORT DEPT. MR./MS.XXXXX

**Notes:**

1. This is a top urgent SWIFT message sent by the remitting bank to the collecting bank asking and tracking the status of the returned documents.
2. **DUBAI** 迪拜
3. **U. A. E: United Arab Emirates** 阿拉伯联合酋长国
4. **DETAIN** 滞留
5. **EXPRESS** 快递
6. **TRACK** 查询

（2）Changing relative terms by OC 变更出口托收的相关条款

**Sample 63**

---

Sequence Number: C3HR21

Message Type: 499

Sender Institution: XXXXCNBJXXX
                    BANK OF CHINA, THE
                    XXX

Receiver Institution: ETHNGRAA
                      NATIONAL BANK OF GREECE S.A.
                      86 AEOLOU STREET
                      ATHENS

Message Status: I

Message Input Date: 2018-08-02

Message Priority: N

——————Message Content : ——————

20:Transaction Reference Number  OC18000066

21:Related Reference  36788808180052009

79:Narrative
   ATTN: NBG KALOCHORIOY BRANCH (839)
   REF OUR DOCS COLLECTION UNDER OUR
   REF NO. OC18000066
   DRAWEE: XYZ CO., LTD
   DRAWER: ABC TRADING CO., LTD

COLLECTION AMT: USD67,500.00.

REFER TO YR MT499 DATED AUG 02, 2018

AS PER THE DRAWER'S INSTRUCTION, PLEASE CHANGE THE PAYMENT TERMS FROM 'CAD AT SIGHT' TO 'DELIVERY DOCUMENTS AGAINST PAYMENT AT 45 DAYS FROM BILL OF LADING DATE (I.E.180722)'

OTHERS REMAIN UNCHANGED.

B.RGDS.

ITPC, EXPORT DEPT. MR./MS.XXXXX

**Notes:**

1. This is a SWIFT message sent by the remitting bank to the collecting bank asking them to change the relative payment terms by substituting TENOR D/P for CAD.
2. **NATIONAL BANK OF GREECE S.A.** 希腊国民银行
3. **ATHENS** 雅典
4. **DRAWEE** 受票人
5. **CAD AT SIGHT**[①]: cash against document at sight 即期凭单付款
6. **DOCUMENTS AGAINST PAYMENT** 付款交单

## Sample 64

Sequence Number: BD78H9

Message Type: 499

Sender Institution: XXXXCNBJXXX

　　　　　　　　　BANK OF CHINA, THE

　　　　　　　　　XXX

Receiver Institution: HDFCINBB

　　　　　　　　　HDFC BANK LTD

---

① CAD at sight（cash against documents at sight，即期凭单付款）的一般做法：卖方在合同中规定在出口地银行提示单据，收取货款。出货后，卖方将装运事实通知买方，买方依约将货款向银行申请汇付，汇款银行将款项汇给出口地的指定付款银行，后者收到后，按照汇款指示通知卖方。卖方提示单据，请求付款。付款银行取得单据后付款，然后将单据寄交进口地的汇款银行，该银行收到单据后，通知买方领取单据。D/P at sight（documents against payment at sight，即期付款交单）的一般做法：出口商在合同中规定支付方式为即期付款交单。出货后，卖方将单据通过出口地的银行（托收行）寄单给买方当地的银行（代收行）。代收行收到单据后，通知买方，买方付款后拿单据。CAD和D/P sight 都是客户付款在先，拿单在后；但前者是发生在国内，后者是发生在国外。

Message Status: I

Message Input Date: 2018-04-08

Message Priority: N

——————Message Content : ——————

20:Transaction Reference Number  OC18000035

21:Related Reference  240BC05180640001

79:Narrative

  ATTN:IMPORT COLLECTION DEPT.

  CONCERNING OUR DOCUMENTARY COLLECTION

  WITH REF NO. OC18000035 FOR USD 27,562.50

  DRAWEE: ABC CO., LTD

  DRAWER: XYZ CO., LTD

  AT THE REQUEST OF DRAWER, PLS DELIVER THE DOCUMENTS AGAINST PAYMENT AT SIGHT FOR USD19,293.75 INSTEAD OF USD 27,562.50.

  OTHERS REMAIN UNCHANGED.

  B.RGDS.

  ITPC, EXPORT DEPT. MR./MS.XXXXX

**Notes:**

1. This is an SWIFT message sent by the remitting bank to the collecting bank asking them to change the amount to USD19,293.75 instead of USD 27,562.50.

2. **HDFC BANK LTD**　　HDFC 银行，印度一家私营银行，由印度住房开发金融公司持股，目前是印度第四大银行，印度最大的抵押放款银行。2009 年 8 月 3 日开始，HDFC 银行获批在中国香港从事持牌商业银行业务。

## Sample 65

Sequence Number: CC4D8E

Message Type: 499

Sender Institution: XXXXCNBJXXX
      BANK OF CHINA, THE
      XXX

Receiver Institution: HANDSESSGBG

SVENSKA HANDELSBANKEN

Message Status: I

Message Input Date: 2018-01-09

Message Priority: N

————Message Content : ————

20:Transaction Reference Number  OC18000245

21:Related Reference  FBCI038165

79:Narrative

   ATTN: COLLECTION DEPT.

   REFER TO YOUR REF. FBCI038165

   UNDER OUR REF. OC18000245 FOR USD80,752.50

   DRAWER: ABC CO., LTD

   DRAWEE: XYZ (PTY), LTD

   AS AUTHORIZED BY THE DRAWER, THE TOTAL COLLECTION AMOUNT

   IS NOW DECREASED TO USD72,677.25 I/O USD80,752.50 AS

   ORIGINALLY STATED.

   ALL OTHER TERMS AND CONDITIONS REMAIN UNCHANGED.

   THANKS FOR YR COOPERATION.

   B.RGDS.

   ITPC, EXPORT DEPT. MR./MS.XXXXX

**Notes:**

1. This is a SWIFT message sent by the remitting bank to the collecting bank asking them to change the amount to USD72,677.25 I/O USD80,752.50 with all other terms unchanged.

2. **SVENSKA HANDELSBANKEN**　瑞典商业银行

（3）**Collecting proceeds by OC**　代收货款

**Sample 66**

---

Sequence Number: C4K8N9

Message Type: 499

Sender Institution: XXXXCNBJXXX

        BANK OF CHINA, THE

        XXX

Receiver Institution: DBSSINBB
　　　　　　　　　DBS BANK LTD, MUMBAI BRANCH
　　　　　　　　　FORT HOUSE FLOOR 3 221, DR. D. N. R-
　　　　　　　　　OAD, FORT
　　　　　　　　　MUMBAI

Message Status: I

Message Input Date: 2018-08-27

Message Priority: N

————————Message Content : ————————

20:Transaction Reference Number　OC18000021

21:Related Reference　811-03-01811752

79:Narrative

　　RE YR REF. NO.:811-03-0181752

　　ATTN IMP COLLECTION DEPT

　　COLLECTING BANK

　　DBS BANK LTD., MUMBAI

　　3RD FL., FORT HOUSE, 221 DR. D. N.

　　ROAD, FORT, MUMBAI-400001, INDIA

　　ATTN:TRADE SERVICES DEPT

　　DRAWEE ABC CO., LTD

　　ADD: ... (INDIA)

　　OUR REF. OC18000021

　　COLLECTION AMT USD38,430.00

　　PLS ADVISE THE PRESENT STATUS OF

　　THE CAPTIONED DOCS.

　　B.RGDS.

　　ITPC, EXPORT DEPT. MR./MS.XXXXX

## Notes:

1. This is a standardized SWIFT message sent by the remitting bank to the collecting bank asking them the status of the proceeds collected.

2. **DBS BANK LTD, MUMBAI BRANCH: The Development Bank of Singapore Limited**　新展银行孟买分行

3. **THE CAPTIONED DOCS**　标题下的单据

# Sample 67

Sequence Number: C434E0

Message Type: 499

Sender Institution: XXXXCNBJXXX

        BANK OF CHINA, THE

        XXX

Receiver Institution: SBININBB582

        STATE BANK OF INDIA

        LHO BUILDING FLOOR 1 C-6, G BLOCK,

        BANDRA KURLA COMPLEX

        MUMBAI

Message Status: I

Message Input Date: 2018-08-20

Message Priority: N

————Message Content : ————

20:Transaction Reference Number  OC18000078

21:Related Reference  0505012GS0004470

79:Narrative

    RE OUR COLLECTION NO. OC18000078

    FOR USD68,550.00

    DRAWEE: ABC TRADING PVT., LTD.

    DRAWER: XYZ CO., LTD

    INVOICE NO.:XPRHJ1278

    TENOR:90 DAYS AFTER B/L DATE

    DUE DATE:180224.

    WE HAVE NOT RECEIVED YR PAYMENT UNTIL NOW.

    PLS URGENTLY ADVISE THE PRESENT STATUS OF

    THE CAPTIONED DOCS IMMEDIATELY.

    B.RGDS.

    ITPC, EXPORT DEPT. MR./MS.XXXXX

**Notes:**

1. This is a non-standardized SWIFT message sent by the remitting bank to the collecting

bank urging them to advise the status of the proceeds collected.

2. **STATE BANK OF INDIA**　印度国家银行

3. **DUE DATE**　到期日

## 4. Import business related to IC (inward collection)（进口托收的相关业务）

### （1）Making payment or nonpayment by drawee　受票人付款或未付款

#### Sample 68

---

Sequence Number: C95678

Message Type: 499

Sender Institution:　XXXXCNBJXXX
　　　　　　　　　　BANK OF CHINA, THE
　　　　　　　　　　XXX

Receiver Institution: BNPAHKHHGCG
　　　　　　　　　　BNP

Message Status: I

Message Input Date: 2018-11-20

Message Priority: N

――――――Message Content : ――――――

20:Transaction Reference Number　IC18000022

21:Related Reference　EDEX8008839HKG

79:Narrative

　　ATTN: COMMODITY FINANCE OPERATIONS
　　YOUR REF: EDEX8008839HKG
　　OUR REF: IC18000022
　　BILL AMOUNT: USD 26,100,390.48
　　DRAWER: ABC TRADING CO., LTD
　　DRAWEE: XYZ EXP.CO., LTD.
　　WE ARE INFORMED BY THE DRAWEE THAT THEY HAVE
　　REACHED AN AGREEMENT WITH THE DRAWER TO PAY
　　AN AMOUNT OF USD5,898,000.00. PLEASE CONTACT THE
　　DRAWER AND CONFIRM IT BY AUTHENTICATED SWIFT
　　AS SOON AS POSSIBLE.

        B.RGDS.
        ITPC, IMPORT DEPT. MR./MS.XXXXX

## Notes:

1. This is a SWIFT message sent by the collecting bank to the remitting bank informing them that the drawee (i.e. importer) is going to make partial payment based on the agreement of the drawer (i.e. exporter) with them.
2. **BNP** 法国巴黎银行
3. **AUTHENTICATED SWIFT** 加密报文

## Sample 69

Sequence Number: CA789S

Message Type: 499

Sender Institution: XXXXCNBJXXX
                    BANK OF CHINA, THE
                    XXX

Receiver Institution: CIBCCATT
                     CANADIAN IMPERIAL BANK OF COMMERCE
                     PAYMENT CENTRE SUITE 700 595 BAY STREET
                     TORONTO

Message Status: I

Message Input Date: 2018-12-10

Message Priority: N

————————Message Content : ————————

20:Transaction Reference Number  IC18000056

21:Related Reference  OUDT422190

79:Narrative

    URGENT+++URGENT+++URGENT

    ……………………

    RE:YOUR REF. OUDT422190 FOR EUR8,311.38

    OUR REF. IC18000056

    DRAWEE: ABC CO., LTD.

    DRAWER: XYZ COMPANY INC.

WE RECEIVED YOUR DOCUMENTS FOR COLLECTION ON DEC. 05 2018.

PLEASE BE ADVISED THAT THE DRAWEE REFUSED TO PAY THE COURIER CHARGES EUR 68.17.

WE WILL HOLD THE DOCUMENTS AT YOUR DISPOSAL PENDING YOUR FURTHER INSTRUCTION.

B.RGDS.

ITPC, IMPORT DEPT. MR./MS.XXXXX

**Notes:**

1. This is an urgent SWIFT message sent by the collecting bank to the remitting bank informing them that the drawee refuses to pay the courier charges as requested by the drawer.
2. **CANADIAN IMPERIAL BANK OF COMMERCE**　加拿大帝国商业银行
3. **COURIER CHARGES**　快递费
4. **AT YOUR DISPOSAL**　听任你方处置
5. **PENDING YOUR FURTHER INSTRUCTION**　等候你方进一步通知

## Sample 70

Sequence Number: B78G15

Message Type: 499

Sender Institution: XXXXCNBJXXX
　　　　　　　　　BANK OF CHINA, THE
　　　　　　　　　XXX

Receiver Institution: HSBCHKHHHKH
　　　　　　　　　　HONGKONG AND SHANGHAI BANKING CORPO
　　　　　　　　　　HONGKONGBANK BUILDING  SUITE 123 1
　　　　　　　　　　QUEEN'S ROAD CENTRAL
　　　　　　　　　　HONG KONG

Message Status: I

Message Input Date: 2018-01-24

Message Priority: N

————Message Content : ————

20:Transaction Reference Number  IC18000056

21:Related Reference   BPPTST159121CCC

79:Narrative

REFER TO YOUR MT499 DATED20180116

YR REF. BPPTST159121CCC

OUR REF. IC18000056

BILL AMOUNT:USD24,200.00.

THE DRAWEE CLAIMED THAT THEY HAVE PAID THE A/M

COLLECTION TO DRAWER DIRECTLY THROUGH

T/T REMITTANCE. PLEASE CONFIRM THIS MATTER

WITH THE DRAWER AND AUTHORIZE US TO DELIVER

THE DOCUMENTS TO THE DRAWEE FREE OF PAYMENT.

B.RGDS.

ITPC, IMPORT DEPT. MR./MS.XXXXX

---

**Notes:**

1. This is a SWIFT message sent by the collecting bank to the remitting bank informing them that the drawee has remitted the proceeds to the drawer by T/T and asking them to authorize to deliver documents free of payment.

2. **HONGKONG AND SHANGHAI BANKING CORP**  汇丰银行

3. **T/T**：**telegraphic transfer**  电汇

## Sample 71

---

Sequence Number: C5CW61

Message Type: 499

Sender Institution: XXXXCNBJXXX

　　　　　　　　BANK OF CHINA, THE

　　　　　　　　XXX

Receiver Institution: COBADEFF360

　　　　　　　　COMMERZBANK AG

　　　　　　　　ESSEN

Message Status: I

Message Input Date: 2018-09-17

Message Priority: N

————Message Content : ————

20:Transaction Reference Number   IC18000063

21:Related Reference   ESEEI101532109

79:Narrative

  RE:YOUR REF. ESEEI101532109

  COLLECTING AMOUNT:EUR3,785.00

  OUR REF. IC18000063

  DRAWER: ABC CO., KG

  DRAWEE: XYZ TRADE CO., LTD

  YOUR COLLECTION ORDER SHOWS THAT THE TENOR IS AT

  SIGHT. HOWEVER, THE INVOICE ENCLOSED SHOWS THAT TENOR IS

  D/P WITHIN 30 DAYS AFTER RECEIPT OF INVOICE.

  PLEASE KINDLY INVESTIGATE AND CONFIRM US THE

  PRECISE INSTRUCTIONS AT YOUR EARLIEST CONVENIENCE.

  B.RGDS.

  ITPC, IMPORT DEPT. MR./MS.XXXXX

**Notes:**

1. This is a SWIFT message sent by the collecting bank to the remitting bank inquiring the precise payment tenor as the collection order gives an uncertain one.

2. **COMMERZBANK AG**　德国商业银行，成立于1870年，德国第二大银行，2004年年底资产总额约为4200亿欧元。公司的业务包括个人客户、国际私人银行、集团公司、国际银行关系、银行投资等方面。2014年11月12日，中国银行和德国商业银行签署协议，以后可以直接从法兰克福为客户提供人民币支付业务。

3. **ESSEN**　埃森，德国西部北莱茵-威斯特法伦州的一个非县辖城市，城市位于鲁尔工业区，所属行政区首府为杜塞尔多夫，是德国第九大城市。

4. **COLLECTION ORDER**　托收委托书，托收指示

5. **AT YOUR EARLIEST CONVENIENCE**　尽快

### Sample 72

Sequence Number: CW1963

Message Type: 499

Sender Institution: XXXXCNBJXXX

BANK OF CHINA, THE
XXX

Receiver Institution: BKCHHKHH
BANK OF CHINA (HONG KONG) LIMITED
BANK OF CHINA CENTER FLOOR 19, OLY
MPIAN CITY 11 HOI FAI ROAD WEST KOW LOON
HONG KONG

Message Status: I

Message Input Date: 2018-05-24

Message Priority: N

————Message Content :————

20:Transaction Reference Number  IC18000037

21:Related Reference  265A18EC002853

79:Narrative

   RE: YOUR REF. 265A18EC002853

      OUR REF. IC18000037

      DRAWEE : XYZ CO., LTD.

      DRAWER : ABC TRADING (HK) LTD.

      AMOUNT : USD8,453,702.19

WE CONFIRM HAVING EFFECTED PAYMENT AS INSTRUCTED FOR USD 8,453,642.19 VALUE DATE 20180521 THROUGH BANK OF CHINA, LONDON WITH DEDUCTION OF OUR CABLE CHARGES USD60.00. REGARDS.

B.RGDS.

ITPC, IMPORT DEPT. MR./MS.XXXXX

## Notes:

This is a SWIFT message sent by the collecting bank to the remitting bank replying to their inquiry of non-receipt of proceeds that the payment has been made as instructed.

## Sample 73

Sequence Number: BM0927

Message Type: 499

Sender Institution: XXXXCNBJXXX
　　　　　　　　　BANK OF CHINA, THE
　　　　　　　　　XXX
Receiver Institution: PNBPUS33PHL
　　　　　　　　　　WACHOVIA BANK, NA
　　　　　　　　　　530 WALNUT STREET
　　　　　　　　　　PHILADELPHIA, PA

Message Status: I

Message Input Date: 180610

Message Priority: N

————Message Content : ————

20: Transaction Reference Number  IC18000055

21: Related Reference TX021837DRU

79: Narrative

　　ATTN:COLLECTION DEPT
　　RE YOUR REF NO. TX021837DRU DATED JUN. 7, 2018
　　FOR AMOUNT: USD13,260.00
　　UNDER OUR REF NO. IC18000055
　　DRAWER: ABC CO., LTD
　　DRAWEE: XYZ TRADE CO., LTD.
　　　　　YOUR COVERING LETTER SHOWS CERT. OF ORIGIN IN
　　　　　FOUR FOLDS BUT WE HAVE ONLY RECEIVED ONE FOLD.
　　　　　KINDLY CLARIFY TO US THE CORRECT DOCUMENT NUMBER.
　　　　　BEST REGARDS.
　　　　　B.RGDS.
　　　　　ITPC, IMPORT DEPT. MR./MS.XXXXX

### Notes:

1. This is a SWIFT message sent by the collecting bank to the remitting bank inquiring the numbers of documents as the real numbers and the ones that indicated in covering letter differ.

2. **WACHOVIA BANK, NA**　美联银行，又称瓦霍维亚银行。于2001年由美联银行同瓦霍维亚银行合并而成，并沿用了后者的名字，是向零售、经纪与公司客户提供金融服务的大公司之一。

3. **NA**　national 的缩写形式，表示美国国民银行，即为联邦注册银行。

# Sample 74

Sequence Number: C76S58

Message Type: 999

Sender Institution: XXXXCNBJXXX
            BANK OF CHINA, THE
            XXX

Receiver Institution: CCOPFRPP
            CREDIT COOPERATIF
            33 RUE DES TROIS FONTANOT
            NANTERRE

Message Status: I

Message Input Date: 2018-10-28

Message Priority: N

————Message Content : ————

20:Transaction Reference Number   IC18000079

21:Related Reference   00098EE0466201

79:Narrative

   ATTN:COLLECTION DEPT.

   REFER TO YOUR REF NO. 00098EE0466201

   FOR EUR44,410.89

   DELIVERY TERM: D/P 30 DAYS AFTER SIGHT.

   PLEASE BE ADVISED THAT WE HAVE PAID AS

   YOUR INSTRUCTION AND THE DETAILS ARE GIVEN

   AS FOLLOWING:

   AMOUNT PAID: EUR44,330.89

   VALUE DATE: 181028

   CHARGES: EUR30 DEDUCTED FOR CABLE FEE AND

   EUR50 DEDUCTED FOR COMMISSION FEE.

   B.RGDS.

   ITPC, IMPORT DEPT. MR./MS.XXXXX

**Notes:**

1. This is a SWIFT message sent in MT999 by the collecting bank to the remitting bank informing them that the payment has been effected with some charges and fees deducted.
2. **CREDIT COOPERATIF**  信（用）贷合作银行
3. **NANTERRE**  楠泰尔，法国巴黎市西郊工业区，位于巴黎盆地，塞纳河曲中

## （2）Returning the relative documents  退单

### Sample 75

Sequence Number: C78912

Message Type: 499

Sender Institution: XXXXCNBJXXX
      BANK OF CHINA, THE
      XXX

Receiver Institution: BOFAUS3N
      BANK OF AMERICA, N. A.
      100 WEST 33RD STREET
      NEW YORK, NY

Message Status: I

Message Input Date: 2018-11-21

Message Priority: N

——————Message Content : ——————

20:Transaction Reference Number  IC18000067

21:Related Reference  81262207SC

79:Narrative

  RE YOUR DOCUMENTS
  UNDER YOUR REF. 81262207SC
  FOR AMOUNT USD 238,096.62
  OUR REF NO. IC18000067.
  WE RETURNED THE A/M DOCUMENTS TO YOU TODAY AS PER
  YOUR INSTRUCTION WITH DHL COURIER NO.: 8642208746.
  PLS PAY THE HANDLING CHGS USD XXXX TO OUR H. O.
  ACCOUNT WITH (H. O. A/C BANK'S SWIFT CODE) QUOTING OUR REF.
  WE HAVE CLOSED OUR FILES.

        B.RGDS.
        ITPC, IMPORT DEPT. MR./MS.XXXXX

**Notes:**

1. This is a SWIFT message sent by the collecting bank to the remitting bank replying to them that relative documents have been returned as instructed by their client/the drawer.
2. **BANK OF AMERICA, N. A.** 美国银行
3. **DHL COURIER** 敦豪快递
4. **HANDLING CHGS** 服务费，手续费（此文中表示退单相关费用）
5. **H. O.: head office** 总行

## Sample 76

Sequence Number: B7MN68

Message Type: 499

Sender Institution: XXXXCNBJXXX
　　　　　　　　　BANK OF CHINA, THE
　　　　　　　　　XXX

Receiver Institution: HSBCHKHHHKH
　　　　　　　　　HONGKONG AND SHANGHAI BANKING CORPO
　　　　　　　　　HONGKONGBANK BUILDING SUITE 123 1
　　　　　　　　　QUEEN'S ROAD CENTRAL
　　　　　　　　　HONG KONG

Message Status: I

Message Input Date: 2018-01-25

Message Priority: N

————Message Content :————

20:Transaction Reference Number  IC18000026

21:Related Reference  BPPKTG733019CCC

79:Narrative
　　RE YOUR DOCUMENTS
　　UNDER YOUR REF. BPPKTG733019CCC
　　FOR AMOUNT USD175,995.48.
　　PLEASE BE INFORMED THAT THE DRAWEE REQUIRES TO RETURN

A/M DOCUMENTS.

PLEASE OBTAIN THE DRAWER'S CONSENT AND CONFIRM US BY AUTHENTICATED SWIFT AS SOON AS POSSIBLE.

B.RGDS.

ITPC, IMPORT DEPT. MR./MS.XXXXX

**Notes:**

1. This is a SWIFT message sent by the collecting bank to the remitting bank informing them that relative documents should be returned as requested by their client/the drawee as the quality of the shipped goods are not up to the required standard.
2. **DRAWER'S CONSENT**　出票人（出口方）的同意
3. **AUTHENTICATED SWIFT**　加密报文

## Sample 77

Sequence Number: C89BBC

Message Type: 499

Sender Institution: XXXXCNBJXXX
　　　　　　　　　BANK OF CHINA, THE
　　　　　　　　　XXX

Receiver Institution: ESSEDE5F
　　　　　　　　　　SEB AG
　　　　　　　　　　ULMENSTRASSE 30
　　　　　　　　　　FRANKFURT AM MAIN

Message Status: I

Message Input Date: 2018-09-12

Message Priority: N

————Message Content :————

20:Transaction Reference Number　IC18000022

21:Related Reference DD3701VC13631218

79:Narrative

　　RE YOUR MT499 WITH REF. NO. DD3701VC13631218

　　PLS BE INFORMED THAT WE WILL RETURN THE

　　A/M DOCUMENTS TO YOU.

PLS CHECK THE MAIL INFORMATION:
THE RECEIVER:SEB AG
MAILING ADDRESS:
HANS-JURGEN WAGNER GOLTSTEINSTR 28
DUSSELDORF 40211 GERMANY
PH:021158340551
IF THE ABOVE MESSAGE IS INCORRECT, PLEASE
GIVE US THE RIGHT MAIL INFORMATION.
B.RGDS.
ITPC, IMPORT DEPT. MR./MS.XXXXX

**Notes:**
1. This is a SWIFT message sent by the collecting bank to the remitting bank asking them to confirm the mail address to which the relative documents are to be returned.
2. **SEB AG** 德国公共经济银行
3. **FRANKFURT AM MAIN** 法兰克福（Frankfurt），正式全名为：美因河畔法兰克福（德语:Frankfurt am Main），以便与位于德国东部的奥得河畔法兰克福（德语:Frankfurt an der Oder）相区别。它是德国第五大城市及黑森州最大城市，德国乃至欧洲重要的工商业、金融和交通中心。

（3）**Making acceptance under OC and IC** 出口托收和进口托收项下的承兑
**Sample 78**

Sequence Number: CE02E9
Message Type: 499
Sender Institution: XXXXCNBJXXX
                BANK OF CHINA, THE
                XXX
Receiver Institution: KASITHBK
                KASIKORNBANK PUBLIC COMPANY LIMITED
                KASIKORNBANK 1 SOI KASIKORNTHAI RA
                TBURANA ROAD
                BANGKOK
Message Status: I

Message Input Date: 2018-02-14

Message Priority: N

————————Message Content : ————————

20:Transaction Reference Number  OC18000025

21:Related Reference  OC1801

79:Narrative

  RE YR MT412 DATED 180213

  UNDER YR REF NO. OC1801

  OUR REF NO. OC18000025.

  PLS BE INFORMED THAT WE HAVE RECEIVED YOUR ADVICE OF

  ACCEPTANCE WITH THE MATURITY DATE 20180414 AND

  THE ACCEPTED AMOUNT USD10,000.00.

  BUT THE ACTUAL AMOUNT OF THIS COLLECTION

  SHOULD BE USD15,000.00, AND THE MATURITY DATE

  (60 DAYS AFTER B/L DATE 20180114) SHOULD BE 20180317.

  PLS CORRECT THE A/M INFORMATIONS AND CONFIRM US

  AS SOON AS POSSIBLE.

  B.RGDS.

  ITPC, EXPORT DEPT. MR./MS.XXXXX

---

**Notes:**

1. This is a SWIFT message sent by the remitting bank to the collecting bank informing them that there are some errors in the accepted amount and the maturity date related to the relative acceptance.

2. **KASIKORNBANK PUBLIC COMPANY LIMITED**  泰华农民银行，是泰国第三大银行，创建于1945年6月，目前在中国及其他国家和地区有多家海外分行。

3. **BANGKOK**  曼谷，泰国的首都

4. **ADVICE OF ACCEPTANCE**  承兑通知

5. **B/L DATE: bill of lading date**  提单日

**Sample 79**

---

Sequence Number: C95628

Message Type: 499

Sender Institution: XXXXCNBJXXX
BANK OF CHINA, THE
XXX

Receiver Institution: ESSEDE5F
SEB AG
ULMENSTRASSE 30
FRANKFURT AM MAIN

Message Status: I

Message Input Date: 2018-11-20

Message Priority: N

————Message Content :————

20:Transaction Reference Number  IC18000065

21:Related Reference DD3701VC18631557

79:Narrative

　　ATTN: COLLECTION DEPT.
　　RE YOUR BILL REF NO. DD3701VC18631557
　　FOR AMOUNT OF USD 608,980.24
　　TENOR: 30 DAYS AFTER SIGHT
　　THE A/M BILL HAS BEEN ACCEPTED TO
　　BE MATURE ON 180120.
　　HOWEVER, IF THE MATURITY DATE FALLS
　　ON OUR NATIONAL PUBLIC DATE,
　　PAYMENT WILL BE POSTPONED ACCORDINGLY.
　　B.RGDS.
　　ITPC, IMPORT DEPT. MR./MS.XXXXX

### Notes:

1. This is a SWIFT message sent by the collecting bank to the remitting bank informing them that the relative bill has been accepted and payment will be postponed if the maturity date falls on national public date.

2. **NATIONAL PUBLIC DATE**　公共假日

## 5. Business related to L/G (letter of guarantee)（担保函业务）

### (1) L/G on advance payment[①]　预付款保函
### Sample 80

Sequence Number: J458TW

Message Type: 760

Sender Institution: XXXXCNBJXXX
　　　　　　　　　BANK OF CHINA, THE
　　　　　　　　　XXX

Receiver Institution: IBKOKRSE
　　　　　　　　　　INDUSTRIAL BANK OF KOREA
　　　　　　　　　　50,ULCHIRO 2-GA,CHUNG-GU
　　　　　　　　　　SEOUL

Message Status: I

Message Input Date: 2018-09-30

Message Priority: N

————Message Content:————

27:Sequence of Total　1/1

20:Transaction Reference Number　DG18000015

23:Further Identification　ISSUE

30:Date　180930

40C:Applicable Rules　URDG

77C:Details of Guarantee
　　　TO: ABC CO., LTD
　　　ADD: …, KOREA
　　　ISSUING DATE: SEP. 30, 2018
　　　DEAR SIRS,

---

[①] 在贸易合同中，预付款保函（advance payment guarantee）也可以是定金保函（down-payment guarantee）。在大额交易中，买方或业主在合约签订后的一定时间内需预先向供货方支付一定比例的款项作为执行合同的启动资金，由于该款项是对供货方在履约之前所作的预付，买方为了避免日后由于供货方拒绝履行义务或者无法履行义务，却不退款而无端遭到损失，通常要求供货方在买方预付之前的若干日内通过其银行开出预付保函，由银行做出承诺，一旦申请人未能履约或者是无法全部履约（不管这种行为是有意的或者是无意造成的），担保行将在收到买方提出的索赔后，向其返还这笔与预付金额等值的款项，或者相当于合约尚未履行部分相当比例的预付金额，使买方能够顺利地收回所预付的款项。

RE: OUR IRREVOCABLE GUARANTEE NO. DG18000015.
WE HAVE BEEN INFORMED THAT XYZ CO., LTD(ADD:…, SHENZHEN, CHINA) (HEREINAFTER CALLED 'APPLICANT') HAS ENTERED INTO THE CONTRACT NO. 123 DATED AUG. 08, 2018 (HEREINAFTER CALLED 'CONTRACT')
WITH YOU. FURTHERMORE, WE UNDERSTAND THAT, ACCORDING TO THE CONDITIONS OF CONTRACT, AN ADVANCE PAYMENT IS TO BE MADE AGAINST AN ADVANCE PAYMENT GUARANTEE. AT THE REQUEST OF THE APPLICANT, WE, BANK OF CHINA LIMITED, SHENZHEN BRANCH (ADDRESS:..,SHENZHEN CHINA) HEREBY ISSUE OUR IRREVOCABLE ADVANCE PAYMENT GUARANTEE NO. DG17000015 (HEREINAFTER REFERRED TO AS 'THE GUARANTEE') IN FAVOR OF ABC CO., LTD.

(ADD:…, KOREA) (HEREINAFTER CALLED 'BENEFICIARY') FOR USD17,400.00 (SAY US DOLLARS SEVENTEEN THOUSAND FOUR HUNDRED ONLY).
WE HEREBY UNDERTAKE TO PAY YOU ANY AMOUNT NOT EXCEEDING USD17,400.00 (SAY US DOLLARS SEVENTEEN THOUSAND FOUR HUNDRED ONLY), UPON RECEIPT OF YOUR COMPLYING DULY SIGNED DEMAND FOR PAYMENT STATING THAT THE APPLICANT IS IN BREACH OF HIS OBLIGATION(S) UNDER THE CONTRACT AND THE RESPECT IN WHICH THE APPLICANT IS IN BREACH. FOR THE PURPOSE OF IDENTIFICATION, YOUR DEMAND FOR PAYMENT MUST BE PRESENTED TO US BY MAIL THROUGH YOUR BANK, WHICH IS REQUESTED TO CONFIRM US THE AUTHENTICITY OF THE SIGNATURE(S) APPEARING ON THE DEMAND BY A SEPERATE AUTHENTICATED SWIFT.

THIS GUARANTEE SHALL ONLY BECOME EFFECTIVE ONCE THE A/M ADVANCE PAYMENT IS RECEIVED BY THE APPLICANT INTO
ACCOUNT NO. 12341100040005863 HELD WITH
BANK OF CHINA LIMITED, SHENZHEN BRANCH
QUOTING THE GUARANTEE NO. DG18000015.

THE AMOUNT OF THIS GUARANTEE SHALL BE AUTOMATICALLY REDUCED BY THE SUM(S) ALREADY PAID BY THE APPLICANT OR BY US AS A RESULT OF A CLAIM, AND BY THE VALUE OF EACH

SHIPMENT/WORKING PROGRESS UNDER CONTRACT UPON PRESENTATION TO US OF COPIES OF THE COMMERCIAL INVOICE
AND ANY RELATED SHIPPING DOCUMENTS/WORK SCHEDULE WHICH WE SHALL BE ENTITLED TO ACCEPT AS CONCLUSIVE EVIDENCE THAT SUCH SHIPMENT/WORKING PROGRESS HAS BEEN EFFECTED.

THE GUARANTEE SHALL BE EXPIRED ONCE IT HAS BEEN REDUCED TO NIL OR SHOULD YOUR WRITTEN DEMAND FOR PAYMENT NOT BE IN OUR POSSESSION AT ABOVE ADDRESS ON OR BEFORE
JAN. 20, 2019(THE EXPIRY DATE), WHICHEVER OCCURS EARLIER.

ALL BANKING CHARGES OUTSIDE THE ISSUING BANK ARE FOR ACCOUNT OF APPLICANT.

THIS GUARANTEE IS SUBJECT TO THE UNIFORM RULES FOR DEMAND GUARANTEES, ICC PUBLICATION NO. 758.

PURSUANT TO THE SANCTIONS AND RELEVANT REGULATION OF PEOPLE'S REPUBLIC OF CHINA, UNITED NATIONS, THE EUROPEAN UNION, THE UNITED STATES OF AMERICA, THE UNITED KINGDOM OR ANY OTHER INTERNATIONAL BODY OR JURISDICTION, WE MAY BE UNABLE TO PROCESS ANY DOCUMENTS, SHIPMENT, GOODS, PAYMENT AND/OR TRANSACTIONS THAT MAY RELATE, DIRECTLY OR INDIRECTLY, TO ANY SANCTION COUNTRIES, ENTITIES AND INDIVIDUALS, AND AUTHORITIES.
MAY REQUIRE DISCLOSURE OF SUCH INFORMATION. ACCORDINGLY, WE SHALL NOT BE LIABLE FOR ANY LOSS, DAMAGE OR DELAY ARISING IN CONNECTION WITH THE ABOVE MATTER.

---

Operator Name: Li Ming
Checker Name: Chen Wei
Authorizer Name: Hu Gui

**Notes:**
1. This is a SWIFT letter of Guarantee Advance Payment sent by the guaranteeing bank or

the exporter's bank, at the applicant's (exporter's) request, to the beneficiary's (importer's) bank undertaking to pay a certain sum of money to them once the applicant (exporter) is in breach of its obligation based on the relative contract.

2. **ADVANCE PAYMENT GUARANTEE** 预付保函，又称还款保函（repayment guarantee）及退款保函。

3. **URDG: UNIFORM RULES FOR DEMAND GUARANTEES** 《见索即付保函统一规则》

4. **ENTERED INTO THE CONTRACT** 签订合同

5. **IS IN BREACH OF HIS OBLIGATION** 违背合同规定的责任和义务，即未履行合同义务

## Sample 81

Sequence Number: J9C567

Message Type: 799

Sender Institution: XXXXCNBJXXX
　　　　　　　　　BANK OF CHINA, THE
　　　　　　　　　XXX

Receiver Institution: IBKOKRSE
　　　　　　　　　　INDUSTRIAL BANK OF KOREA
　　　　　　　　　　50, ULCHIRO 2-GA, CHUNG-GU
　　　　　　　　　　SEOUL

Message Status: I

Message Input Date: 2018-10-12

Message Priority: N

————Message Content :————

20:Transaction Reference Number
　　410319DG18000001

79:Narrative
　　RE YR MT799 DATED 181010
　　FOR OUR GUARANTEE NO. DG18000016
　　AMOUNT USD17,400.00.
　　WE NOW OFFER YOU THE INFORMATION ABOUT THE

BENEFICIARY, PLS ADVISE THE A/M GUARANTEE WITHOUT ALL YOUR LIABILITIES AND RISKS ASAP.

BENEFICIARY: XYZ CO., LTD

(ADD:… , KOREA)

TEL:

MOBILE:

EMAIL:

WEBSITE: WWW.JEONG-AM.CO.KR

ACCOUNT NO.:216-033720-56-00016

ACC.BANK: INDUSTRIAL BANK OF KOREA, NOKSAN-GONGDAN BRANCH(SWIFT: IBKOKRSE).

RGDS

---

Operator Name: Li Ming

Checker Name: Chen Wei

Authorizer Name: Hu Gui

**Notes:**

This is a SWIFT message sent by the guaranteeing bank to the beneficiary's (importer's) bank asking them to advise the L/G to the beneficiary based on the detailed information provided as soon as possible.

## （2）L/G on financing　融资类保函

### Sample 82

---

Sequence Number: J4CH78

Message Type: 760

Sender Institution: XXXXCNBJXXX
　　　　　　　　　　BANK OF CHINA, THE
　　　　　　　　　　XXX

Receiver Institution: XXXXCNBJXXX
　　　　　　　　　　　BANK OF CHINA, THE
　　　　　　　　　　　XXX

Message Status: I

Message Input Date: 2018-10-09

Message Priority: N

————Message Content : ————

27:Sequence of Total    1/1

20:Transaction Reference Number  DS18000017

23:Further Identification  ISSUE

30:Date    181009

40C:Applicable Rules  ISP

77C:Details of Guarantee

 TO: BANK OF CHINA LIMITED, SHANGHAI PILOT FREE TRADE ZONE BRANCH

 ADD:..., SHANGHAI, CHINA

 ISSUING DATE: 20181009.

 RE OUR IRREVOCABLE STANDBY L/C NO. DS18000017.

 AT THE REQUEST OF ABC COMPANY LIMITED, (ADD:... , SHENZHEN, CHINA) (HEREINAFTER CALLED 'THE APPLICANT').

 WE, BANK OF CHINA LIMITED, SHENZHEN BRANCH (ADD:..., SHENZHEN 510000, P. R. CHINA) HEREBY ISSUE OUR IRREVOCABLE STANDBY LETTER OF CREDIT NO. DS17000017 (HEREINAFTER REFERRED TO AS 'STANDBY L/C') IN YOUR FAVOR

 FOR YOUR GRANTING THE FACILITY TO XYZ CO. LTD (ADD: ...HONG KONG, CHINA) (HEREINAFTER CALLED 'BORROWER'),

 A COMPANY INCORPORATED UNDER THE LAWS OF CHINA

 WITH ITS REGISTERED OFFICE AT... HONG KONG FOR THE MAXIMUM AMOUNT OF CNY150,000,000.00(SAY CNY ONE HUNDRED AND FIFTY MILLION ONLY), WHICH INCLUDES THE PRINCIPAL SUM, ACCRUED INTEREST AND DEFAULT INTEREST, DUTIES, TAXES PAID OR PAYABLE AND OTHER COST INCURRED WHICH THE BORROWER OWES TO YOU

 AS ITS INDEBTEDNESS PURSUANT TO THE FACILITY BETWEEN THE BORROWER AND YOU.

 WE HEREBY UNDERTAKE TO PAY YOU ANY AMOUNT NOT EXCEEDING CNY150,000,000.00 (SAY CNY ONE HUNDRED AND FIFTY MILLION ONLY) UPON RECEIPT OF YOUR COMPLYING WRITTEN DEMAND ON OR BEFORE THE EXPIRY DATE BY AUTHENTICATED SWIFT MESSAGE STATING

AS BELOW:

1. THE NUMBER AND ISSUING DATE OF THE STANDBY L/C UNDER WHICH THE CLAIM IS MADE, AND
2. THE AMOUNT YOU CLAIM, AND
3. THE DATE OF THE FACILITY IN RELATION TO WHICH THE CLAIM IS MADE, AND
4. THE BORROWER HAS DEFAULTED ON ITS OBLIGATIONS TO YOU UNDER THE BANKING FACILITIES GRANTED BY YOU TO THE BORROWER.

THE STANDBY L/C IS AVAILABLE BY SIGHT PAYMENT FROM THE ISSUING DATE 20181009 UNTIL 20191008(EXPIRY DATE) AT THE COUNTER OF THE ISSUING BANK. YOUR DEMAND UNDER THE STANDBY L/C MUST BE RECEIVED BY US ON OR BEFORE 20191008. OUR LIABILITY TOWARDS YOUR BANK UNDER THE STANDBY L/C SHALL EXPIRE ON 20191008 IN FULL AND AUTOMATICALLY IF YOUR DEMAND HAS NOT BEEN RECEIVED BY US ON OR BEFORE EXPIRY DATE.

THE AMOUNT OF THE STANDBY L/C SHALL BE AUTOMATICALLY REDUCED BY THE SUM(S) ALREADY PAID BY THE BORROWER PURSUANT TO THE FACILITY OR BY US AS A RESULT OF CLAIM.
MULTIPLE DRAWINGS AND PARTIAL DRAWINGS ARE ALLOWED.
ALL BANKING CHARGES OUTSIDE THE ISSUING BANK ARE FOR ACCOUNT OF APPLICANT.
THE STANDBY L/C IS SUBJECT TO THE INTERNATIONAL STANDBY PRACTICES1998(ISP98), ICC PUBLICATION NO. 590.

PURSUANT TO THE SANCTIONS AND RELEVANT REGULATION OF PEOPLE'S REPUBLIC OF CHINA, UNITED NATIONS, THE EUROPEAN UNION, THE UNITED STATES OF AMERICA, THE UNITED KINGDOM OR ANY OTHER INTERNATIONAL BODY OR JURISDICTION, WE MAY BE UNABLE TO PROCESS ANY DOCUMENTS, SHIPMENT, GOODS, PAYMENT AND/OR TRANSACTIONS THAT MAY RELATE DIRECTLY OR INDIRECTLY, TO ANY SANCTION COUNTRIES, ENTITIES AND INDIVIDUALS, AND AUTHORITIES MAY REQUIRE DISCLOSURE OF SUCH INFORMATION. ACCORDINGLY, WE SHALL NOT BE LIABLE FOR ANY LOSS,

DAMAGE OR DELAY ARISING IN CONNECTION WITH THE ABOVE MATTERS.

Operator Name: Zhu Li

Checker Name: Chen Wei

Authorizer Name: Hu Rong

**Notes:**

1. This is a SWIFT Standby Letter of Credit sent by the issuing bank to the lending bank, which provides credit facility to the borrower, undertaking to pay them a certain sum of money within the expiry date once the borrower is in breach of its obligations.

2. **ISPR: THE INTERNATIONAL STANDBY PRACTICES** 《国际备用惯例》

3. **STANDBY L/C: standby letter of credit** 备用信用证，又称担保信用证，是指不以清偿商品交易的价款为目的，而以贷款融资，或担保债务偿还为目的所开立的信用证。备用信用证的种类也非常多。

4. **IRREVOCABLE** 不可撤销的

5. **GRANTING THE FACILITY TO** 提供信贷便利给

6. **PRINCIPAL SUM** 本金总额

7. **ACCRUED INTEREST AND DEFAULT INTEREST, DUTIES** 所产生的利息、违约利息和关税

8. **MULTIPLE DRAWINGS AND PARTIAL DRAWINGS** 多次索偿和部分索偿

（3）**L/G on payment** 付款保函

**Sample 83**

Sequence Number: J89765

Message Type: 760

Sender Institution: XXXXCNBJXXX
                      BANK OF CHINA, THE
                      XXX

Receiver Institution: BKAUATWW
                      UNICREDIT BANK AUSTRIA AG
                      SCHOTTENGASSE 6-8
                      VIENNA 1010 AUSTRIA

Message Status: I

Message Input Date: 2018-10-25

Message Priority: N

——————Message Content : ——————

27:Sequence of Total  1/1

20:Transaction Reference Number  DG18000012

23:Further Identification  ISSUE

30:Date  181025

40C:Applicable Rules  URDG

77C:Details of Guarantee

 TO: XYZ CO. LTD

 ADD: … LEOBEN, AUSTRIA

 ISSUING DATE:

 DEAR SIRS,

 RE: OUR IRREVOCABLE GUARANTEE NO. DG18000012.
 WITH THE REFERENCE TO THE CONTRACT NO. 180123
 DATED JULY 20180807(HEREINAFTER CALLED 'CONTRACT')BETWEEN
 ABC CO., LTD(ADD: … , ANHUI, CHINA) (HEREINAFTER CALLED
 'APPLICANT') AND YOU, A PAYMENT GUARANTEE IS REQUIRED.
 AT THE REQUEST OF THE APPLICANT, ABC CO., LTD
 (ADD: … , ANHUI, CHINA) WE, BANK OF CHINA LIMITED, ANHUI BRANCH
 (ADD: … , HEFEI, ANHUI, 230000, P. R. CHINA) HEREBY ISSUE OUR
 IRREVOCABLE PAYMENT GUARANTEE NO. DG18000012
 IN FAVOUR OF XYZ CO., LTD (ADD:… , LEOBEN, AUSTRIA)
 (HEREINAFTER CALLED 'BENEFICIARY')FOR EUR144,392.00
 (SAY EUR ONE HUNDRED AND FORTY-FOUR THOUSAND THREE HUNDRED
 AND NINETY-TWO ONLY).

 WE HEREBY UNDERTAKE TO PAY YOU ANY AMOUNT NOT EXCEEDING
 EUR144,392.00 (SAY EUR ONE HUNDRED AND FORTY-FOUR THOUSAND
 THREE HUNDRED AND NINETY-TWO ONLY). UPON RECEIPT OF YOUR
 COMPLYING DULY SIGNED DEMAND STATING THAT THE
 APPLICANT HAS NOT FULFILLED ITS CONTRACTUAL PAYMENT
 OBLIGATIONS AS STIPULATED IN THE CONTRACT NO. 180123.

 FOR THE PURPOSE OF IDENTIFICATION, YOUR DEMAND FOR PAYMENT

MUST BE PRESENTED TO US BY COURIER SERVICE THROUGH YOUR BANK, WHICH IS REQUESTED TO CONFIRM US THE AUTHENTICITY OF THE SIGNATURE(S) APPEARING ON THE DEMAND BY A SEPERATE AUTHENTICATED SWIFT. THE GUARANTEE IS EFFECTIVE ON. DD…

THE AMOUNT OF THE GUARANTEE SHALL BE AUTOMATICALLY REDUCED BY THE SUM(S) ALREADY PAID BY THE APPLICANT OR BY US AS A RESULT OF A CLAIM.

YOUR DEMAND AND THE AUTHENTICATED SWIFT UNDER THE GUARANTEE MUST BE RECEIVED BY US ON OR BEFORE 20190331 AT THE ABOVE ADDRESS. OUR LIABILITY TO YOU UNDER THE GUARANTEE SHALL EXPIRE ON 20190331 IN FULL AND AUTOMATICALLY IF YOUR DEMAND HAS NOT BEEN RECEIVED BY US ON OR BEFORE THAT DATE.

ALL BANKING CHARGES OUTSIDE ISSUING BANK ARE FOR THE ACCOUNT OF BENEFICIARY.

THIS GUARANTEE IS SUBJECT TO THE UNIFORM RULES FOR DEMAND GUARANTEES(URDG) 2010 REVISION, ICC PUBLICATION NO. 758.

PURSUANT TO THE SANCTIONS AND RELEVANT REGULATION OF PEOPLE'S REPUBLIC OF CHINA, UNITED NATIONS, THE EUROPEAN UNION, THE UNITED STATES OF AMERICA, THE UNITED KINGDOM OR ANY OTHER INTERNATIONAL BODY OR JURISDICTION, WE MAY BE UNABLE TO PROCESS ANY DOCUMENTS, SHIPMENT, GOODS, PAYMENT AND/OR TRANSACTIONS THAT MAY RELATE, DIRECTLY OR INDIRECTLY, TO ANY SANCTION COUNTRIES, ENTITIES AND INDIVIDUALS, AND AUTHORITIES MAY REQUIRE DISCLOSURE OF SUCH INFORMATION. ACCORDINGLY, WE SHALL NOT BE LIABLE FOR ANY LOSS, DAMAGE OR DELAY ARISING IN CONNECTION WITH THE ABOVE MATTERS.

Operator Name: Zhu Li

Checker Name: Chen Wei

Authorizer Name: Hu Rong

**Notes:**

1. This is a SWIFT Letter of Payment Guarantee sent by the guaranteeing bank or the importer's bank, at the applicant's (importer's) request, to the beneficiary's (exporter's) bank undertaking to pay a certain sum of money to them once the applicant (importer) has not fulfilled the contractual payment obligation based on the relative contract.

2. **UNICREDIT BANK AUSTRIA AG** 奥地利信贷联合银行，也被称为奥地利银行，该银行是一家中欧和东欧银行，意大利联合信贷银行集团拥有其96.35%的权益。该银行网络枢纽是中欧和东欧的市场领导者，在全球19个国家拥有约3900家分行。根据2008年的数据，奥地利信贷银行85%的员工为奥地利人。

3. **VIENNA** 维也纳

4. **PAYMENT GUARANTEE** 付款保函是指担保银行应买方的申请而向卖方出具的，保证买方履行购买商品、技术、专利或劳务合同项下的付款义务的书面文件。付款保函应买方、业主等申请，向卖方、施工方保证，在卖方、施工方按合同提供货物、技术服务及资料或完成约定工程量后，如买方、业主不按约定支付合同款项，则银行接到卖方、施工方索偿后代为支付相应款项。

（4）L/G on performance  履约保函

**Sample 84**

Sequence Number: J1E6R9

Message Type: 760

Sender Institution: XXXXCNBJXXX

     BANK OF CHINA, THE

     XXX

Receiver Institution: BKTWTWTP

     BANK OF TAIWAN

Message Status: I

Message Input Date: 2018-09-15

Message Priority: N

————Message Content :————

27:Sequence of Total   1/1

20:Transaction Reference Number   DG18000015

23:Further Identification  ISSUE
30:Date  180915
40C:Applicable Rules  URDG

   77C:Details of Guarantee
   TO:ABC TRADING CORP.
   ADD: …, TAIPEI, TAIWAN, CHINA
   ISSUING DATE:SEP. 15, 2018.
   DEAR SIRS,
   RE:OUR IRREVOCABLE GUARANTEE NO. DG18000015.
   WE HAVE BEEN INFORMED THAT XYZ CO., LTD (ADD:…, ANHUI, CHINA) (HEREINAFTER CALLED 'APPLICANT') HAS ENTERED INTO THE CONTRACT NO. 234, DATED AUG. 08, 2018(HEREINAFTER CALLED THE 'CONTRACT') WITH YOU FOR ADDITIONAL SPECIAL TRACK COMPONENT MATERIALS. FURTHERMORE, WE UNDERSTAND THAT, ACCORDING TO THE CONTRACT, A PERFORMANCE GUARANTEE IS REQUIRED.

   AT THE REQUEST OF THE APPLICANT, WE, BANK OF CHINA LIMITED, ANHUI BRANCH (ADDRESS: …, ANHUI, 230061, P. R. CHINA), HEREBY ISSUE OUR IRREVOCABLE PERFORMANCE GUARANTEE NO. DG18000015 (HEREINAFTER CALLED 'THE GUARANTEE')IN FAVOR OF ABC CORP. (ADD:…, TAIPEI, TAIWAN, CHINA) (HEREINAFTER CALLED 'BENEFICIARY') FOR USD2,900.00(SAY US DOLLARS TWO THOUSAND AND NINE HUNDRED ONLY).
   WE HEREBY UNDERTAKE TO PAY YOU ANY AMOUNT NOT EXCEEDING USD2,900.00(SAY US DOLLARS TWO THOUSAND AND NINE HUNDRED ONLY), UPON RECEIPT OF YOUR COMPLYING DULY SIGNED DEMAND FOR PAYMENT STATING THAT THE APPLICANT IS IN BREACH OF HIS OBLIGATION(S) UNDER THE CONTRACT AND THE RESPECT IN WHICH THE APPLICANT IS IN BREACH. FOR PURPOSES OF IDENTIFICATION, YOUR DEMAND FOR PAYMENT MUST BE PRESENTED TO US BY COURIER SERVICE THROUGH YOUR BANK, WHICH IS REQUESTED TO CONFIRM US THE AUTHENTICITY OF THE SIGNATURE(S) APPEARING ON THE DEMAND BY A SEPERATE AUTHENTICATED SWIFT.

THE AMOUNT OF THE GUARANTEE SHALL BE AUTOMATICALLY REDUCED BY THE SUM(S) ALREADY PAID BY THE APPLICANT OR BY US AS A RESULT OF A CLAIM.

YOUR DEMAND AND THE AUTHENTICATED SWIFT UNDER THE GUARANTEE MUST BE RECEIVED BY US ON OR BEFORE AUG. 30, 2018 AT THE ABOVE ADDRESS. OUR LIABILITY TO YOU UNDER THE GUARANTEE SHALL EXPIRE ON AUG. 30, 2019 IN FULL AND AUTOMATICALLY IF YOUR DEMAND HAS NOT BEEN RECEIVED BY US ON OR BEFORE THAT DATE.

ALL BANKING CHGS OUTSIDE ISSUING BANK ARE FOR THE ACCOUNT OF BENEFICIARY. THIS GUARANTEE IS SUBJECT TO THE UNIFORM RULES FOR DEMAND GUARANTEES(URDG) 2010 REVISION, ICC PUBLICATION NO. 758.

PURSUANT TO THE SANCTIONS AND RELEVANT REGULATION OF PEOPLE'S REPUBLIC OF CHINA, UNITED NATIONS, THE EUROPEAN UNION, THE UNITED STATES OF AMERICA, THE UNITED KINGDOM OR ANY OTHER INTERNATIONAL BODY OR JURISDICTION, WE MAY BE UNABLE TO PROCESS ANY DOCUMENTS, SHIPMENT, GOODS, PAYMENT AND/OR TRANSACTIONS THAT MAY RELATE, DIRECTLY OR INDIRECTLY, TO ANY SANCTION COUNTRIES, ENTITIES AND INDIVIDUALS, AND AUTHORITIES MAY REQUIRE DISCLOSURE OF SUCH INFORMATION. ACCORDINGLY, WE SHALL NOT BE LIABLE FOR ANY LOSS, DAMAGE OR DELAY ARISING IN CONNECTION WITH THE ABOVE MATTERS.

ALL DOCS SHOULD BE SENT TO US IN ONE LOT AT: BANK OF CHINA LIMITED, XXX BRANCH, INT'L DEPT. ADD: … , XXX, XXX, CHINA.

Operator Name: Zhu Li
Checker Name: Chen Wei
Authorizer Name: Hu Rong
**Notes:**

1. This is a SWIFT Performance Guarantee sent by the guaranteeing bank, at the applicant's request, to the beneficiary's bank undertaking to pay a certain sum of money to them once the applicant has not fulfilled the contractual obligation based on the relative contract.
2. **PERFORMANCE GUARANTEE** 履约保函，是合约一方或承包方向另一方或业主提出的保证认真履行合同义务的一种经济担保。履约保函一般有三种形式，即银行保函（Bank Guarantee）、履约保函（Performance Guarantee）和履约保证金（Performance Bond）。
3. **IN ONE LOT** 一次

（5）L/G on tender  投标保函
**Sample 85**

Sequence Number: IM9Y78

Message Type: 760

Sender Institution: XXXXCNBJXXX
　　　　　　　　　BANK OF CHINA, THE
　　　　　　　　　XXX

Receiver Institution: HDFCINBBDEL
　　　　　　　　　　HDFC BANK LIMITED
　　　　　　　　　　H T HOUSE  FLOOR 5 18/20 KASTURBA G
　　　　　　　　　　HANDHI ROAD
　　　　　　　　　　NEW DELHI

Message Status: I

Message Input Date: 2018-08-09

Message Priority: N

────Message Content :────

27:Sequence of Total   1/1

20:Transaction Reference Number   DG18000016

23:Further Identification   ISSUE

30:Date   180809

40C: Applicable Rules URDG

77C:Details of Guarantee
　　　TO: ABC. CO., LTD
　　　NEW DELHI-110002, INDIA

ISSUING DATE: AUG. 09, 2018
DEAR SIRS,
RE: OUR IRREVOCABLE GUARANTEE NO. DG18000016.
WE HAVE BEEN INFORMED THAT XYZ CO., LTD
(ADD:… , ANHUI CHINA)(HEREINAFTER CALLED 'APPLICANT')
SUBMITTED THE EXECUTION OF HYDRAULIC PRESS BRAKE
UNDER YOUR BID INVITATION NO. G789 DATED AUG. 08, 2018.
FURTHERMORE, WE UNDERSTAND THAT, ACCORDING TO THE TENDER
CONDITION, A BID BOND IS REQUIRED.

AT THE REQUEST OF THE APPLICANT, WE, BANK OF CHINA LIMITED, ANHUI BRANCH(ADDRESS: … , HEFEI, ANHUI, 230000, P. R. CHINA), HEREBY ISSUE OUR IRREVOCABLE BID BOND NO. DG18000016
(HEREINAFTER CALLED 'THE GUARANTEE')
IN FAVOR OF ABC CO., LTD, ADD: … , NEW DELHI–110002, INDIA
(HEREINAFTER CALLED 'BENEFICIARY') FOR USD7,700.00(SAY US DOLLARS SEVEN THOUSAND AND SEVEN HUNDRED ONLY).

WE HEREBY UNDERTAKE TO PAY YOU ANY AMOUNT NOT EXCEEDING USD7,700.00(SAY US DOLLARS SEVEN THOUSAND AND SEVEN HUNDRED ONLY), UPON RECEIPT OF YOUR COMPLYING DULY SIGNED DEMAND FOR PAYMENT STATING THAT:
I. THE APPLICANT AFTER SUBMITTING HIS TENDER, MODIFIES THE RATES OR ANY OF THE TERMS AND CONDITIONS THEREOF, EXCEPT WITH THE PREVIOUS WRITTEN CONSENT OF BENEFICIARY, OR
II. THE APPLICANT WITHDRAWS THE SAID BID WITHIN 180 DAYS AFTER OPENING OF BID, OR
III. THE APPLICANT HAVING NOT WITHDRAWN THE BID, FAILS TO FURNISH THE CONTRACT PERFORMANCE GUARANTEE WITHIN THE PERIOD PROVIDED IN THE GENERAL CONDITIONS OF CONTRACT.

FOR PURPOSES OF IDENTIFICATION, YOUR DEMAND FOR PAYMENT MUST BE PRESENTED TO US BY POST THROUGH YOUR BANK, WHICH IS REQUESTED TO CONFIRM US THE AUTHENTICITY OF THE SIGNATURE(S)

APPEARING ON THE DEMAND BY A SEPERATE AUTHENTICATED SWIFT.

THE GUARANTEE IS EFFECTIVE ON AUG. 09, 2018.
THE AMOUNT OF THE GUARANTEE SHALL BE AUTOMATICALLY REDUCED BY THE SUM(S) ALREADY PAID BY THE APPLICANT OR BY US AS A RESULT OF A CLAIM.

YOUR DEMAND AND THE AUTHENTICATED SWIFT
UNDER THE GUARANTEE MUST BE RECEIVED BY US ON OR BEFORE MAY. 04, 2019 AT THE ABOVE ADDRESS. OUR LIABILITY TO YOU UNDER THE GUARANTEE SHALL EXPIRE ON MAY 04, 2019 IN FULL AND AUTOMATICALLY IF YOUR DEMAND HAS NOT BEEN RECEIVED BY US ON OR BEFORE THAT DATE.
ALL BANKING CHGS OUTSIDE ISSUING BANK
ARE FOR THE ACCOUNT OF BENEFICIARY.

THIS GUARANTEE IS SUBJECT TO THE UNIFORM RULES FOR DEMAND GUARANTEES(URDG) 2010 REVISION, ICC PUBLICATION NO. 758.

PURSUANT TO THE SANCTIONS AND RELEVANT REGULATION OF PEOPLE'S REPUBLIC OF CHINA, UNITED NATIONS, THE EUROPEAN UNION, THE UNITED STATES OF AMERICA, THE UNITED KINGDOM OR ANY OTHER INTERNATIONAL BODY OR JURISDICTION, WE MAY BE UNABLE TO PROCESS ANY DOCUMENTS, SHIPMENT, GOODS, PAYMENT AND/OR TRANSACTIONS. THAT MAY RELATE, DIRECTLY OR INDIRECTLY, TO ANY SANCTION COUNTRIES, ENTITIES AND INDIVIDUALS, AND AUTHORITIES MAY REQUIRE

DISCLOSURE OF SUCH INFORMATION. ACCORDINGLY, WE SHALL NOT BE LIABLE FOR ANY LOSS, DAMAGE OR DELAY ARISING IN CONNECTION WITH THE ABOVE MATTERS.

---

Operator Name: Zhu Li
Checker Name: Chen Wei
Authorizer Name: Hu Rong

**Notes:**

1. This is a SWIFT Bid Bond sent by the guaranteeing bank, at the applicant's request, to the beneficiary's bank undertaking to pay a certain sum of money to them once the applicant has not fulfilled the contractual obligation based on the relative bid contract.

2. **HDFC BANK LIMITED** 一家印度私营银行，由印度住房开发金融公司持股，是目前印度第四大银行。

3. **NEW DELHI** 新德里，印度的首都。

4. **BID BOND** 投标保函（Bid Bond, Tender Guarantee），指在投标中，招标人为防止中标者不签订合同而使其遭受损失，要求投标人提供的银行保函，以保证投标人履行招标文件所规定的义务①。

5. **HYDRAULIC PRESS BRAKE** 液压制动

6. **TENDER CONDITION** 招标条件

7. **WITHDRAWS THE SAID BID** 撤标

8. **OPENING OF BID** 开标

9. **DISCLOSURE OF SUCH INFORMATION** 信息披露

## III. Commonly Used Sentences on Banking SWIFT（银行SWIFT业务常用句型）

（1）THE AMENDMENT FEE USD35.00 OR EQUIVALENT IS FOR ACCOUNT OF BENEFICIARY, IT WILL BE DEDUCTED FROM PROCEEDS UPON PAYMENT.

（2）PLS ADVISE US WHETHER THE BEN ACCEPT THIS AMENDMENT OR NOT, THIS AMENDMENT IS SUBJECT TO UCP600.

（3）ALL DOCUMENTS TO BE PRESENTED WITHIN 15 DAYS AFTER L/C ISSUING DATE BUT WITHIN THE VALIDITY OF THE CREDIT.

（4）PLS CONVERT THE CURRENCY AND AMOUNT OF THE A/M L/C TO USD7,475,000.00 BEFORE ADVISING IT TO BENEFICIARY.

（5）ALL YOUR BANKING CHARGES ARE FOR ACCOUNT OF THE APPLICANT.

（6）PLEASE TREAT THIS MESSAGE AS A CORRECTION ONLY

---

① 义务如下：
（1）在标书规定的期限内，投标人投标后，不得修改原报价，不得中途撤标。
（2）投标人中标后，必须与招标人签订合同并在规定的时间内提供银行的履约保函。若投标人未履行上述义务，则担保银行在受益人提出索赔时，须按保函规定履行赔款义务。
（3）担保银行的责任是：当投标人在投标有效期内撤销投标，或者中标后不能同业主订立合同或不能提供履约保函时，担保银行就自己负责付款。菲迪克（FIDIC）条款中，投标保证金又译作 TENDER SECURITY。

AND ADVISE IT TO THE BENEFICIARY ACCORDINGLY.

(7) PLS BE INFORMED THAT WE WILL REIMBURSE YOU DIRECTLY.

(8) PLS GIVE US YR CLEAR PAYMENT INSTRUCTIONS BY MT799 ASAP SO THAT PAYMENT CAN BE EFFECTED WITHOUT DELAY.

(9) PLS BE ADVISED THAT WE HAVE INSTRUCTED ABOCHKHH TO REMIT THE PROCEEDS TO YOU AS PER YR PAYMENT INSTRUCTION VALUE ON 20180104.

(10) AFTER RECEIVING YOUR CONFIRMATION MESSAGE, WE WILL CLOSE OUR FILES ACCORDINGLY.

(11) THE MATURITY DATE 180611 FELL ON OUR NATIONAL PUBLIC HOLIDAY, SO PAYMENT SHOULD BE POSTPONED TO 180613 ACCORDINGLY.

(12) THE A/M BILL HAS BEEN ACCEPTED TO BE MATURE ON 18102.

(13) WE WILL REMIT THE A/M AMOUNT TO YOU ACCORDING TO YOUR INSTRUCTION DEDUCTING OUR CHARGES.

(14) PLEASE INVESTIGATE IT AND CONFIRM THE CORRECT AMOUNT BY AUTHENTICATED SWIFT ASAP.

(15) AT THE REQUEST OF APPLICANT, WE TODAY RETURNED THE DOCUMENTS TO YOU BY DHL.

(16) WE CONFIRM THAT WE HAVE PAID THE PROCEEDS OF CNY1,977,974.27 AS PER YOUR INSTRUCTIONS.

(17) WE HEREBY ACKNOWLEDGE RECEIPT OF ABOVE-MENTIONED L/C, BUT WE ARE CONFUSED ABOUT THE FOLLOWING CLAUSES:

(18) PLS VERIFY THE AUTHENTICITY OF THE ABOVE-MENTIONED LETTER OF CREDIT BY MT799 TO US.

(19) PLS BE ADVISED THAT THE BENEFICIARY HAS ACCEPTED THE ABOVE-MENTIONED AMENDMENT.

(20) WE HEREBY CLAIM REIMBURSEMENT FROM YOUR GOOD BANK AS INSTRUCTED BY THE L/C.

(21) PLEASE BE INFORMED THAT WE WILL CLAIM REIMBURSEMENT FROM THE REIMBURSING BANK FOR USD122,070.00 ON DUE DATE(DD…).

(22) PLS RECONSIDER THE DISCREPANCY AND PAY US ASAP WITHOUT ANY DEDUCTION OF DISCREPANCY FEE.

## IV. Exercises（练习）

**1. Write a SWIFT message based on the following:**

发文：旧金山，美国银行

主送：成都，中国银行

日期：2018年2月23日

事由：

我行信用证号：

你行案号：

受益人：

账目：

金额：

称呼：

现将贵行2018年2月12日寄来的本金为……的提示单证退还贵行。

我行客户拒绝为这些单据付款，原因如下：

（1）货运起点不是成都而是上海。

（2）发票商品名称与信用证要求不符。

（3）空运提单没有签字。

（4）给买方的电文无副本案号。

我们建议买卖双方直接联系。现我行即将勾销这笔业务。

附件如文。

**2. Translate the following into SWIFT message:**

据4月5日报文证实书，东京银行通知我行，他们已经该行伦敦分行向你行汇出……款额，以抵补我行4月1日开具给……，……号的电汇款，现谨奉告贵行。我行至今并未收到你行有关借贷通知书，敬希查证；如该项资金尚未收悉，请代我行向东京银行的伦敦分行联系，并将结果告我行。

# PART IV

## LETTERS ON OTHER ITEMS
## 第四部分　其他业务函件样例

| | |
|---|---|
| Unit Nine | Other Items |
| 第 9 单元 | 其他业务函件 |
| Appendix I | Opening Sentences and Closing Sentences Commonly Used in Banking Communication |
| 附录 I | 国际金融函电常用开头语和结束语 |
| Appendix II | Commonly Used Abbreviations in Banking Communication |
| 附录 II | 国际金融函电常用缩略词 |
| Appendix III | Keys to Exercises |
| 附录 III | 练习参考答案 |

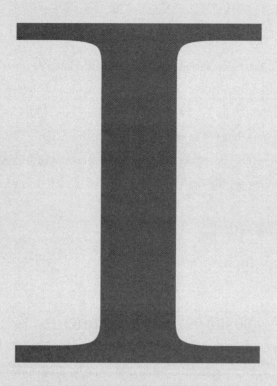

## Unit Nine   Other Items

## 第9单元   其他业务函件

**After studying this unit, you will be able to:**
- Understand there are many kinds of letters related to other affairs between international banks
- Recognize the features of this kind of letter in format and style after learning sample letters
- Learn how to write letters related to other affairs
- Master the language skills of this respect
- Evaluate your writing skills by completing the self-test checklists in the unit

## I. Introduction（概述）

Except for business letters, there are various kinds of letters related to other affairs intra-banks and between international banks, which are notice, advertisement, letter of thanks, letter of invitation, letter of congratulation, letter of condolence, resume etc., which contain many aspects of contents in varieties of forms, but not as specific as the business letter. When writing, they are to be written concisely and clearly based on the different features of different contents, and most importantly to the point in the opening sentence regardless of the letter in what kinds of formats.

## II. Specimen Letters（样例信件）

### 1. Notice（通知）

**Sample 1**

**BOARD OF DIRECTORS NOTICE**

Dear Shareholder,

    You are cordially invited to attend the Annual Meeting of Shareholders to be held at … a. m., local time, on (Friday)…, 2018, at the …Conference and Training Center,…. We look forward to seeing many shareholders at the meeting.

    By attending the meeting, you will have an opportunity to hear a report on 2018 operations, to meet your directors and executive officers, and to participate in the meeting. Information regarding the business of the meeting is set forth in the formal Notice of Annual Meeting and Proxy Statement. There will be an opportunity for shareholders to ask questions about our business and to comment on any aspect of bank affairs properly brought before the meeting.

    We cannot stress strongly enough that the vote of every shareholder, regardless of the number of shares owned, is important. Therefore, after reading the Notice of Annual Meeting and Proxy Statement, even if you plan to attend the meeting, you are urged to complete and return promptly the enclosed for your convenience. Since mail delays may occur, it is important that the proxy be returned well in advance of the meeting. If you decide to attend the meeting and wish to vote your shares personally, you may revoke your proxy at any time before it is exercised.

    We are expecting to receive your vote and see you at the meeting.

    … (Signature)                     … (Signature)
    Chairman of the Board          President and
    and Chief E. Officer             Chief E. Officer

**Notes:**

1. This is a Notice of Board of Directors on the Annual Meeting of Shareholders.

2. **shareholder** *n.* 股东

   [同义词语] stockholder

3. **Annual Meeting** 年会

4. **conference** *n.* 会议，讨论会

   e.g. The conference on international economic problems met in Geneva.

5. **participate** *vi.* 参加

   后面接用介词 in

   e.g. You are warmly welcomed to participate in our Seminar.

6. **set forth** 陈述，列举

   e.g. Your L/C reached us much behind the time limit as set forth in Contract No. 1234.

7. **proxy statement** 代表权声明书

8. **comment** *vi.* 评论

   常接用 on, upon

   e.g. The owner shall approve and/or comment on the Contractor's documents within the time stipulated in the Contract.

9. **vote** *n./v.* 投票表决，选举，表决

   e.g. John made a motion to take a vote.

   They all voted against changing the law.

   They voted that this clause should be canceled.

10. **regardless of** *prep.* 不管，不论

    e.g. All payments of commissions shall be made monthly on all money collected from customers, regardless of whether such amounts are in full or partial fulfillment of the entire obligation to the Principal.

11. **urge** *vt.* 催促，奉劝

    常用结构为：

    1) urge sb. for sth.

       e.g. For some time past they have been urging us for immediate payment of this amount.

    2) urge sb. to do sth.

       e.g. We urge you to make decision as early as possible.

       You are urged to effect payment promptly.

12. **revoke** *vt.* 撤销，取消

    e.g. In view of the above reasons, we cannot but revoke the contract.

[同义词语] rescind, cancel 等

## 2. Certificate（证书）

**Sample 2**

---

**CERTIFICATE**

Whereas, after due examination it appears that the… Bank having its principal place of business in Shenzhen —the Special Economic Zone, has complied with all the provisions of the Banking Law of the Special Economic Zone of P. R. China, and with all other necessary requirements of law relating thereto.

Now therefore, I, the undersigned, Superintendent of Commercial Bank of China, do certify that the said bank is qualified and is hereby authorized to transact commercial banking business and to accept savings deposits at… Street in Shenzhen, the Special Economic Zone of P. R. China.

IN TESTIMONY WHEREOF witness my head office seal this… day of…, 2018 at…, P. R. China.

Superintendent of Commercial<br>Bank of China

---

**Notes:**

1. This is a Certificate issued by Superintendent of Commercial Bank of China.

2. **principal place**　主要地位

3. **comply with**　依从，照办

   e.g. You should comply with the terms of the Agreement.

4. **superintendent** *n.*　总监

5. **qualified** *adj.*　合格的，有资格的

   常用结构为：

   1）be qualified + to do/for doing sth.

   　e.g. We are qualified to do/for doing import and export business in this district.

   2）qualified 作定语

   　e.g. The lowest bona fide bid received from a qualified bidder for any or all of such work shall be accepted.

6. **the undersigned**　签字人，签名者

7. **savings deposit**　储蓄存款

8. **IN TESTIMONY WHEREOF witness my head office seal this …day of …, 2018 at …, P. R. China.**（法律用语）于2018年×月×日在中华人民共和国×地在本文

（证明书）签名盖印作证。

## 3. Advertisement（广告）

**Sample 3**

Advertisement for a Commercial Line of Credit
WANTED
US$...

1. We are a wholly-owned subsidiary whose parent has a history of long-term, first-class relationships.
2. We are a well-capitalized mortgage lending bank with audited financial and a "real" net worth in excess of US$....
3. Our business is making high equity/high return/"hard money" (equity) loans from US$... to US$....
4. We have been profitable each of the three years of our existence.
5. We want to (carefully) expand and are looking for a revolving commercial line of credit secured by our net worth and loan portfolio.

...

**Notes:**

1. This is an Advertisement for a Commercial Line of Credit Wanted, which is worded sincerely based on the facts.
2. **wholly-owned subsidiary**　全资子公司
3. **a well-capitalized mortgage lending bank**　资本充足的抵押贷款银行
4. **line of credit**　信贷额度
5. **audited** *adj.*　审核的，审计的
6. **net worth**　资本净值
7. **in excess of**　超过

    e.g. Party A agrees to pay Party B a 4% commission on the purchased amount in excess of US$1000.

    ［同义词语］more than, above, over（in excess of 不及其他三个词语通俗、简明）

8. **high equity** *n.*　高收益
9. **high return** *n.*　高回报
10. **hard money**　高利润
11. **profitable** *adj.*　有益的，有利的

    e.g. We hope this transaction may lead to a mutually profitable connection between us.

12. **a revolving commercial line of credit**　循环商业信贷额度

13. **loan portfolio**　贷款组合

## Sample 4

<u>Advertisement of Bank of China</u>

Bank of China with its Head Office in Beijing is the largest transcontinental/national bank in China designated by the Chinese Government to specialize in the international banking business. Bank of China with nationwide network and overseas branches and correspondent banks is engaged in foreign exchange transactions, foreign and local currency deposits and loans as well as inter-bank lending both at home and abroad, settlement of trade-related payments, financial leasing, guarantee on many respects such as: tender; foreign currency dealings etc.

Bank of China has enjoyed high prestige at home and abroad for its wide business scope and fine reputation and can offer best services to its clients.

Address: …, Beijing, China　　　　　　Tel: …
Telex: …　　　　Cable: …　　　　Fax: …　　　　SWIFT…

**Notes:**

1. This is an advertisement of Bank of China.

2. **transcontinental bank**　跨国银行

3. **designated** *adj.*　指定的

4. **nationwide network**　全国联网

5. **engaged** *adj.*　从事于

   常用结构为：be engaged in sth.

   e.g. We have been engaged in this business for past 20 years.

6. **inter-bank lending**　同业银行间借贷

7. **financial leasing**　融资性租赁

8. **prestige** *n.*　声誉，声望

   常与动词 enjoy, gain 等搭配

   e.g. The said bank enjoys high prestige all over the world for its best service.

   Our Renminbi is gaining more and more international prestige.

## 4. Invitation（请帖和邀请函）

### Sample 5

> Mr. Li Ming, the President of
> Bank of China and his colleagues
> Request the pleasure of
> Mr. and Mrs. John Smith's presence
> At a reception in White Cloud Hotel
> on Tuesday, July the first, 2018
> at six o'clock p.m.
> R. S. V. P.
>                             Telephone:
>                                 …

**Notes:**

1. This is an Invitation Card.
2. **request the pleasure of** 谨邀（请帖用语）
3. **presence** *n.* 出席
4. **reception** *n.* 招待会
5. **R. S. V. P.** 请答复（是 repondez s'il vous plait 的缩写）（请帖用语）

### Sample 6

> Mr. and Mrs. John Smith
> accept with pleasure
> Mr. Li Ming, the President of
> Bank of China and his colleagues' kind invitation
> for the reception in White Cloud Hotel
> on Tuesday, July the first, 2018
> at six o'clock p.m.

**Notes:**

1. This is an acknowledge receipt to accept an invitation of Sample 5.
2. **accept with pleasure** 欣然接受

## Sample 7

> Mr. and Mrs. John Smith
> regret that a previous engagement
> prevents their acceptance of
> Mr. Li Ming, the President of Bank of China
> and his colleagues' kind invitation
> to the reception in White Cloud Hotel
> on Tuesday, July the first, 2018
> at six o'clock p.m.

**Notes:**

1. This is an acknowledge receipt to decline an invitation due to a previous engagement.

2. **previous engagement** 之前有约

## Sample 8

5th June, 2018

Dear Mr. John Smith,

  I'm very delighted to hear from your Embassy in Beijing that you would visit China next month this year. May I take the opportunity to invite you to come here to have a meeting at our bank during your stay in Beijing?

  We trust that through this meeting we can renew our friendship and exchange views on further expansion of business between our two banks.

  Please let me know as soon as possible whether you will be able to come and visit our bank, and if so, tell me when it is convenient to you so that we can make a better arrangement for you.

  We are awaiting your early reply.

Yours sincerely,
Li Ming
President of Bank of China

**Notes:**

1. This is a letter of invitation based on Sample 5.

2. **opportunity** *n.* 机会

 常用结构为：

1）take this/the opportunity to do sth.

  e.g. We take this opportunity to express our wish to enter into business relations with you.

2）take this/the opportunity of/for doing sth.

 e.g. We take this/the opportunity of/for expressing our appreciation for your cooperation in training our personnel.

3. **renew** *vt.* 重温

 e.g. We invite you to attend the party in the hope that we can renew our friendship.

## Sample 9

Dear Mr. Li Ming,

 I accept with great pleasure your kind invitation by your letter dated 5th June, 2018, to come to your bank and have a meeting with you. I am very pleased to recall our last meeting with you in Beijing on…, 2018, and I think it was constructive since then the business volume between us has been increasing.

 I am looking forward to meeting you and thank you very much for your kind invitation.

Yours sincerely,<br>John Smith

**Notes:**

1. This is a letter of accepting an invitation based on Sample 6.

2. **recall** *vt.* 回忆，想起

2. **constructive** *adj.* 建设性的

3. **call on** 拜访，访问

 e.g. We called on Mr. Li Ming the president of Bank of China last week.

## Sample 10

Dear Mr. Li Ming,

 Thank you very much for inviting me to come to your bank and have a meeting with you. I should be pleased to visit your bank and have a meeting with you if time permits, I regret to inform you that owing to a limit of time and a previous engagement in Beijing, we shall be unable to come this time.

 I hope you will give me your understanding and trust there may be another opportunity to call upon you. Thank you once again for your kind invitation.

Yours sincerely,<br>John Smith

**Notes:**

1. This is a letter of declining an invitation based on Sample 7.

2. **call upon**  拜访

## Sample 11

> Dear Sirs,
>
> Formal Invitation
>
> As previously discussed with you by Mr. Anderson Smith, our Chief Representative in Beijing, we are pleased to formally extend an invitation for your bank to send two participants to attend our three-week Overseas Bankers Training Course.
>
> Our course has been designed to study all respects of International Banking, as well as an introduction to other major areas of activity of our bank. We trust it will be proved beneficial to your selected officers in their development and deployment within your fine bank.
>
> Next year's course will commence on Monday, March 1st, 2018 and close on Friday, March 22nd, 2018. We suggest that participants arrive on weekend Feb. 27/28th and depart Mar. 23th /24th to return their home countries.
>
> We will meet all costs associated with the course incurred within Australia including accommodations and meals, and ask for your bank to cover the cost of airfares, personal accident insurance and a daily allowance, for your trainees.
>
> We look forward to receiving your formal acceptance along with the information requested and assure you that your colleagues' stay in Australia will be both comfortable and enjoyable. We believe that after completion of the course your trainees will have made new friends at the … Bank and gained valuable experience for their future banking career.
>
> Yours sincerely.<br>(Signature)

**Notes:**

1. This letter is a formal invitation on personnel training.
2. **Overseas Bankers Training Course**  海外银行职员培训课程
3. **deployment** *n.*  施展（才华等）
4. **commence** *vi.*  开始

    e.g. This Agreement should commence on this date and may be terminated on June 15, 1996.

    [同义词语] begin  commence 较 begin 正式，多用于书面语中。

5. **accommodations and meals**  膳宿
6. **airfares**  机票费
7. **personal accident insurance**  个人意外险
8. **a daily allowance**  日常开支

## 5. Letter of thanks（感谢信）

### Sample 12

Dear Mr. Peterson William,

  Many thanks for your kind hospitality and the honor you showed me during our recent visit to your bank. During our stay in your bank, it was thoughtful of you to introduce me and my colleague to meet with Mr. …, President of your Bank and many famous senior officers, and give us a chance to visit your Electronic Data Processing Center and attend a very important seminar entitled on Internet Banking Services.

  There is no doubt that we shall benefit from this arrangement, and we believe our visit to your bank will be to the benefit of the development of our banking business.

  We returned to China safe and sound last Saturday and hope you will some day visit our country. Please do not hesitate to write to me should you need me to do something for you in China.

  With best regards.

Sincerely yours,

Zhou Jianwei

Vice-president of Bank of China

**Notes:**

1. This is a letter of thanks for hospitality.
2. **Electronic Data Processing Center**　电子数据处理中心
3. **Internet Banking Services**　互联网银行业务
4. **safe and sound**　平安地
5. **hesitate** *vi.*　犹豫不决

  常用结构为：

  1）hesitate + to do…

    e.g. Do not hesitate to write to us if you require further information.

  2）hesitate + about/over + *n.* /*v*-ing.

    e.g. We are still hesitating about accepting the invitation to the Fair.

      They hesitated over the choice between the two optional ports.

### Sample 13

Gentlemen:

  I wish to express sincere thanks to you and your fine university in my own name and on behalf of the Commercial Bank of China for the efforts you have made in training our personnel.

    Thanks to your careful arrangement, Mr. Liu Wei and his colleagues have an opportunity last year to make advanced study in Financial English. Not only are their English and professional skills improved but their ability of self-teaching is enhanced, which has certainly laid down a good foundation for their future banking career.

    While appreciating once again your efforts in the training courses, I hope you will extend our thanks to the Foreign Language Department for their great support and close cooperation in this respect.

    I look forward to a continuous development of the long-existing friendly relationship and cooperation between our two institutions.

Sincerely yours,<br>(Signed)

**Notes:**

1. This is a letter of thanks for personnel training.

2. **thanks to** 由于，因为

    e.g. Thanks to mutual efforts, we were able to enter into the business relations between us smoothly.

    ［同义词语］because of, owing to。 thanks to 用以接受褒义的词语；而其他词则侧重讲原因，可以是褒义，也可以是贬义。

3. **make advanced study in**… 在……方面深造

4. **professional skills** 职业技能

5. **enhance** *vt.* 加强

    e.g. Through foreign trade, we can enhance the friendship between the Chinese people and the people of other countries.

6. **lay down a foundation for**… 为……打下基础

    e.g. We believe that the study of the banking course will lay down a good foundation for their future banking career.

## 6. Letter of Congratulation（祝贺信）

**Sample 14**

Dear Mr. Green,

    My warm congratulation to you on your selection as President of the Eastern Bank Ltd., London. It is a fine tribute from your colleagues, and a reward you richly deserve for your unusual abilities and many years of splendid service to the profession. I can't think of any man who would have been a better choice.

Our two banks keep very friendly business relationship, which has been developed rapidly in recent years. I believe, under your excellent guidance, your bank will do even better than ever. I expect with great confidence for continuous cooperation between our two banks in more business areas in future.

My very best wishes to you!

Sincerely yours,

(Signature)

**Notes:**

1. This is a letter of Congratulation on Promotion.

2. **tribute** *n.* 评价

3. **reward** *n.* 奖赏

4. **deserve** *vt.* 应得

   e.g. This is a reward you richly deserve for your many years of sincere/splendid service to the profession.

5. **a better choice** 最恰当的人选

### 7. Letter of condolence（吊唁信）

### Sample 15

Dear Sirs,

We are shocked by the painful news of the passing away of your President Mr. …, who was our good friend admired by all who knew him and who was also our good cooperator, contributed greatly to promoting the friendship and cooperation between our two banks.

We deeply grieve over his death. I would, in my own name and on behalf of the board of directors of …Bank, express our deepest condolence.

Please accept our deepest sympathy.

Sincerely yours,

(Signature)

**Notes:**

1. This is a letter of condolence.

2. **pass away** 逝世

3. **admire** *vt.* 敬慕，仰慕

   e.g. Mr. John Smith was an old gentlemen who was admired by his colleagues and neighbors.

4. **promote** *vt.* 促进

   e.g. We believe we shall be able, by joint efforts, to promote friendship as well as business.

5. **grieve over one's death**　为……逝世而悲伤

6. **condolence** *n.* 吊唁

## 8. Curriculum vitae（简历）

**Sample 16**

---

**CURRICULUM VITAE**

NAME:　　　　Robert Cortex

ADDRESS:　　55 Rue St. Louis

　　　　　　　Strasbourg 67000, France

OBJECTIVE:

EDUCATION: 2004—2007. George Manson university (one of the leading business universities in France ).

M.B.A. emphasis on International Business.

2008, EDP International:

Work experience in market research. Conducted field surveys in the Netherlands and France.

PROFESSIONAL ACTIVITY

　　2009—2011. Demont S. A. Financial controller responsible for:

　　——organizing bank credits for civil engineering work

　　——visit Latin American and Asian subsidiaries

　　——designing data processing, accounting, cost control and reporting systems

　　——hiring and training local staff for subsidiaries

　　2011—present. Phoenix properties investment officer responsible for:

　　——checking feasibility studies and predicting returns on investment

　　——solving legal problems related to investments

　　——negotiating contracts with property developers

PERSONAL DATA: (date and place of birth; language; nationality etc.)

REFERENCE AND SUPPORTING DOCUMENTS: Available on request.

Resume Submitted in Confidence

---

**Notes:**

1. This is a chronological resume.

2. **MBA (master of business administration)** 工商管理硕士
3. **emphasis on** 专修

   e.g. She has gained the Master Degree emphasis on international banking.
4. **international business** 国际商务
5. **EDP(electronic data processing)** 电子数据处理
6. **market research** 市场调研/调查
7. **conducted field survey** 进行试验调查
8. **financial controller** 财务主管
9. **civil engineering work** 民用工程项目
10. **cost control** 成本控制
11. **property** *n.* 财产
12. **investment** *n.* 投资
13. **feasibility** *n.* 可行性
14. **available on request** 承索即寄

## Sample 17

<u>C.V.</u>

Name: Glends St. Johns
Add:　Box 6671, College Station
　　　 Iowa City, Iowa 52240
　　　 (515) 545-9876

OBJECTIVE: To obtain a position in corporate public relations where my technical and interpersonal skills and experience will be of use.

WRITING/EDITING:

Wrote arts and entertainment articles for college newspaper

Edited University of Iowa Handbook, guidebook mailed to all incoming freshmen

Published guest editorial on student attitudes in Des Moines Register

Wrote prize-winning script for sorority skit in Fall Follies talent show

PUBLIC SPEAKING:

Participated in over 100 debates as member of college debating team led seminars to teach job-search skills to underprivileged teenagers as part of campus outreach program

Performed in summer theater production in Clear Lake, Iowa

MANAGING:

Created and administered summer parts and recreation program for city of Osaqe, Iowa

Developed budget, schedule, and layouts for college handbook; assigned work to photographers and copywriters

Developed publicity campaign for Fall Follies, a three-hour talent show that raised $7000 for The University of Iowa's Panhellenic Council

EDUCATION:

The University of Iowa, Iowa City, September 1984—June 1989 B.A. Journalism; Speech minor; Two courses in Public Relations

EXPERIENCE:

June 2008—April 2009, Editor, University of Iowa Handbook

Summer 2007, Director, Summer Recreation Program, Osage, Iowa Summer 2006, Actress, Cobblestone Players, Clear Lake, Iowa

PERSONAL DATA:

Excellent health; willing to relocate

REFERENCES AND SUPPORTING DOCUMENTS: Available from Placement Office, The University of Iowa, Iowa City, IA 52242

**Notes:**

1. This is a functional C.V. which is different in format and focus from the chronological curriculum vitae.
2. **public relations** 公共关系
3. **interpersonal skill** 人际能力
4. **entertainment articles** 公共娱乐文章
5. **edit** *vt.* 主编（杂志、报刊等）
6. **handbook** *n.* 手册，指南
7. **editorial** *n.* 评论，社论
8. **Des Moines Register** 地蒙（爱阿华州一城市）记录
9. **script** *n.* 手稿
10. **sorority skit** 女生联谊会幽默短剧
11. **debates** *n.* 辩论
12. **underprivileged teenager** 没有机会受教育的少年
13. **campus outreach program** 校外节目
14. **budget** *n.* 预算
15. **assign** *vt.* 指派，分配

    常用结构为：

    1) assign sb. to do sth.

e.g. I assign you to wash the plates.

2）assign sb. sth.

e.g. I assigned you the job.

16. **publicity campaign**　宣传活动
17. **B. A. Journalism**　新闻学士（B. A. 是 bachelor 的缩写）
18. **Speech, minor**　副修演讲专业
19. **Director** *n.*　导演
20. **Cobblestone players**　鹅卵石剧团演员
21. **actress** *n.*　女演员
22. **willing to relocate** *v.*　愿意再分配

## Sample 18

**RESUME**

Name: Liu Kai

Sex: Male

Age: 36 ( Date of Birth: April 10, 1970)

Hometown: Changsha, Hunan

Marital status: Married

Health:

Family background: Intellectual family; both father and mother are teachers in Hunan University

Education: 1978—1983 Enrolled in the Primary School attached to Normal University

　　　　　　1983—1988 Enrolled in the No. 1 Middle School

　　　　　　1988—1992 Enrolled in Beijing Foreign Trade University, Major in English Language; Minor in International Banking.

Working Experience:

　　　　　　1992—1998 An English teacher in Hunan College of Finance and Economic

　　　　　　1998—2002 On the staff of the International Clearing Department of Bank of China

　　　　　　2002—present Manager of the International Clearing Center of Bank of China

Remarks:

**Notes:**

1. This is a curriculum vitae in Chinese style.
2. **enroll** *vt.* 注册，登记（指入伍，上学等）

　　常用结构为：

1）enroll + *n.*

   e.g. The secretary enrolled our names.

2）be enrolled in

   e.g. He was enrolled in army.

3）enroll for

   e.g. He enrolled for a cookery class.

   I like the school but I don't want to enroll.

3. **attached to**　附属的

## 9. Diploma（文凭）

**Sample 19**

---

　　Li Zhigang, male born on July 2nd, 1996, native of Changsha, Hunan, was an undergraduate student majoring in International Banking in the College of Finance of Hunan University during September, 2014 to July, 2018. He has completed all the prescribed four-year undergraduate courses, passed all the examinations and is entitled to be a graduate of Hunan University.

　　No. 9010082　　　Duan Xianzhong

　　　　　　　　　　President of Hunan University

　　　　　　　　　　Issued in: July 6th, 2018

---

**Notes:**

1. This is a diploma of an undergraduate student from Hunan University.

2. **major in**　主修

3. **prescribed** *adj.*　必修的

## 10. Other Daily Business Letters（其他商务信函）

**Sample 20**

---

Dear Sirs,

N. Z. Forests Products Shares

　　At the request of our clients, we are forwarding to you the following documents pertaining to the above shares:

　　1. One sheet of 5.5% Cumulative Preference Share Certificate No.…for…shares in the name of…

　　2. One sheet of Ordinary Share Certificate No.…for…shares in the name of…

　　3. One Sworn Declaration of the identity of the registered shareholders.

> 4. Two Deeds of Transfer duly signed and witnessed.
>
> Upon receipt of above documents, you are requested to:
>
> 1. Sell all the shares, both Preference and Ordinary, on your local market.
>
> 2. Convert the proceeds thus obtained, less all charges, into transferable Sterling and credit it to our account with you under your usual advice to us.
>
> For your reference, we would inform you that the owner of the shares, Mr…, resides at Shanghai, whose address is…Shanghai, China, and the above shares were bought by him with his own funds.
>
> We thank you in advance for your kind cooperation.
>
> Yours sincerely,
>
> (Signature)

**Notes:**

1. This letter refers to entrusting business on shares transactions.

2. **entrust** vt. 委托

   常用结构为：

   1）entrust sb. with sth.

   e.g. We have decided to entrust you with the sole agency for the shares on your local market.

   2）entrust sth. to sb.（或 sth.）

   e.g. We entrust the collection of this amount to your careful attention.

3. **N. Z.（New Zealand）Forests Products Shares** 新西兰木材公司股票

4. **pertain** vi. 关于，有关

   常接用介词 to。

   e.g. All the accounts, books and reports of the operator so far as they pertain to the business shall be opened to the inspection by the company.

5. **Cumulative Preference Share Certificate** 累积优先股凭证

6. **Ordinary Share Certificate** 普通股票凭证

7. **Sworn Declaration of the identity** 共同誓言

8. **Deeds of Transfer** 转户凭证

9. **witness** vt. 证明

   e.g. In order to check and witness the guaranteed performance of the plant, acceptance tests and inspections at site shall be carried out by contractor in the presence of purchaser.

10. **convert** vt. 兑换（货币）

    常与介词 into 搭配使用。

    e.g. At what rate does the dollar convert into pounds?

11. **transferable Sterling**　可转让的英币

12. **less** *prep.*　减除

   e.g. We wish to inform you that we have credit your account with the amount less all the commissions and charges due to us.

13. **reside (at/in …)**　居住

   e.g. We suggest that the credit be settled in China as the beneficiary resides at Shanghai, China.

## Sample 21

Dear Sirs,

<u>Check No.…for…</u>

　　We are sending you herewith the captioned check drawn by your depositor Mr.… on your Bank and request you to kindly issue, in placement, a demand draft payable to our order in its equivalent Pounds Sterling and send same to us.

　　We confirm the correctness of the drawee's signature on the check and look forward to receiving your reply at an earlier date.

Yours truly,

(Signature)

**Notes:**

1. This letter is a request for check in Pounds Sterling.

2. **depositor** *n.*　储户

3. **in placement**　另外（替换）

4. **demand draft**　即期汇票

5. **equivalent** *n.*　等价物，相同价值的东西

   e.g. The total invoice value must be paid in RMB or its equivalent in Euro.

6. **outstanding balance**　未达余额，未偿清余额

7. **regulations**　规则，规定

8. **close the account**　注销账户

9. **considering** *prep.*　考虑到，鉴于

   e.g. Considering the friendly business reasons between us, we decide not to charge the overdue interests on you.

   ［同义词语］in consideration of，in view of

10. **Specimen T/C**　旅行支票样本（其中 T/C 是 Traveler's Check 的缩写形式）

## III. Sentences Commonly Used on Other Items（其他业务函件的常用句型）

1）This is to certify that the said bank registered with the undersigned … on the date of …, 2018 and was issued this Business License No.…thereby having acquired the status of a legal person.

2）The People's Bank of China, responsible for supervising banks in the People's Republic of China, hereby certifies that …Bank is an organization under the direct leadership of the State Council and is a bank authorized by the State to engage specially in international banking.

3）…Chairman of the Board and Chief Executive Officer of …Bank, the undersigned, hereby makes, constitutes and appoints Mr. …Chief Representative, …Bank Representative Office in the P. R. China, his true and lawful attorney for him and in his name, place and stead and for his use and benefits.

4）The specific duties and responsibilities are to fail within the scope of business applied for, and approved, by the People's Bank of China.

5）If you are planning to do business in China, you should look for a bank that understands a bit more than just Chinese business.

6）An international bank not only help you with the complexities of the Chinese market, its laws and regulations, but also appreciate the implications for your international business.

7）We are the second largest bank of China, with …domestic branches and over…offices worldwide.

8）Our bank is large enough to offer you all the financial services you need, yet flexible enough to produce detailed solutions to specific national problem.

9）We are the fifth largest bank in North America, with over US$ 90 billion in assets.

10）You can trust your foreign exchange dealings to us.

11）Our electronic banking system can provide the most imaginative cash management support for your American operations.

12）Industrial and Commercial Bank of China is the largest bank in China specializing in urban banking business such as saving deposit, loans for industrial and commercial purposes and settlement of their account.

13）The balance of all its deposit ending 2018 stood at …billion yuan and that of various loans at …billion yuan.

14）The Industrial and Commercial Bank of China handles both local and foreign currency business.

15）Whenever you work and whatever you do, the … Bank can always offer you its best services to your satisfaction in the light of your unique financial conditions.

16）The…Bank with its branches and sub-branches at home and abroad can provide perfect services to customers by means of its advanced telecommunication networks and operational tactics adaptable to all market requirements.

17) I am very delighted to hear from your Embassy in Beijing that you will join your government delegation in a study visit of a month to China in the next month.

18) On behalf of …Bank I am very pleased to confirm our invitation to you to attend the Seminar for …that we are organizing in …during…(date).

19) We are looking forward to receiving confirmation of your attendance and to seeing you in…

20) I am very happy to learn that you have been newly appointed chairman of the Board of Directors of …Bank. I wish to extend to you my hearty congratulations.

## IV. Exercises（练习）

### 1. Write a letter based on the following situations:

Suppose you work in CITIBANK, N. A. Hong Kong Branch ( locate in 17/F, West Tower Bond Center 189 Queens Way, Central H. K. ). Your colleague Mr. Zhang paid a visit to Bank of China Head Office Beijing ( at 410 Fuchengmen Nei Dajie Beijing 100828 ) last month and received a kind reception.

Now you are asked to write on behalf of your manager a letter of thanks to Deputy Manager in Bank of China according to the following particulars:

（1）张先生上个月拜访时受到了中行的友好接待，在此谨致深切的谢意。

（2）我行始终期待同贵行保持友好互利的业务关系。

（3）再次感谢中行对张先生的热忱款待。

### 2. Write a letter base on the following situations:

Suppose you work in Investment Bank of China who intends to expand its overseas business. You are requested to write an advertisement within 120-150 words with the following particulars:

（1）中国投资银行是一家由中国政府指定的为国内建设从国外筹资的专业银行。

（2）中国投资银行所筹集的资金来自国际金融机构、外国政府、国际国内的货币贷款以及其他方面。

（3）中国投资银行所从事的业务有：再贷款业务、同业银行间的借贷、往来贸易的结算、融资租赁、外汇交易担保和外汇交易等。

（4）中国投资银行总部地址在北京，拥有分行达……家之多，遍及全国各省。

（5）中国投资银行愿为各客户提供最佳服务。

### 3. Imagine you are the president of Bank of China, Beijing. Now you, in your own name and on behalf of your bank write a letter of invitation to Mr. John Smith—the Director of the

Chartered Bank with the followings:

(1) You are told by your mutual friend Mr. Anderson that the Director of the Chartered Bank will visit China in October 2018.

(2) You wish to take opportunity to invite him to a dinner party at the restaurant of the Chang Cheng Hotel.

(3) The purpose you are going to entertain him is to express your thanks for his great efforts in training your personnel and to enhance your relationship and expand the business between your two banks.

(4) You write to ask him to answer when it is convenient by telex if acceptable, so that a better arrangement can be made.

**4. Write two replies to Letter 3 with an affirmative and/or negative tone.**

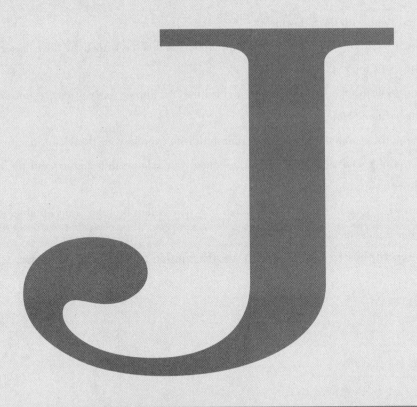

**Appendix Ⅰ** Opening Sentences and Closing Sentences Commonly Used in Banking Communication

附录 I 国际金融函电常用开头语和结束语

## （一）开始语（Opening Sentences）

1. 奉告……

   （1）We are pleased to inform you that…

   （2）We have the pleasure in informing you that…

   （3）We take the pleasure of informing you that…

   　　很高兴告知……

   （4）We wish to inform/advise you that/of…

   （5）We wish to notify you that/of…

   （6）We would inform/advise/notify you that…

   （7）We would like to inform/advise/ you that…

2. 请予惠告……

   （1）Please inform us that/of…

   （2）Kindly inform us that/of…

   （3）Be good enough to inform us that/of…

   （4）Please let us know that…

   　　请告知……

   （5）We should be obliged if you would inform us that/of…

   （6）We shall appreciate it if you will inform us that/of…

   （7）We should be indebted if you would inform us that/of…

   （8）We shall be thankful if you will let us know that…

   　　如蒙惠告……则不胜感激。

   （9）We should be pleased if you would let us know that…

   （10）We should be glad if you would inform us that/of…

   （11）We shall be pleased to have your information on…

   　　如蒙告知……不胜荣幸。

3. 确认收悉对方函电

   （1）Thank you for your letter/cable of (date) Ref. …

   （2）We have received your letter/cable/telex dated…Ref. … with thanks.

   （3）We acknowledge with thanks the receipt of your letter dated…Ref. …

   （4）Many thanks for your letter of…

   （5）We thank you for your letter dated…

   　　感谢贵行×月×日案号为××的来函。

   　　贵行×月×日案号××的来函收悉，谨致谢意。

(6) We are in receipt of your letter of… Ref. …

(7) Your letter dated… Ref. …has just reached us.

### 4. 答复对方来函或提及某事

(1) We reply to your letter dated …
我行谨回复贵行×日来函

(2) Replying to your letter of (date) about…we have the pleasure to inform you that…
兹回复贵行×日关于……的来函，我行很高兴地奉告贵行……

(3) In reply/answer/response to your letter of… we wish to inform/advise you that…
兹回复你行×日来函，我行谨通知/建议……

(4) In answer to your letter dated…, we would reply as follows:
兹就你行×日来函，我行谨答复如下：

(5) Referring to your letter of (date) Ref. …, we wish to inform you that…
兹就×日案号为……来函事，现奉告贵行……

(6) With reference to your captioned mail transfer, we have to inform you that…
我行谨就上述信汇事通知贵行……

(7) In response to the captioned collection, we are informed by…that…
关于上述托收事，……行已通知我行……

### 5. 遵照对方指示或应对方要求办事

(1) In compliance with your request as contained in your letter of (date), we take pleasure in…
按照贵行×日来函所提出的要求，我们很高兴……

(2) In accordance with your clients' instruction, we paid you…
按我客户的指示，我行已向贵行支付……

(3) According to the directions contained in your letter of…, we…
按照贵行×日来函指示，我们……

(4) In conformity with your instructions of…, we…
依从贵行×日指示，我们……

(5) To comply with your request as put forward in your letter of…, we…
按照贵行×日来函所提出的要求……我们……

(6) At the request of your clients, we are forwarding to you…/we enclose the above-mentioned…
应我行客户之请求，现寄上……/现随函附寄上述……

(7) At the request of your clients, we would ask your assistance in…
应贵行客户之请求，我行谨请贵行在……方面予以协助。

(8) As requested in your letter of…, we…

应你行×日来函要求，我们……

### 6. 向对方表示遗憾

（1）We regret to inform you that/of…

（2）We regret to advise you that/of…

（3）We regret to announce that…

　　遗憾……，特此通知。

（4）We are sorry to say that…

（5）It is most regrettable that…

（6）We feel regretful that…

（7）It is with our greatest regret that we must inform you that…

（8）Much to our regrets we have to inform you that…

（9）It is our regret…

（10）We feel our regret for…

　　我方必须通知贵行……深感遗憾。

### 7. 随函附上……请查收

（1）We are enclosing…

（2）Enclosed please find…

（3）Enclosed are our…

（4）Herewith we have the pleasure in sending you…

（5）We take the pleasure of enclosing…

（6）We are pleased to enclose…

（7）You will find enclosed herewith…

## （二）结尾语（Closing Sentences）

### 1. 盼望对方早日函复

（1）We are looking forward to receiving your early reply.

（2）We are expecting your early reply.

（3）We are awaiting your early reply.

（4）We are looking forward to hearing from you at an early date.

（5）We are expecting your reply soon.

（6）We are anxious to your early reply.

　　盼早复。

（7）We are awaiting your favorable reply.

静候佳音。

（8）Please write to us as early as possible.

（9）Please reply immediately.

（10）Please let us know as soon as possible.

（11）Please reply at your earliest convenience.

敬希早日回函。

（12）Your early reply will be highly appreciated.

（13）Your prompt reply will be greatly obliged.

（14）We shall appreciate it very much if you will give us your early reply.

致盼早日函复为感。

（15）We await your reply by cable/telex/fax.

盼电复。

（16）Please confirm by cable/telex/fax.

请电确认。

（17）Please cable us your decision without delay.

请电告你方决定不误。

2. 感谢对方……

（1）We thank you in anticipation.

（2）We thank you in advance.

预致谢意。

（3）We thank you in advance for your kind cooperation/your valuable service.

对贵行友好的合作/有益的帮助预致谢意。

（4）We reiterate our thanks for your kind cooperation.

谨对你们的友好合作再次致谢意。

（5）Your assistance in this regard would be greatly appreciated.

对你们为此所给予的帮助深表感谢。

（6）Your kind cooperation in this respect will be highly appreciated.

对贵行的友好合作再次致以谢意。

（7）We shall much appreciate it if you will complete enclosed list and return it to us in due course.

如蒙贵行填好附件并按时退还我行则不胜感激。

（8）We would express our sincere thanks to you for your kind assistance.

对贵行的友好帮助在此表达我行忠诚的谢意。

（9）Please accept our thanks for your kind invitation.

对贵行的友好邀请在此表达感谢。

3. 请求对方的谅解

（1）We regret trouble you may have been caused in this regard.

对由此给贵行造成的麻烦深感抱歉。

（2）We apologize for any inconvenience you may be caused in this respect.

此事可能给贵行造成不便，谨致歉意。

（3）We apologize for the inconvenience caused to you in this regard.

我行谨对此引起的不便致以歉意。

（4）Please accept our apology for the inconvenience caused to you in this respect.

对因此引起的不便，谨致歉意。

4. 敬希查明

（1）Please look into the matter and give us an early reply.

敬希查明此事并早日复函。

（2）We would ask you to investigate the matter and give us an early reply.

请贵行查证此事，并早日复函。

（3）You are requested to look into the matter and inform us of the result by returning airmail.

请查证此事，将结果空邮我行。

（4）We shall appreciate it if you will look into the matter and let us know by returning mail.

如贵行能查证此事并函告我行，我们将不胜感激。

5. 随时为对方服务

（1）We assure you of our best services at all times.

（2）We shall be pleased of best service to you at all times.

（3）We are always ready to render you our sincere services.

（4）We shall at all times be willing to reciprocate your goodwill.

（5）We shall be pleased to offer you our best services at your disposal.

（6）We wish to assure you that our services will be entirely at your disposal.

我们愿随时竭诚为您服务。

# Appendix II  Commonly Used Abbreviations in Banking Communication

# 附录II  国际金融函电常用缩略词

# A

| | | |
|---|---|---|
| AUD; A$ | Australian Dollar | 澳元（货币单位） |
| A. A. R. | Against All Risks | 保综合险 / 一切险 |
| ABBR | abbreviation | 缩写字；略语 |
| ABT | about | 大约；约 |
| ACC | acceptance; accepted | 承兑；已承兑；承兑汇票 |
| A/C; ACCT | account; account current | 账户；账号；往来账户 |
| ACK | acknowledge; acknowledgement | 确认收悉 |
| A/D; a/d | after date | 出票后；……日后 |
| AD | advertisement | 广告 |
| ADP | automated date processing | 自动化数据处理 |
| ADV | advice | 通知书 |
| A. F. | advanced freight | 预付运费 |
| AGD | agreed | 同意的 |
| AGST | against | 凭借；对 |
| AGT | agent | 代理人 |
| A1 | A one; first-class | 一等；一流；一级 |
| AMB | ambassador | 大使 |
| AMT | amount | 金额 |
| ALDY | already | 已经 |
| A. N. | arrival notice | 到货通知 |
| ANS | answer; answered | 答复 |
| A/O; a/o | account of; at once | （某人）账内；立即 |
| ACC/O | account of | 入某账户 |
| A/OR | and/or | 和 / 或 |
| APR | April | 四月 |
| APP | appendix | 附录 |
| APPOX | approximately | 大约 |
| A/P | additional premium | 附加保险费 |
| A/R | all risks | 一切险；综合险 |
| ARR | arrangement | 安排；协定；商定 |
| ART | article | 商品；条款 |
| A/S | at sight; after sight | 见票后付；即付 |

| | | |
|---|---|---|
| ASAP | as soon as possible | 尽快 |
| ASS; ASSN | association | 协会；公司 |
| ASST | assortment | 类别；花色品种 |
| ATTY | attorney | 代理人；律师（美） |
| ATTN | attention | 经办；请……注意 |
| AUCT | auction | 拍卖，竞价 |
| AUG | August | 八月 |
| AV; A/V | average | 平均数；海损 |
| A/W | actual weight | 实际重量 |
| A. W. B. | air way bill | 空运提单 |
| A. W. G. | American Wire Gauge | 美国标准线规 |

## B

| | | |
|---|---|---|
| B | bag; bale; be | 包；袋；是 |
| B/ | second class | 二等（船） |
| B1 | B one | 二级 |
| B. A. | Bachelor of Arts | 文学士 |
| BAL | balance | 平衡量；余额 |
| BANKY | bankruptcy | 破产；倒闭 |
| BARGN | bargain | 交易；买卖 |
| B. B. | bill book; bank book | 票据薄；银行存折 |
| B. B. | back to back account | 对开账户；背靠背帐户 |
| B/C | bill for collection | 托收票据 |
| B. COM. | Bachelor of Commerce | 商学士 |
| B/D | bank draft; bill discounted | 银行汇票；已贴现票据 |
| BD | bond | 公债；债券；契约 |
| B/E | bill of exchange | 汇票 |
| BIS | Bank for International Settlement | 国际结算银行 |
| BK | bank | 银行 |
| BKG | banking | 银行业务；银行的 |
| B/L | bill of lading | 提单 |
| B/N | bank note | 钞票；银行承兑的汇票 |

| | | |
|---|---|---|
| B. O. | branch office | 分公司；分行 |
| BLK | blank | 空白的 |
| BP | bill payable, | 应付票据 |
| | bill purchased | 押汇 |
| BR | bill receivable | 应收票据 |
| B. P. B | bank post bill | 银行邮政汇票 |
| B. S. | balance sheet | 资产负债表 |
| BRKGE | brokerage | 佣金；经纪费用 |
| BTT | bank telegraphic transfer | 银行电汇 |
| BUS | business | 生意；业务 |
| B/V | book value, | 账面价值 |
| | back value | 倒期计息 |

## C

| | | |
|---|---|---|
| C; c | cent; currency | 分；货币 |
| C. A. | chartered accountant | 会计师 |
| | credit advice | 贷记通知书 |
| C/A | capital account | 资本；现金账 |
| | current account | 往来账；现金账；经常账户 |
| | credit account | 贷方账户 |
| C. A. D. | cash against documents | 交单付现 |
| CANC | canceled; cancellation | 注销 |
| CAP | capital | 资本 |
| CARR. PD | carriage paid | 运费付讫 |
| CAT | catalogue | 商品目录 |
| C/B | cash book | 现金账 |
| C. B. D. | cash before delivery | 交货前付款 |
| C. C; c. c | carbon copy | 抄送件 |
| | cash credit | 现金贷款 |
| | casher's check | 现金支票 |
| | Chamber of Commerce | 商会 |
| CERT | certificate | 证明书 |

323　　附录Ⅱ　国际金融函电常用缩略词

| | | |
|---|---|---|
| CFR | cost and freight | 成本加运费价 |
| CFP | cost freight price | 交货收款价 |
| CGE. PD | charges paid | 费用已付 |
| CGE | carriage | 运费 |
| C. H. | custom house | 海关 |
| CH. PD | charges paid | 费用预付 |
| C/I | certificate of insurance | 保险凭证 |
| C. I. A. | cash in advance | 预付现金 |
| CIC | China Insurance Clause | 中国保险条款 |
| CIF | cost, insurance, freight | 到岸价 |
| CIFC | cost, insurance, freight and commission | 到岸价加佣金 |
| C. I. O. | cash in order | 订货时付款 |
| CKS | checks | 支票 |
| CLD | cleared | 清算 |
| C/M | certificate of manufacture | 生产证明 |
| | credit memo | 贷项债单 |
| C/N | credit note | 贷记通知 |
| C. O. | certificate of origin | 原产地证明书 |
| CO. | company | 公司 |
| COD | cash on delivery | 货到付现 |
| COLL | collection | 托收 |
| COMM | commission | 佣金 |
| CNTR | contract | 合同 |
| CORP | corporation | 公司；企业 |
| CR | credit; creditor | 贷方；债权人 |
| C/P | charter party | 租船契约 |
| C. R. S. | cash by return steamer | 回船付款 |
| CTD | combined transport documents | 联合运输单据 |
| CUR | currency | 货币 |
| CWO | cash with order | 订货时付现 |

# D

| | | |
|---|---|---|
| D | draft | 汇票 |
| D/A | documents against acceptance | 承兑交单 |
| | deposit account | 存款账户 |
| | documents attached | 单据附上 |
| | days after acceptance | 承兑后数天 |
| | discharge afloat | 船上卸货 |
| | debit advice | 借记通知书 |
| DAF | delivered at frontier | 边境交货价 |
| D/B | day book | 流水账 |
| DC | documentary credit | 跟单信用证 |
| D/D | demand draft; documentary draft | 即期汇票；跟单汇票 |
| | days after date | 开票日后……天 |
| | delivered | 交货 |
| | deadline | 截止日期 |
| DE | deferred | 延期 |
| DEB | debenture | 债券 |
| DEC | December | 十二月 |
| DFT | draft | 汇票 |
| DEM | demurrage | 滞期费 |
| DEP | deposit | 存款 |
| DEPT | department | 部门 |
| DES | Delivered Ex Ship | 船上交货价 |
| DESTN | destination | 目的港 |
| D. F. | dead freight | 空仓费 |
| DHL Express | Dalsey, Hillblom & Lynn Express | 敦豪快递 |
| DIFF | difference | 差额 |
| DIR | director | 董事 |
| DIS | discount | 贴现；折扣 |
| DIV | division | 部门；科；处 |
| | dividend | 股息 |
| D/N | debit note | 借记通知 |
| D/O | delivery order | 提货单货物出仓凭单 |

| | | |
|---|---|---|
| DOA | date of arrival | 到达日期 |
| DOC | documents | 单据 |
| DLS | dollars | 美元 |
| DOZ | dozen | 一打 |
| D/P | documents against payment | 付款交单 |
| DR | debtor; debit | 债务人；借方；欠款 |
| D/R | deposit receipt | 存款收据 |
| DRT | draft | 汇票 |
| D/S; d. s. | day's sight; days after sight | 见票后……天 |
| D/T | delivery time | 交货期 |
| DUP; DUPL | duplicate | 副本 |
| D/W | dead weight | 重货；载重量 |
| D/Y | delivery | 交货 |
| D/W | dock warrant | 码头 |
| DZ | dozen | 一打 |

# E

| | | |
|---|---|---|
| EA | each | 每一；各 |
| ECOM | economy | 经济 |
| E&O. E | error and omissions excepted | 错漏当查 |
| E. C. | exempli cause = for example | 例如（拉） |
| ED | ex dividend | 无红息；除息 |
| E/D | export declaration | 出口申报表 |
| EDP | electronic data processing | 电子数据处理 |
| E. E | errors excepted | 错误不在次限 |
| EEC | European Economic Community | 欧洲经济共同体 |
| EFTA | European Free Trade Association | 欧洲自由贸易协会 |
| EFT | electronic fund transfer | 资金电子转账 |
| EG | exempli gratia = for example | 例如（拉） |
| EMA | European Monetary Agreement | 欧洲货币协会 |
| EMF | European Monetary Fund | 欧洲货币资金 |
| EMS | European Monetary System | 欧洲货币体系 |

| | | |
|---|---|---|
| ENC(S); ENCL | enclosure(s) | 附件 |
| ENTD | entered | 入账 |
| END | endorse; endorsement | 背书 |
| E. O. M. | end of month | 月底；月末 |
| E. O. S. | end of season | 季末 |
| EQ | equivalent | 相等于；同值 |
| ESQ | Esquire | 先生（尊称） |
| EST | established | 创立；设立 |
| ETA | estimated time of arrival | 估计到达时间 |
| ETD | estimated time of departure | 估计离港时间 |
| EX | exchange; example; exception | 外汇；例子；除外 |
| EXCL | exclusive; excluding | 除外；不包括 |
| EX CONT | from contract | 从合同 |
| EX. CP | ex coupon | 无息票（除息票） |
| EX DIV | without dividend | 无股息（除利息） |
| EXQ | Ex Quay | 码头交货价 |
| EXP | express; expenses; export | 快件；费用；出口 |
| EXS | Ex Ship | 船上交货价 |

## F

| | | |
|---|---|---|
| F | franc | 法郎 |
| F. A. A | free of all average | 一切海损均不赔 |
| F. A. Q. | fair average quality | 大路货；中等品 |
| F. A. S. | Free Alongside Ship | 船边交货价 |
| F. B | freight bill | 运费单 |
| F. B. E. | foreign bill of exchange | 外汇汇票 |
| F. C. | fixed capital; future contract | 固定资本；期货合约 |
| FCL | full container load | 整箱装 |
| F/D | Free Docks | 码头交货；船坞交货 |
| F. F. A. | Free From Alongside | 船边交货 |
| FF | French Franc | 法国法郎 |
| F. F. D. | free from duty | 免税 |

| | | |
|---|---|---|
| F. G. A. | free of general average | 共同海损不担保 |
| F. I. | for instance | 例如 |
| FIGS | figures | 数字 |
| FIN | financial | 财务的；金融的 |
| FIN STAT | financial statement | 财务报表 |
| FIN. STNDG | financial standing | 财务状况 |
| F. M. | force majeure | 不可抗力 |
| FOB | Free on Board | 离岸价 |
| FOC | free of charge | 免费 |
| FOBST | free on board stowed and trimmed | 包括清理仓位费在内的离岸价 |
| FOQ | free on quay | 码头交货价 |
| F. O. I. | free of interest | 免息 |
| FOR | free on rail | 铁路交货价 |
| FOS | free on steamer | 船上交货价 |
| FOT | free on trucks | 卡车上交货价 |
| FPA | free of particular average | 平安险 |
| FRT | freight | 运费 |
| FRT. PPD | freight prepaid | 运费已预付 |
| FUT | futures | 期货 |
| F. W. | fresh water | 淡水 |
| FY | fiscal year | 财政年度；会计年度 |
| FX | foreign exchange | 外汇 |
| FYR | for your reference | 供你方参考 |
| FYI | for your information | 供你方参考 |

# G

| | | |
|---|---|---|
| G/A | general average | 共同海损 |
| GATT | General Agreement on Tariffs & Trade | 关贸总协定 |
| G. B. O. | goods in bad order | 货物损坏 |
| GBP | Great Britain Pound | 英镑 |
| GDS | goods | 货物 |
| G. N. | gross for net (pay on gross weight) | 以毛作净 |

| | | |
|---|---|---|
| G/N | guarantee notes | 承诺保证 |
| GR | gross revenue | 总收入 |
| GR. WT | gross weight | 毛重 |
| GP | gross profit | 毛利 |
| GSP | generalized system of preferences | 普惠制 |
| G/T | gross ton | 英吨；毛重吨 |
| GSW | gross shipping weight | 总载货量 |
| GUAR | guarantee | 担保 |

## H

| | | |
|---|---|---|
| H. I. D. C. | hold in due course | 正当持票 |
| H | hour | 时 |
| HNDCHGS | handling charges | 处理/经营费 |
| HK | Hong Kong | 香港 |
| HKD | Hong Kong Dollars | 港元 |
| HO | head office | 总行；总部 |
| HT | height | 高 |
| HUND | hundred | 百 |
| H. Q. | head quarter | 总部；总公司 |

## I

| | | |
|---|---|---|
| I. A. | inactive account | 不活动账户 |
| IAS | International Accounting Standard | 国际会计标准 |
| I. B. | invoice book | 发票簿 |
| I. B. R. D | International Bank for Reconstruction and Development (World Bank) | 国际复兴开发银行(世界银行) |
| ISBP | International Standard Banking Practice for the Examination of Documents Under Documentary Credits | 关于审核跟单信用证项下单据的国际标准实务 |
| I/C | inward collection | 进口托收 |

| | | |
|---|---|---|
| I. C. U. | International Code Used | 国际使用的电码 |
| ICC | Institute Cargo Clause | 协会货物条款 |
| | International Chamber of Commerce | 国际商会 |
| ID | identification | 身份证 |
| IDA | International Development Association | 国际开发协会 |
| IE | id est. (that is) | 即（拉） |
| IFC | International Finance Corporation | 国际金融公司 |
| IMF | International Monetary Fund | 国际货币基金组织 |
| IMO | International Money Order | 国际汇款单 |
| IMP | import | 进口 |
| IN | inch | 英寸 |
| INC | incorporated | 合并；有限责任 |
| I/L | Import License | 进口许可证 |
| INCOTERMS | International Chamber of Commerce Terms | 国际(商会)贸易术语 |
| IND | indent | 合同；订单 |
| INS | insurance | 保险 |
| INSTR | instructions | 指示 |
| INST | instant=of the present month | 本月 |
| INV | invoice | 发票 |
| INVT | inventory | 财产目录；盘存 |
| I. O. U | I owe you | 借据 |
| I/O | inspecting order; in order | 检验单；良好；整齐 |
| I/P | insurance policy | 保险单 |
| I/R | inward remittance | 汇入汇款 |
| IRR | irrevocable | 不可撤销的 |
| ISS | issue | 发行；开立 |
| IT | item | 项；条 |
| I. V. | invoice value | 发票金额 |
| IVO | in view of | 鉴于 |

## J

| | | |
|---|---|---|
| J | journal | 日记账；分类账 |
| J. A.; J/A | joint account | 共同账户 |
| JAN | January | 一月 |
| J. F. | journal folio | 日记账页数 |
| JS | Japanese Yen | 日元 |
| JSC | joint stock company | 股份联合公司 |
| JV | joint venture | 合营企业；合资经营 |

## K

| | | |
|---|---|---|
| K | kilo; karat | 千克；克拉 |
| K. D. | knock down price | 成交价格 |
| KP | keep | 保持记账 |
| LL | Letter | 信 |
| P | Pounds | 英镑 |
| L/A | letter of authority | 授权书 |
| L/C | letter of credit | 信用证 |
| L. C. L. | less-than-car-load lot | 零星货运 |
| LCL | less than container load | 拼箱装 |
| L. D. T | long-distance telephone | 长途电话 |
| L/G | letter of guarantee | 担保函；保证书 |
| L/H | letter of hypothecation | 押质权书 |
| L. I. P. | life insurance policy | 人寿保险单 |
| LME | London Metal Exchange | 伦敦金属交易所 |
| LNG | liquified natural gas | 液化天然气 |
| L/T | long ton | 长吨 |
| L. T. | letter telegram | 信电 |
| LTD | limited | 有限公司 |

## M

| | | |
|---|---|---|
| M | meter | 米 |
| M/A | my account | 我的账户 |
| MAR | March | 三月 |
| MAX | maximum | 最大 |
| M. B. | memorandum book | 备查簿；备忘录 |
| M/D | months after date | 发票后……月 |
| MDSE | merchandise | 商品 |
| MEMO | memorandum | 备忘录 |
| MESSRS | Messieurs (p) | 尊称：先生（法） |
| MFG | manufacturing | 制造 |
| MIN | minimum | 最少量 |
| M. I. P. | marine insurance policy | 海运保险单 |
| MKS | marks | 标记；印章 |
| MKT | market | 市场 |
| M. O. | money order; mail order | 邮汇汇票 |
| MO | month | 月 |
| M/R | mate's receipt | 收货单 |
| M/S | month after sight | 见票后……月 |
| M/T | Mail Transfer | 信汇 |
| | metric ton | 公吨 |
| | multimodal transport | 联运 |
| MTG | mortgage | 抵押 |

## N

| | | |
|---|---|---|
| NA | non-available | 无效的；不祥；无法提供的 |
| N/A | no account | 无账户 |
| | no advice | 未通知 |
| | new account | 新开账户 |
| | non-acceptance | 拒绝承兑 |

| | | | |
|---|---|---|---|
| N. B. | nata bene (take notice) | 注意,留心(拉) | |
| | new bond | 新公债 | |
| N/F | no funds | 无资金;存款不足 | |
| NEG | negotiable | 可转让的;可议付的 | |
| N/G | net gain | 纯利益;净利益 | |
| NO | number | 数,数字 | |
| N/M | no marks | 无唛头 | |
| N/O | no order | 无抬头人 | |
| NOV | November | 十一月 | |
| N/P | no payment | 拒绝支付 | |
| | net proceeds | 净收入 | |
| | net profit | 纯利 | |
| N. P. | notary public | 公证人 | |
| N. R. | no risk | 无险 | |
| N/R | no responsibility | 无责任 | |
| NSF | not sufficient funds | 存款不足 | |
| NWT | net weight | 净重 | |
| NYC | New York City | 纽约 | |

## O

| | | |
|---|---|---|
| O | order | 通知,票据 |
| ORD | to order of | 指定…… |
| O/A | open account | 赊销账户 |
| | on account | 赊账 |
| | our account | 我账 |
| O/B | order book | 订货簿 |
| O. B/L | order bill of lading | 指示提单 |
| OC. B/L | ocean bill of lading | 海运提单 |
| O. C. | overcharge | 多收;多载 |
| O/C | outward collection | 出口托收 |
| OCT | October | 十月 |
| O/D | on demand; overdraft | 即期;透支 |

| | | |
|---|---|---|
| OEEC | Organization for European Economic Co-operation | 欧洲经济合作组织 |
| OK | all correct | 全部正确 |
| OG | ordinary goods | 普通商品 |
| ON A/C | on account | 记账 |
| O/O | order of | 抬头人 |
| O/P | open policy | 预定保险单 |
| OPEC | Organization of Petroleum Exporting Countries | 石油输出国组织 |
| O. R. | owner's risk | 业主风险 |
| OT | on truck | 上卡车 |
| OZ | ounce | 盎司 |

## P

| | | |
|---|---|---|
| P | per; page | 每；页 |
| P. A. | per annum (per year) | 每年 |
| | particular average | 单独海损 |
| | power of attorney | 委托书 |
| | personal account | 私人账户 |
| PC | percent | 百分比 |
| | price | 价格 |
| PCL | parcel | 包裹 |
| PD | paid | 已付 |
| PER PRO | per procuration | 代理；委托代办 |
| PL | partial loss | 部分损失 |
| P&L | profit and loss | 损益类 |
| PM | premium | 保险费 |
| P. M. O. | postal money order | 邮政汇票 |
| P. N.; P/N | promissory note | 本票 |
| POB | post office box | 邮政信箱 |
| POD | pay on delivery | 交货付款 |

| | | |
|---|---|---|
| PPD | prepaid | 预付 |
| PR | price | 价格 |
| PRES | president | 行长；董事长；总经理 |
| PRIN | principal | 委托人 |
| PS | postscript | 附言 |
| PTY | proprietary | 企业公司 |
| PX | please exchange | 请交换 |

## Q

| | | |
|---|---|---|
| Q | quantity | 数量 |
| QC | quality control | 质量控制；质量管理 |
| Q. V. | Quod vide =PLS REFER TO | 请查阅（拉） |
| QLY | quality | 质量 |
| QTN | quotation | 行情表；估价表 |
| QY | quay | 码头 |

## R

| | | |
|---|---|---|
| R | response; registered | 回答；注册的；挂号 |
| R/A | referred to acceptor | 请与承兑人接洽 |
| RB | regular budget | 正常预算 |
| R/D | referred to drawer | 请与出票人接洽 |
| R/E | refer to endorser | 请与背书人接洽 |
| RE; REF | regarding; with reference to | 关于 |
| RCVD | received | 收到 |
| RECT | receipt | 收据 |
| RED B/L | red bill of lading | 划红线提单 |
| REM | remittance | 汇款 |
| REP | representative | 代表 |
| Rev. A/C | revenue account | 出纳账 |
| R. O. | receiving office | 收入行 |

| | | |
|---|---|---|
| R. O. D. | refused on delivery | 拒绝交货 |
| R. O. | remittance order | 汇款委托书 |
| RYT | referring to your telex | 关于你方电传 |

## S

| | | |
|---|---|---|
| S | sale; Sunday | 销售；星期日 |
| S/A | special authority | 特别代理权 |
| S/A | societe anonym (incorporated) | 股份有限公司（法） |
| S. B. | savings bank | 储蓄银行 |
| S/C | sales contract | 销售合同书 |
| S/C | sale confirmation | 销售确认书 |
| S/D | sea-damage (grain trade) | 海水损 |
| | short delivery | 交货不足 |
| | sight draft | 即期汇票 |
| SDRS | special drawing rights | 特别提款权 |
| SEC | Security and Exchange Commission | 证券交易委员会 |
| SEPT | September | 九月 |
| SF | sinking fund | 偿债基金 |
| | Swiss Frank | 瑞士法郎 |
| SGD | signed | 签字；签署 |
| SH; SHR | share | 股份；股票 |
| SIG | signature | 签字；签名 |
| S/N | shipping note | 装运通知单 |
| S/O; S. O. | seller's option; shipping order | 卖主的选择；发运单 |
| S. R. | shipping receipt | 装船收据 |
| SRCCR | strike, riots and civil commotion risks | 罢工、暴动民变险 |
| S/S | steamship | 轮船；蒸汽船 |
| STR | street | 街 |
| S/T | short ton | 短吨 |
| STG | sterling | 英镑 |
| STK | stock | 股票 |
| S. W. G | standard wire gauge | 标准线规 |

## T

| | | |
|---|---|---|
| T | ton; tare | 吨；皮重 |
| T/A | telegraphic address | 电挂地址 |
| T/C | traveler's check | 旅行支票 |
| Tel | telephone number | 电话号码 |
| THRO | through | 通过；经由 |
| T. L. | total loss | 全损险 |
| T. L. O. | total loss only | 只保全损险 |
| T. M. | trade mark | 商标 |
| T. M. O. | telegraphic money order | 电汇票 |
| TONN | tonnage | 吨位 |
| TPND | theft, pilferage & non-delivery | 偷窃、提货不着险 |
| TR | transfer | 过户；转让 |
| T/R | trust receipt | 信托收据 |
| TRIP | triplicate | 一式三份 |
| T/T | telegraphic transfer | 电汇 |

## U

| | | |
|---|---|---|
| U/A | underwriting account | 承保账户 |
| ULT | ultimo (last month) | 上月 |
| UCC | Uniform Commercial Code | （美国）统一商法典 |
| UCP | Uniform Customs and Practice for Documentary Credits | 跟单信用证统一惯例 |
| UK | United Kingdom | 联合王国（英国） |
| UNCONF | unconfirmed | 未保兑的 |
| UNDSGD | undersigned | 签字人 |
| U/W | underwriters | 承销商；承保人；保险人 |

## V

| | | |
|---|---|---|
| V/A | value analysis | 价值分析 |

|  |  |  |
|---|---|---|
|  | voucher attached | 附传票 |
| VAT | value added tax | 增值税 |
| VES | vessel | 船舶 |
| VID | videlicet (namely) | 即；就是 |
| VOL | volume | 量；容积；卷 |
| VOY | voyage | 航程 |
| V. P. | vice-president | 副行长 |

## W

|  |  |  |
|---|---|---|
| W. A. | with average | 单独海损赔偿 |
| WB | water-book | 流水账 |
|  | waybill | 货运单 |
| WHF | wharf | 码头 |
| WK | week | 周；星期 |
| W. E. | warehouse entry | 仓库登记 |
| W. P. A. | With Particular Average | 水渍险 |
| W. R. | warehouse receipt | 仓库收据 |
|  | War Risks | 战争险 |
| WT | weight | 重量 |
| W/W | warehouse to warehouse (Risks) | 仓至仓(险) |

## X

| X. C. | Ex Coupon | 除息票 |
|---|---|---|
| X. D. | Ex dividend | 无股息 |
| X. I. | ex interest | 无利息 |
| X. N. | ex new | 无权要求新股 |
| XM | Christmas | 圣诞节 |

# Y

| | | |
|---|---|---|
| Y | year | 年 |
| Y/A | York-Antwerp Rules | 约克·安特卫普规则 |
| YD | yard | 码 |
| YR | your | 你方 |
| Y | yen | 日元 |

Appendix Ⅲ　Keys to Exercises

附录Ⅲ　练习参考答案

# Unit 1

1. Seven "Cs" refers to: completeness, courtesy, consideration, clarity, concreteness, conciseness and correctness.

2. One should follow closely the following suggestions:

   (1) Be sincerely tactful, thoughtful and appreciative;

   (2) Take a personal, friendly and modest tone;

   (3) Omit expressions that irritate, hurt or belittle.

   (4) Be prompt in reply.

# Unit 2

1. A complete banking letter usually consists of 14 parts:

   Letterhead, date, reference, inside address, attention note, salutation, subject line, body of letter, complementary close, signature, enclosure, reference initials, carbon copy and postscript.

2. In full block style, all parts contained in a banking letter should be typed from the left margin to the right without any blanks left. e.g.

   (1) BANK OF CHINA, HUNAN BRANCH
   
   71 Wuyi East Road DongDistrict
   
   Changsha 410000
   
   P. R. China
   
   Phone: (0731)84422312
   
   Telex: 98107 HNBOC CN
   
   Cable Add.: CHUNGKUO CHANGS
   
   Fax: 0086 731 82299846

   (2) March 5th, 2018

   (3) Our Ref.: L/C1234

   (4) CITIBANK, N. A.
   
   339 Park Ave.
   
   New York, N. Y. 10021
   
   U. S. A.

   (5) ATTN: Mr. Johnson Smith, Int'l Dept.

   (6) Gentlemen:

   (7) Re: Your Reference Number:
   
   Our letter of credit number: 25910

Draft Amount: USD 61812.50

a) We have accepted the above-mentioned draft maturing on 06/01/18:

—— The draft is held in our portfolio.

—— The draft is attached kindly acknowledge receipt by signing and returning the copy of this advice.

——We shall effect payment at maturity per your instructions.

b) Very truly yours,

c) (signature)

International Department

Bank of China, Hunan Branch

d) GW/dp

e) Enc. ...

f) C.C. ...

P. S.

3.

BANK OF CHINA, HUNAN BRANCH                    Stamp

71 Wuyi East Road Changsha 410000

P. R. China

Cable:

Telex:

Fax:

                                        Citibank. N. A. New York

                                        34 Main Ave

                                        New York N. Y. 10022

                                        U. S. A.

                                        ATTN: Clearing Center

# Unit 3

1.

FM:

TO:

Date:

Dear Sirs,

Agency Relationship

We are pleased to receive your letter of Apr. 12, 2018 in which you propose to establish a direct agency relationship with us, which is in agreement with our desire.

In order to cope with the increase trade volume between us, it is necessary for us to conclude such kind of agreement with your bank.

Enclosed you will find our control documents and a draft agreement for your consideration.

We trust the conclusion of the agreement will lead to a consistent development of business between our two banks.

Faithfully yours,

(Signature)

Encl as stated:

2.

Bank of China, Beijing
410 Fuchengmen NeiDajie
Beijing 100818
P. R. China
Cable:
Telex:
Fax:

8 March, 2018

Barclays Bank PLC
12 Barclays House, Windborne Road
Poole Dorset BH15 2BB
England

ATTN:

Dear Sirs,

Amendment of Agency Relationship

It is our pleasure to see that the business transaction between your fine bank and ourselves have been increasing steadily since the establishment of a direct correspondent relationship in 2008.

In view of the fact that a big increase has been seen in the volume of transactions between China and your country, we consider this to be a good time to propose an amendment to the existing Agency Relationship to enable us to do business directly with your following branches:

… …, … …

We trust the inclusion of your above branches will further develop our mutually beneficial relationship existing between our two banks.

We shall send you our control documents including the Fixed Number to your branches upon receipt of your letter of consent.

Thank you in advance for your kind cooperation in this matter and we look forward to hearing from you at an early date.

Yours sincerely,

(Signature)

3.

(1) We are informed by our Head Office in Beijing that they agree to your suggestion as contained in your letter of June 2, 2018, to use our test key for authentication of cable messages exchanged between our two banks. Accordingly we send you herewith a list of serial and rotation numbers to be used for authentication of your cables dispatched to us. Please note that the fixed number remains the same as that we send you on May 5, 2017, which is now in your possession.

Please acknowledge receipt.

(2) We are asked by our clients, … to authenticate the Advice of your Milan Branch L/C No. … for…, which was sent directly by you to them. As we are not in possession of your List of Specimen Signatures, you are requested to have the signatures appearing thereon verified by our London Office. In this connection, the beneficiaries ask us to convey their opinion that it will be more convenient to them if your future credits be routed through this bank.

# Unit 4

1.

BANK OF CHINA, HUNAN BRANCH
71 Wuyi East Road Dong District
Changsha 410000
P. R. China
Cable:

Telex:

Fax:

16th May, 2018

Midland Bank, London

53 Golden House, Midland Road

London BB1 5HM

England

Dear Sirs,

    We refer to your letter of 4th May, 2018, Ref. ... written at the request of your clients,...

    Inquiries have been made in this connection and we are pleased to introduce you China National Animal By-Products-Import & Export Corporation, ... Branch which deal in the import and export of leather products. The Corporation is reliable in reputation and abundant in resources with registered capital of CNY..., Please advise your clients to communicate with them direct, stating our recommendation.

    For your reference, we enclose a credit report on the above corporation which is passed on to you for your private use only.

Yours sincerely,

(Signature)

2.

BANK OF CHINA, HUNAN BRANCH

71 Wuyi East Road Dong District

Changsha 410000

P. R. China

Cable:

Telex:

Fax:

24th Apr., 2018

Eastern Bank Ltd. London

605 Hard Building, Eastern Road

London AB4 5WZ
England

Dear Sirs,

Our value clients, China National Textile Import & Export Corporation, ... Branch, specializing in all sorts of textiles, wish to enter into business connection with customers at your end who are interested in the import of textiles, especially woolen textiles.

Besides, they should be very much pleased if you would be able to furnish them with information as to the annual demand of the said commodity in your market, the import exchange control, customs regulations, and the necessary formalities in connection with the importation into your place of woolen textiles.

We should much appreciate it if you would forward to us the names and addresses of any of your clients who are interested in this inquiry, together with such information as you may give in respect of these above points.

For your information we enclose a report on this corporation.

Yours sincerely,

(Signature)

## Unit 5

1.

From: Main Bank, Hong Kong
To: Bank of China, Hong Kong

May 20, 2018

Re: Bill No. BP12345 of Bank of China, Ningbo
Drawn on: East-Asia Bank, Hong Kong
under our L/C No. 5678 for HK$125,600.00
(charges HK$280 include )
(our Bill No. 6789)

Dear Sirs,

At the request of the above bank, we enclose our cashier's Order/Demand Draft No....for HK$125,600.00 in settlement of the captioned bill.

Please credit the account of the captioned bank under cable/airmail advice to them quoting their above reference.

Yours faithfully,

(signed)

Encl.: 1 C/O

C.C.Bank of China,

Ningbo

2.

    We are informed by our Beijing Head Office that in your statement of account appears the following debit entry, which is not shown in our books:

    "Feb. 6th… in cover of charges in respect of return of goods to Shanghai as well as our charges in this connection US Dollar 2,400.25."

    As we do not seem to have received the relative advice from you, and besides, no reference number of ours is given in your statement, we are unable to reconcile this item, and would request you to furnish us with additional information for our guidance.

    Thank you in advance.

# Unit 6

1.

BANK OF CHINA, HUNAN BRANCH

71 Wuyi East Road Dong District

Changsha 410000

P. R. China

Cable:

Telex:

Fax:

April 4th, 2018

Commercial Bank, Chicago

204 Haide Ave

Chicago 20032

Attn: clearing Dept.

Gentlemen:

<u>Your L/C's 2314&2315</u>

<u>f/o China Nat'l Tea &Native Produce Imp. & Exp. Corp, Hunan Branch</u>

    In reply to your letter of 26th March, 2018, instructing us to transfer the balance of your L/C 2315, we wish to advise that it is done accordingly.

We are, however, informed by the beneficiaries that while they are in agreement with your request for transfer of the balance, they should like to state that the new balance under L/C 2315 at the end of February, 2018 should be US$8,387.15 instead of US$7,732.00 as mentioned in your letter. We are informed that this difference of US$655.15 arises from your exclusion of the increased amount of your cable amendments of 19th November, 2017 and 11th February, 2018 for US$300.50 and US$355.10 respectively.

Please confirm us at your earliest convenience the correct balance of the said Credit on 28th February, 2018.

Faithfully yours,

(Signature)

2.

(1)

CITIBANK N. A., HONG KONG BRANCH

30 Main Street, Hong Kong

Tel:

Telex:

Cable:

April 15, 2018

Midland Bank Ltd, London

4 Midland Street

London BH45WA

Dears sirs,

Your L/C No. … for… Dated…

We refer to your L/C No. …which contains the clause "this credit expires on 15th May, for negotiation in Hong Kong."

In view of the fact that the beneficiaries are domiciled at…, China and our Bank is authorized, in accordance with the stipulations of the Credit, to claim reimbursement from… Bank Ltd, Overseas Department, London, we should think that negotiation should be made in Mainland of China instead of in Hong Kong, China. Therefore, we have taken the liberty to make due correction on your behalf before advising the Credit to the beneficiaries.

Kindly take note.

Yours sincerely,

(Signature)

(2)

BANK OF CHINA, SHANGHAI BRANCH

54 Huangxing Road Dong District

Shanghai 220000

P. R. China

Cable:

Telex:

Fax:

December 26th, 2018.

Chase Lincoln First Bank, N. A.

Lincoln First Square

Rochester, New York N. Y. 14634

U. S. A.

Attn: Clearing Dept.

Gentlemen:

Your L/C No. …Dated …

　　The above Credit stipulates that the unit price of the goods is on FOB basis, but it goes on to require that the Bills of Lading be marked "Freight Paid". The two stipulations apparently do not tally.

　　After communicating with the beneficiaries, we are given to understand that the relative goods are contracted on FOB terms, and we have, therefore, taken the liberty of Changing …"Freight Collected at Destination", and have advised the credit to the beneficiaries.

　　Please look into the matter and confirm to us our action is in order.

Yours faithfully,
(Signature)

3.

Your L/C No. …Our BP…Dated…

　　Upon our claiming on Lloyds Bank Ltd., London through our London Office reimbursement of our negotiation under the above Credit, we are informed that payment was effected by them under reserve for the reason that the Credit expired on 31st October.

　　We wish to point out that according to your cable amendment of 10th November the shipment and validity dates of the Credit were extended up to 31st December. We presume that it might possibly be due to the failure on your part to advise the reimbursing bank in time of the said amendment, or the advise having gone astray. Your are now requested to immediately authorize to Lloyds Bank Ltd., London to release the revise. It is hoped that similar cases will not occur in the future.

Yours sincerely,
(Signature)

# Unit 7

1.

OURBPNO…UNDER YRL/CNO…

HVRECVD YRLTR DD6THOCT AND CREDITADV INFORMGUS YOU HVCREDITD THENEGS INTO OURA/C WITH OURHO BEIJING ONSAMEDAY STOP

WE HAVETO POINTOUT PAYMENT DELAYED TWOWEEKS MUCH LONGERTIME THANUSUAL PLS LOOKINTO THEMATTER AND LETUSHAVE YR REASON FOR THISDELAY. THKS REGARDS.

2.

FM:…, Hong Kong

TO:

DD:

OUR DC NO …

UR BP NO …

V HV RECVD UR LTR DD N RELATIVE DOCS UNDER THE A/M L/C

IN SETTLEMENT OF THIS NEGOTIATIONS, YOU MAY CHOOSE ONE OF THE REIMBURSG METHODS IN THE FOLLOWGS:

1. YOU MAY DEBIT OUR A/C WZ UR BEIJING HO.

2. WE CREDIT UR A/C WITH US

3. WE REIMBURSE U BY REMITG THE AMT OF … TO …BANK

RGDS

…HONG KONG

# Unit 8

1.

Sequence Number: C12345

Message Type: 7XX

Sender Institution: XXXXXXXXXXX
BANK OF AMERICA, THE
SAN FRANCISCO

Receiver Institution: XXXXXXXXXXX
BANK OF CHINA, THE
CHENGDU

Message Status: I

Message Input Date: 2018-02-23

Message Priority: N

————Message Content:————

20:Transaction Reference Number  XXXXXXXX

21:Related Reference XXXXXXXXXXX

79:Narrative

 RE OUR L/C NO…

 YOUR REF.: …

 F/O…

 A/C NO…

 AMOUT…

ENCLOSED PLEASE FIND DOCUMENTATION OF USD…PRESENTED TO US BY YOU DD FEB 12 2018.

OUR CUSTOMER REFUSES PAYMENT ON THESE DOCS DUE TO THE FOLLOWG DISCREPANCIES:

(1) SHIPMENT FROM BEIJING I/O CHENGDU.

(2) DISCRIPTION OF MERCHANDISE ON INVOICE DIFFERS FROM L/C.

(3) AIR WAYBILL NOT SIGNED.

(4) COPY OF SWIFT TO BUYER DOES NOT SHOW FLIGHT NUMBER.

WE SUGGEST BENEFICIARY CONTACT BUYER DIRECT. WE ARE CLOSING OUR FILE ON THIS TRANSACTION.

B.RGDS.

ENCLS, AS STATED

ITPC, IMPORT DEPT. MR./MS.XXXXX

2.

NARRATIVE:

BY THEIR SWIFT CONFIRMATION OF 5TH APRIL, THE BANK OF TOKYO LTD, TOKYO INFORM US THAT

THEY HAD REMITTED THROUGH THEIR LONDON OFFICE TO YOU THE SUM OF … TO COVER OUR PAYMENT OF THEIR TT NO… DD 1ST APR. F/O …

HOWEVER WE WISH TO ADV THAT WE DO NOT APPEAR UP TP THE PRESENT TIME TO HAVE RECEIVED THE RELATIVE CREDIT ADVICE FM YOU.

  KINDLY LOOK INTO THE MATTER AND IN CASE THAT THE FUNDS HAVE NOT YET BEEN  RECEIVED, PLS CONTACT THE SAID BANK ON OUR BEHALF AND INFORM US THE RESULT.

# Unit 9

1.

CITIBANK N. A., Hong Kong Branch

17/F, West Tower Bond Center

189 Queen's Way, Central H. K.

April 2, 2018

Bank of China, Beijing. H. O.

410 Fuchengmen NeiDajie

Beijing 100828

ATTN: Mr. …

We thank you indeed for your kind reception extended to Mr. Zhang… when he visited your fine bank last month.

It is always our desire to maintain a pleasant and mutually beneficial business relationship with your bank.

May we reiterate our thanks to your cordial reception extended to Mr. Zhang …

Yours Sincerely,

  (Signature)              (Signature)

Li Ming                    Zhang …
Deputy General Manager     Manager China Dept.

2.

### Advertisement of China Investment Bank

China Investment Bank is a specialized bank designated by Chinese Government to raise funds from abroad for domestic construction. The CIB handles relending with loans borrowed from international financial institutions, foreign governments and international and local currency deposits and loans as well as investment, interbank lending both at home and abroad, settlement, interbank lending both at home and abroad, settlement of trade related payment, financial leasing, guarantee on foreign exchange transactions and foreign currency dealings.

China Investment Bank with its Head Office in Beijing has… branches all over the country. We can offer our best services at your disposal.

Address: …

SWIFT: …

3.

To: Chartered Bank

ATTN: Mr. John Smith,
      Director

Dear Mr. John Smith,

### A Letter of Invitation

I am delighted to hear from our mutual friend Mr. Anderson that you will visit China in the coming October.

It will be a great honor for me to meet you during your stay in China. So I take this opportunity to invite you to a dinner party at the restaurant of Chang Cheng Hotel to express our sincere thanks to you for your great efforts in training our personnel. I hope this meeting will enhance our relationship and expand our business.

Please let us know by telex when it is convenient to you so that we can make a better arrangement for you.

Yours sincerely,

(Signature)

Li Ming

President of Bank of China, Beijing

## 教辅申请说明

北京大学出版社本着"教材优先、学术为本"的出版宗旨，竭诚为广大高等院校师生服务。为更有针对性地提供服务，请您按照以下步骤在微信后台提交教辅申请，我们会在1~2个工作日内将配套教辅资料，发送到您的邮箱。

◎手机扫描下方二维码，或直接微信搜索公众号"北京大学经管书苑"，进行关注；

◎点击菜单栏"在线申请"—"教辅申请"，出现如右下界面：

◎将表格上的信息填写准确、完整后，点击提交；

◎信息核对无误后，教辅资源会及时发送给您；如果填写有问题，工作人员会同您联系。

**温馨提示：**如果您不使用微信，您可以通过下方的联系方式（任选其一），将您的姓名、院校、邮箱及教材使用信息反馈给我们，工作人员会同您进一步联系。

**我们的联系方式：**

北京大学出版社经济与管理图书事业部

北京市海淀区成府路205号，100871

联 系 人：周莹

电　　话：010-62767312 / 62757146

电子邮件：em@pup.cn

Q　Q：5520 63295（推荐使用）

微信：北京大学经管书苑（pupembook）

网址：www.pup.cn